Adjustment, Poverty and Employment in Mexico

ARACELI DAMIÁN
El Colegio de México

Ashgate
Aldershot • Burlington USA • Singapore • Sydney

© Araceli Damián 2000

All rights reserved. No part of this publication may be reproduced, stored in a retrieval system or transmitted in any form or by any means, electronic, mechanical, photocopying, recording or otherwise without the prior permission of the publisher.

Published by
Ashgate Publishing Limited
Gower House
Croft Road
Aldershot
Hampshire GU11 3HR
England

Ashgate Publishing Company
131 Main Street
Burlington VT 05401-5600 USA

Ashgate website: http://www.ashgate.com

British Library Cataloguing in Publication Data
Damián, Araceli
    Adjustment, poverty and employment in Mexico
    1. Structural adjustment (Economic policy) - Mexico
    2. Poverty - Mexico 3. Labor market - Mexico 4. Mexico - Economic conditions - 20th century
    I. Title
    330.9'72'09048

Library of Congress Control Number: 00-134008

ISBN 0 7546 1369 0

Printed and bound by Antony Rowe Ltd, Chippenham, Wiltshire

ADJUSTMENT, POVERTY AND EMPLOYMENT IN MEXICO

To my beloved León and Julio

Contents

List of Figures	*ix*
List of Tables	*x*
List of Abbreviations	*xiv*

1 STRUCTURAL ADJUSTMENT: AN OVERVIEW — 1

1. Introduction — 1
2. Structural Adjustment: the End of a National Economic Project — 3
3. The World Bank Structural Adjustment Packages — 7
4. Government and Control of Economic Process — 8
5. Adjustment and Poverty — 10
6. Methodological Issues of the Relationship of Adjustment and Poverty — 13
7. Summary — 17

2 ADJUSTMENT POLICIES IN MEXICO — 20

1. **Background to the 1982 Economic Crisis** — 20
   1.1 Evolution Before 1982 — 20
   1.2 The 1982 Debt Crisis — 22
2. **The Mexican Economic Reform 1982-1994** — 24
   2.1 The Stabilisation Period (1982-1985) — 24
   2.2 The Structural Adjustment Period (1986-1994) — 26
3. **The Impact of Adjustment Policies on Poverty** — 29
   3.1 Debt Renegotiations and Social Spending — 30
   3.2 Reduction of Subsidies — 35
   3.3 Prices of Public Sector Goods and Services — 42
   3.4 Tax Reform — 43
   3.5 Poverty Alleviation Programmes — 43
   3.6 Wage Controls — 45

4	**Summary**	48

3 POVERTY AND HOUSEHOLD LIVING STANDARDS — 53

1	Introduction	53
2	Problems of Data Sources Used to Measure Poverty	54
3	Methods Used in Mexico to Measure Poverty	60
4	The Measurement of Poverty in Mexico	62
	4.1 The INEGI-CEPAL Study	62
	4.2 The COPLAMAR Study	65
	4.3 The Integrated Poverty Measurement Method (IPMM)	68
5	Trends in Poverty in Mexico after the 1982 Economic Crisis	69
6	Improvement in Some Wellbeing Indicators	75
	6.1 Health Related Indices	75
	6.2 Education	80
	6.3 Housing	81
	6.4 The Paradox: Income Poverty Increases and UBN Poverty Decreases	82
7	Poverty and Living Conditions in Mexico City	84
	7.1 Evidence from Partial Surveys or Micro-Social Studies	84
	7.2 Evidence from Representative Household and Expenditure Surveys	86
8	Changes in Household Living Conditions in Xalpa, Mexico City	93
	8.1 Public Services and Dwelling Improvements	95
	8.2 Household Appliances	98
	8.3 Social Life	101
	8.4 Household Borrowing Capacity	103
	8.5 Education	103
9	Summary	105

4 LABOUR FORCE PARTICIPATION TRENDS (1979-1994) — 115

1	Introduction	115
2	Employment Data Sources and Employment Definitions	116
	2.1 Population Censuses	116

	2.2 Employment Surveys (ECSO, ENE, and ENEU)	118
	2.3 Other Sources to Measure Employment	122
3	**Labour Force Participation Rates I (Employment Surveys)**	124
	3.1 Mexico	124
	3.2 Mexico City	127
4	**Women's Work**	131
5	**Work by Adolescents**	138
6	**Labour Force Participation Rates II (Income and Expenditure Surveys)**	141
	6.1 Mexico	141
	6.2 Mexico City	148
7	**Interaction Between Income Poverty and Working Effort**	151
8	**Summary**	158
	Appendix 1. The Labour Survival Strategies	169
	1. The Counter-Cyclical Nature of the Labour Survival Strategies	170
	2. The Social Sectors that Responded with LSS	173
	3. Young and Women Actors of Survival Strategies	176
	4. The Limits to the Labour Survival Strategies	177
	5. Concluding Remarks	179
	Appendix 2. Employment Data	182

5	**LABOUR MARKETS IN MEXICO CITY AND XALPA**	190
1	**Employment by Occupational Categories in Mexico City**	190
	1.1 Salaried vs. Non-Salaried Employment	190
	1.2 Employment Structure by Economic Sector	199
2	**Xalpa: Household Members Participation in the Labour Markets**	209
3	**Summary**	217
	Appendix 1. Labour Force and Income Data for Mexico City	221

6 CONCLUSIONS 230

1 Introduction 230
2 Criticisms of the Washington Consensus and the Mexican Case 231
3 Stabilisation, Adjustment and Poverty 235
4 Poverty and the Labour Market 238

APPENDIX: THE METHODOLOGY FOR MEASURING POVERTY 245

1 The Integrated Poverty Measurement Method (IPMM) 245
2 The Poverty Line (PL) Method based on a Normative Basket of Essential Satisfiers (NBES) 249
3 Adjusting Household Income to National Accounts (NA) 251

Bibliography 255
Sources of Data 268

List of Figures

4.1 Mexico: Plausible net flows, given empirical results, 1984-1992   155

4.2 "Labour Survival Strategy Current of Thought" logical flows   156

List of Tables

1.1	Latin America and the Caribbean: Selected social indicators, 1970-1990	12
2.1	Mexico: Selected macroeconomic indicators (1970-1981)	21
2.2	Mexico: Growth rate of imports and exports (per cent) (1970-1981)	23
2.3	Mexico: Selected macroeconomic indicators (1982-1988)	25
2.4	Mexico: Total debt and interest payments (as per cent of GDP)	27
2.5	Mexico: Selected macroeconomic indicators (1989-1994)	28
2.6	Mexico: Social spending using different deflationary indices, 1982-1992 (thousands of pesos of 1980)	31
2.7	Educational resources, total and primary school, Mexico, 1977-1978 to 1994-1995	33
2.8	Mexico: Human and physical resources in public health care services. Rates of growth, 1981-1994	34
2.9	Mexico: Amount of subsidies on foodstuff products, 1983-1989 (billions of pesos of 1983)	36
2.10	Mexico: E- and F-mistakes in targeted tortilla programme (per cent)	41
2.11	Mexico: Minimum wage, average earnings and private consumption, 1981-1994 (1981=100)	46
2.12	Mexico: Gini index of monetary and total income, 1977-1994	48
3.1	Operational definitions of rural/urban for sample design in 1984, 1989, 1992, 1994 and 1996 ENIGHs	55
3.2	Evolution of rural and urban population according to ENIGHs	57
3.3	Functional distribution of income in ENIGH surveys and in National Accounts (per cent)	60
3.4	Mexico: Different poverty estimates	72
3.5	Mexico: Selected wellbeing indicators, 1970-1994	76
3.6	Mexico City: Consumption of proteins and calories per capita, June 1985 and February 1988	78

List of Tables   xi

3.7	Poverty incidence in Mexico and Mexico City. Integrated Poverty Measurement Method (IPMM), 1984, 1989 and 1992	89
3.8	IPMM poverty decomposition. Mexico City, 1984, 1989, 1992. Average deprivation gaps	90
3.9	Xalpa: Household socio-economic characteristics by income strata	93
3.10	Household demographic characteristics	95
3.11	Period at which dwelling improvements were carried out (per cent of all dwellings)	97
3.12	Period at which furniture and household appliances were bought	99
3.13	Mexico: Selected household expenditure in urban (high density) areas, 1977, 1984, 1992 (per cent)	102
3.14	Educational level of household members	104
4.1	Mexico: Percentage of workers by position at work, 1979, 1991-1996	121
4.2	Mexico: Economically active population (EAP) and labour force participation rates (LFPR), 1979, 1991, 1993, 1995 and 1996	125
4.3	Mexico: Percentage of workers according to number of hours worked in the reference week, 1979-1996	127
4.4	Mexico City: Labour force participation rates, 1979-1994	128
4.5	Mexico City: Average number of hours worked in the reference week, 1979, 1986-1994	130
4.6	Mexico City: Labour force participation rates (LFPR) and equivalent LFPR, 1979, 1987-1993	131
4.7	Mexico: Employment growth rate by sex, 1980-1985, 1985-1988 and 1988-1993 (per cent)	133
4.8	Mexico City: Income per hour and employment growth rates by sex, 1986-1994	134
4.9	Mexico: Evolution of female and male participation rates and equivalent participation rates, 1979, 1991, 1993, 1995, 1996 (per cent)	136
4.10	Mexico City: Equivalent labour force participation rates by sex, 1979 and 1987-1993	137
4.11	Mexico: Monetary income per capita and earners per household by decile, 1977, 1984, 1989 and 1992	143
4.12	Mexico: Selected household demographic features, 1977, 1984, 1989, 1992, 1994 and 1996	144

4.13	Mexico City: Number of occupied members per household, 1977, 1989 and 1992	149
4.14	Changes in income of the household head, income per capita and household LFPR in a group of households of Mexico City, June 1985-February 1988	150
4.15	Mexico City: Time deprivation evolution, 1984, 1989 and 1992	152
4.16	Mexico: Time and income poverty matrix, 1984, 1989 and 1992. Percentage of population (H) and income-time poverty gap	153
4.17	Mexico City: Time and income poverty matrix, 1984, 1989 and 1992. Percentage of population (H) and income-time poverty gap	154
4.18	Identification of cells for tables 4.16 and 4.17	154
4.A.1	Mexico: Number of workers by employment categories and by sex, 1979-1993	182
4.A.2	Mexico: Employment rate of growth by employment categories and by sex, 1979-1993 (per cent)	183
4.A.3	Mexico: Labour force participation rate of the population of between 12 and 19 years of age, 1979-1991 (per cent)	184
4.A.4	Mexico: Percentage of workers by economic activity, 1979, 1991, 1993, 1995 and 1996	184
4.A.5	Mexico: Number of unpaid workers by economic activity and by sex, 1979, 1991, 1993, 1995 and 1996	185
4.A.6	Mexico: Unpaid workers rate of growth by economic activity and by sex, 1979-1995 (per cent)	185
4.A.7	Mexico: Number of workers by number of hours worked in the reference week, 1979, 1991, 1993, 1995 and 1996	186
4.A.8	Mexico City: Economic active population and number of occupied workers by sex, 1979 and 1986-1994	187
4.A.9	Mexico City: Percentage of workers by number of hours worked in the reference week and by sex, 1979, 1986-1994	188
4.A.10	Mexico City: Average number of hours worked in the reference week. All workers. 1986, 1989, 1992-1994	188
4.A.11	Mexico City: Labour force participation rate by age and sex, 1979, 1987-1994	189
5.1	Mexico City: Percentage of workers by position at work and by sex, 1979, 1986-1994	191
5.2	Mexico City: Percentage of equivalent workers by position at work and by sex, 1986, 1989 and 1994	193

5.3	Mexico City: Income per hour by position at work and by sex, 1986-1994 (Pesos of 1994)	196
5.4	Mexico City: Income per hour growth rate by employment categories and by sex	197
5.5	Mexico: Percentage of workers by economic activity, 1979, 1991, 1993, 1995 and 1996	199
5.6	Mexico City: Percentage of workers by economic activity, 1979, 1986, 1989, 1992 and 1993	200
5.7	Mexico: Growth rate (per cent) of total and waged employment in specialised establishments by economic branch, 1980-1994	201
5.8	Xalpa: Percentage of workers according to the period at which they entered the labour market	210
5.9	Xalpa: Age at which household members entered the labour market	212
5.10	Xalpa: Educational level of workers according to the period at which household members entered the labour market	213
5.11	Xalpa: Educational level of household workers	214
5.12	Xalpa: Skill qualifications of household workers in 1995	215
5.13	Xalpa: Position of household members in the labour market in 1995	216
5.A.1	Mexico City: Percentage of workers by economic branch, 1979 and 1986-1993	221
5.A.2	Mexico City: Rate of growth in occupation by economic branch, 1979-1986, 1986-1994	222
5.A.3	Mexico City: Percentage of male workers by economic activity, 1986-1994 (per cent)	223
5.A.4	Mexico City: Employment growth rate of male workers by economic branch, 1986-1993 (per cent)	224
5.A.5	Mexico City: Percentage of female workers by economic activity, 1986-1994 (per cent)	225
5.A.6	Mexico City: Employment growth rate of female workers by economic branch 1986-1993 (per cent)	226
5.A.7	Mexico City: Average income per hour by economic activity and rate of growth, 1986-1994	227
5.A.8	Mexico City: Income per hour and employment growth rate of male workers by economic activity, 1986-1994	228
5.A.9	Mexico City: Income per hour and employment growth rate of female workers by economic activity, 1986-1994	229
M.1	Adjustment coefficients for income sources in the ENIGH surveys to make them equal to National Accounts estimates	252

List of Abbreviations

CENIET	Centro Nacional de Información y Estadística del Trabajo – National Centre for Employment Statistical Data
CEPAL	Comisión Económica para América Latina – Economic Commission for Latin America and the Caribbean
CONAPO	Consejo Nacional de Población – National Population Council
COPLAMAR	Coordinación General del Plan de Zonas Deprimidas y Grupos Marginados – General Coordination of the National Plan for Depressed Zones and Marginalized Groups
EA	Equivalent Adult
EAP	Economically Active Population
ECLAC	Economic Commission for Latin America and the Caribbean
ECSO	Encuesta Continua sobre Ocupación – Continued Occupational Survey
ELFPR	Equivalent Labour Force Participation Rate
ENE	Encuesta Nacional de Empleo – National Employment Survey
ENEU	Encuesta Nacional de Empleo Urbano – National Survey of Urban Employment
ENIGH	Encuesta Nacional de Ingresos y Gastos de los Hogares – Household Income and Expenditure National Survey
EPL	Extreme Poverty Line
EWT	Excess Working Time
HLFPR	Household Labour Force Participation Rate
ILO	International Labour Organisation
IMF	International Monetary Fund
IMSS	Instituto Mexicano del Seguro Social – Mexican Institute of Social Security
INCO	Instituto Nacional del Consumidor – National Consumer Institute
INEGI	Instituto Nacional de Estadística, Geografía e Informática – National Institute of Statistics, Geography and Informatics

List of Abbreviations xv

INNSZ	Instituto Nacional de Nutrición Salvador Zubirán – National Institute of Nutrition Salvador Zubirán
IPMM	Integrated Poverty Measurement Method
LFPR	Labour Force Participation Rate
LSS	Labour Survival Strategies
LSSCT	Labour Survival Strategies Current of Thought
MAMC	Metropolitan Area of Mexico City
NA	National Accounts
NBES	Normative Basket of Essential Satisfiers
OECD	Organisation of Economic Cooperation and Development
PL	Poverty Line
PNUD	Programa de Naciones Unidas para el Desarrollo – United Nations Development Project
SBSS	Standard Basket of Subsistence Satisfiers
SFB	Standard Food Basket
SPP	Secretaría de Programación y Presupuesto – Secretariat of Programming and Budget
STPS	Secretaría del Trabajo y Previsión Social – Secretariat of Labour and Social Welfare
UBN	Unsatisfied Basic Needs
UNDP	United Nations Development Project
YT	Income – Time

1 Structural Adjustment: an Overview

1. INTRODUCTION

The 1992 World Development Report estimated that the absolute number of poor increased by more than 100 million during the five-year period from 1985 to 1990 (World Bank, 1992:30). The increase in the number of poor during the 1980s took place in parallel with the implementation of structural adjustment reforms, especially in Sub-Saharan African countries and in many Latin American countries. The increase in poverty in the context of adjustment programmes has given rise to the question of whether or not these programmes were the cause of, or even a major contribution to, this increase in poverty.

The relationship between structural adjustment policies and the increase in poverty has become the subject of a vigorous policy debate. Some scholars have suggested that adjustments have had "social costs" in employment and in income losses (increasing the number of the working poor), as well as in regard to a deterioration of social indicators, such as school enrolment, nutrition and health (see Cornia, *et al.*, 1987 and Stewart, 1995). Other writers postulate that the results of structural adjustment policies have been generally encouraging, in the sense that adjustment has contributed to a more rapid GDP growth in many countries, and, consequently, the poor have benefited (see Please, 1996; and World Bank, 1995 and 1996a).

This book is concerned with the changes in the living conditions of the Mexican population and, in particular, of the population living in Mexico City, including a sample survey conducted in one of its poor neighbourhoods.[1] The period of analysis covers 1982 until 1994, that is, when stabilisation and structural adjustment policies were implemented in Mexico.

The present chapter discusses the almost universal process of structural adjustment implemented in many developing countries during the 1980s and the main arguments concerning the implications of that process for poverty and economic growth. I will also examine the main methodological problems involved in the measurement of the impact of adjustment policies on the economy and on poverty.

Chapter 2 presents the evolution of the Mexican economy in terms of growth during the period of stabilisation and adjustment, followed by a review of the main features of specific policy reforms carried out by the Mexican government between 1982 and 1994. It also discusses some of the most likely effects of policy reform on poverty in Mexico.

Chapter 3 analyses whether there is enough evidence to support the idea that poverty increased during the stabilisation and structural adjustment period. This chapter will also discuss the conceptual and methodological problems in defining and measuring poverty. I will begin by presenting the evidence on changes in the level of poverty as measured by income and other social indicators in Mexico and Mexico City. For Mexico City, I will examine the evolution of poverty according to the results obtained by my own calculations applying a new methodology to income and expenditure surveys.[2] The chapter ends with an analysis of the transformation in the living conditions of a group of poor households in Xalpa.

This book is also concerned with whether or not the economic changes generated by policy reform have modified the extent to which people are engaged in the labour market. In chapter 4 I will assess, both at the national level and for Mexico City, the arguments that contend that the increase in the labour force participation rate in Mexico during adjustment (particularly with respect to women and children) is explained by the deterioration in the living conditions of urban households in Mexico. In order to do this, I will introduce two methodological innovations. In the first place, participation rates are re-calculated by standardising the number of workers based on the hours worked. This is done both for Mexico and Mexico City. In the second place, based on the methodology used in chapter 3 to measure poverty, I will look at the interaction between income poverty and extra-domestic working time at the level of households in Mexico City.

Chapter 5 looks at another set of evidences, derived from the ENEU[3] survey databases for Mexico City and from my survey in Xalpa, to contrast the additional thesis propounded by scholars regarding the impact of the crises on the labour and the policies adopted to confront them. I will examine the growth in the proportions, for Mexico and Mexico City, of self-employed workers, of unpaid workers and of tertiary workers, which have been interpreted as symptoms of deterioration in living standards. According to some scholars, children's work, the abandonment of school as a result of involvement in work and a rising proportion of workers performing unskilled activities are among the negative symptoms which ensued the 1982 crisis. All such symptoms are examined for Xalpa.

Chapter 6 is the concluding chapter. In addition to summarising the main conclusions of my book, I will look at the growing body of criticism of the so-called Washington Consensus, which was the general framework that guided the implementation of structural adjustment policies.

2. STRUCTURAL ADJUSTMENT: THE END OF A NATIONAL ECONOMIC PROJECT

From the mid-1940s on, up until the 1970s, it was widely held that the abolishment of dependency in developing countries implied encouraging a process of industrialisation. Import substitution policies were seen as the means to achieve economic development.[4] The highly influential structuralist school of development theory postulated that free-market economies would lead to an "unequal exchange" between developed and underdeveloped countries. This unequal relationship, it was said, had been the result of a long-term trend of growing trade inequalities. It was argued that the monopoly of industrialised countries of the supply of manufactured goods, coupled with competition among developing countries, which drove down commodity prices, led to trade inequalities.

According to this view, in order to overcome underdevelopment, poor countries needed to foster industrialisation, among other measures, by deliberately protecting "infant" industries from foreign competition. To that end, governments had to impose "moderate" and "selective" protection practices and other types of government incentives (Prebisch, 1984:79). In other words, it was thought necessary to impose a strict control of the economic and political boundaries of the nation. This approach saw the State as the powerful economic agent, whose role was to dictate the shape and pattern of the economies of developing countries according to "national" priorities.

After 1945, the fostering of industrialisation became a major economic policy objective of governments in developing countries. At the same time, the prosperity of the post-war world economy offered a highly favourable environment for growth in the newly industrialised countries. Developing countries were able to adopt import substitution policies as the demand for their exports increased. The foreign exchange from exports enabled the developing countries to finance the imports that were needed to sustain the industrialisation process. Many developing countries achieved steady economic growth, with some of them achieving rates of growth of between 5 per cent and 10 per cent a year between 1950 and 1980.

The economic achievements in some developing countries were impressive. Certain governments were able to develop systems of welfare, education and health that protected an increasing number of workers. This process was embodied in the alliance of the government and some social groups (e.g., commercial agriculture, state bureaucracy, national capital devoted to expanding the country's industrial base, urban merchants, and the urban middle- and working-classes). In many cases, governments introduced public-assistance programmes in exchange for political loyalty, based on patron-client relationships (Walton and Seddon, 1994:49). Despite the economic success brought about by import substitution, by the late 1960s and the early 1970s this strategy had become exhausted and began to have a negative impact on economic efficiency.

Overvalued currencies made it almost impossible for developing countries to export manufactured goods. The availability of loans at low interest rates, to encourage industrial investment, in fact encouraged an overabundance of investment in capital-intensive industrial production, often with excess capacity. Excess capacity was observed in heavy industries (for the most part, built by governments), which require an optimum size of plant well beyond the size of the domestic market. As a result, heavy industries became technically obsolete and production became very costly. Other manufacturing industries also operate at an utilization rate far below their capacity, which much exceeded the potential demand of the domestic market. Limited competition, by excluding imports, led to monopoly pricing, to poor quality of local output and to stagnated local technology (Harris, 1990:127-128).

The world-wide economic recession of the 1970s forced some developing countries (as well as virtually all governments in developed countries) to institute or expand " ... programmes of reform both to reduce and reorganise the State domestically and open their economies to world market" (Harris, 1995:111). Even before this recession, there were early examples of economic reform in developing countries. This may be observed in Indonesia (1965) and in Chile (1973), where, following military coups, "authoritarian" governments introduced policies of stabilisation and radical economic restructuring along free-market lines.[5]

Despite the fact that other developing countries needed to adjust their economies, some governments, by keeping public spending up through greater borrowing, postponed economic reform. During the 1970s, with the support of external borrowing, many governments increased State intervention in the economy in order to sustain growth.[6] At the time, there was abundant financial liquidity, resulting from the surplus of funds available for loans built up by the oil producers. The need to recycle the so-called petrodollars gave rise to a new supply of international credit at low rates of interest. Governments in developing countries took advantage of a period of low interest rates by borrowing and investing more than normal (Little et al., 1993:29-34).

Additionally, governments in the developing world were advised by international financial organisations to increase public spending by means of borrowing. The World Bank (1981:13), based on a forecast of consistently strong commodity prices and low international interest rates, promoted huge syndicated loans to developing countries in order to offset the sharp reduction in the pace of growth in 1973-5. This enabled many developing countries to sustain high levels of economic growth during the 1970s, despite the severity of the worldwide crisis.

In Latin America, additional external indebtedness made it possible to prolong a process of import substitution that was already showing clear signs of exhaustion (ECLAC, 1992:30). By the end of the 1970s, many developing countries were running unsustainable current account deficits, a situation that was made worse (for oil importer countries) by the two OPEC oil shocks of 1973 and of 1979-80. Moreover, deflationary policies in industrial countries undermined the growth of exports of developing countries, and commodity prices fell significantly (Toye, 1995:3). This worsened the terms of trade for many of these countries. However, the OPEC oil shocks did not affect all developing countries in the same way. The shocks provided economic benefits for oil-exporting countries (e.g., Nigeria, and, later on, Mexico), which continued borrowing heavily in order to finance expansionary policies.

The period of abundant financial liquidity came to an end at the beginning of the 1980s. As part of the fight against inflationary pressures in the developed world, short-term interest rates were increased. Real interest rates rose from an average of 1.3 per cent in the period from 1973-1980 to an average of 5.9 per cent between 1980 and 1986. A high proportion of bank loans carried a floating interest rate, causing many debtors to face higher interest payments as well as higher oil prices. As a result, total external indebtedness increased sharply. The appreciation of the US dollar during the first half of the 1980s also had a negative effect on the external debt burden of developing countries, since an important percentage of such debts was undertaken in US dollars.

These developments precipitated the 1980s debt crisis, led by Mexico's default on debt repayment. Confidence in international lending was undermined and commercial banks virtually ceased all lending to developing countries. Current account deficits in most developing countries grew, and debt servicing mounted to very high levels, e.g., over 42 per cent of total exports in Latin American countries in 1983 (Stewart, 1995:2-5). The imbalance in the current account of the balance of payments, coupled with the lack of financing from commercial sources, led many countries to approach the International Monetary Fund (IMF) and the World Bank (WB) for rescue loans. However, new loans and debt rescheduling had policy conditions attached for the improvement of trade prospects and the reduction of public expenditure. According to Walton and Seddon (1994:17), in the Bank's view, while during the 1970s external financing had been used as a substitute for structural adjustment, it was now to be used to support structural adjustment.

At the time that the debt crisis surfaced, the economic policies of nationalism (such as import substitution) were under a growing challenge by the neoclassical school, the new orthodoxy. As protectionism and import substitution policies were the norm in highly indebted countries, the poor economic performance of these countries (and in particular of African countries) was attributed to State interventionist and protectionist practices (and, to a much lesser degree, to external factors).

Based on the economic success of Asian economies and on the criticism of the failure of internal policy strategies adopted in Sub-Saharan Africa, the new orthodoxy in aid postulated that regulations governing trade, industrial investment, money and credit, had been the causes of the poor economic performance of developing countries (Toye, 1995:7-8). It was said that State intervention was creating distorted prices, bottlenecks, and rigidities in the economy.[7] This school saw market-oriented economies and structural reform as conducive to economic growth and poverty reduction, whereby it was implicitly assumed that poor countries were not inherently different from rich ones, and that they were able to adjust in the same way that developed countries had done so (Toye, 1995:4-5).

Based on the idea that what prevented economic growth and increased poverty in many developing countries was bad policy and the wrong type of government intervention, the World Bank and the IMF designed stabilisation and structural adjustment policies. By the 1980s, the new orthodoxy postulated that little progress was possible as long as economic policies were governed by economic nationalism. Therefore, the policy package attempted to "depoliticise" the economy (i.e., to put an end to public discretion). The World Bank Report (1981) provided a new policy reform agenda to reduce government intervention in the economy. According to the Banks' view, there were many vested interests in import substitution, and the pressures of conflicting groups had an overbearing influence on government policy decision-making. Hence, policy reform became the principal aim of international aid.

The purposes of adjustment policies, according to the IMF/World Bank view, were to reduce imbalances in external payments and in the public budget, and to shift economic policies that were biased against exports. Policy-based lending was seen as an instrument to demolish those structures of policy which the World Bank blamed both for the increasing incidence of failures in its projects and for the widening gap in economic performance between the Far East and the rest of the developing world (Mosley, *et al.*, 1995:305).

3. THE WORLD BANK STRUCTURAL ADJUSTMENT PACKAGES

Structural reform programmes had two main components. On the one hand, stabilisation policies, which focused on the demand side of the economy, were designed to restore equilibrium in the short run, as a precondition for economic growth. The stabilisation policies were aimed at controlling inflationary trends and at correcting disequilibria in the balance of payments through expenditure-reducing policies. The key policy instruments with which the World Bank/IMF sought to achieve equilibrium were the following: the imposition of domestic credit ceilings and the adoption of a more flexible exchange-rate policy. On the other hand, structural adjustment policies, which concentrated on the supply side of the economy. The structural adjustment policies were aimed at improving the efficiency of resource allocation, at expanding output and at restoring economic growth in the longer term. Such policies involved a deliberate effort to adjust the economy in order to overcome the negative effects of internal and external shocks. The most common policy prescriptions were, and still are, the following: the liberalisation of imports and the promotion of exports, deregulation, privatisation, greater reliance on markets to set prices, reforms of the financial system, and the removal of obstacles to savings (Ajayi, 1995:55 and Krugmann, 1995:139).

Aside from macroeconomic stabilisation, another aim of structural adjustment was to reduce the intervention of the State in the economy, particularly in production and in financial activities. According to the Bank's view, the role of the State in the economy is to provide a framework for the facilitation of production and the promotion of efficient prices. Fiscal prudence, deregulation, privatisation, and free markets were seen as the appropriate economic policies for development.

It should be noted that there is a growing stream of criticism of the theoretical foundations and practical consequences of the IMF/World Bank policy reform package. For example, the IMF/World Bank approach overlooked the contribution of governments to the economic success in Asian countries (see Harris, 1990; Stewart, 1998; and Stiglitz, 1998). In the light of this criticism, the 1997 World Development Report recognised that "governments have helped to deliver substantial improvements in education and in health and in reducing social inequality" (World Bank, 1997: 1). The Bank's new perception of the role of the state is that it "is vital for the provision of the goods and services -and the rules and institutions -that allow markets to flourish and people to lead healthier happier lives. The state is central to economic and social development, not as a direct provider of growth, but as partner, catalyst, and facilitator" (Ibid).

Despite that the Bank's perception of the role of the state in economic and social development has changed, the 1998 World Bank Country Report on Mexico recommends the deepening of policy reform based on the original structural adjustment proposal. This important issue is broached in the closing chapter.

4. GOVERNMENT AND CONTROL OF ECONOMIC PROCESS

As noted, during the 1980s, the debt crisis forced governments committed to long-standing policies of economic nationalism (e.g. Mexico) to adjust their economies if they were to participate in the new economic order. Since then, questions have been raised regarding the capacity of governments to choose specific policy reforms. The question has also been raised as to what extent governments are able to prevent the deterioration in economic growth and welfare of the population or are able to decide which groups in the population are to carry the burden of adjustment.

Harris (1990:190) has asserted that governments may have a capacity for deliberate intervention; however, this would vary enormously depending on the economic power of the government (e.g., the Government of the United States vs. the Government of Mexico). This scholar has also asserted that governments may reverse economic reform, no matter how disastrous this may turn out to be economically; sometimes, from a political standpoint, the reversal of economic reform could be done in order to solicit votes (*Ibid.*: 191).[8]

However, in terms of the global system, governments have a limited capacity to intervene (Harris 1990:191).[9] The changes in worldwide economic conditions of the 1970s precipitated an almost universal trend of policy reforms. In the resulting new economic order, the power of governments to determine what happens in their domestic economies has decreased. Harris has explained that this situation is due to the fact that the changes in the world that impel economic adjustments are not under the control of governments. Policy reform became the response of the government to changes that have come about from the increasingly international integration of production and distribution of commodities, manufactured goods, and services, as well as from the integration of capital and financial markets, and, to a much more limited extent, of labour markets. These changes have undermined the old certainties of national policy. While economic nationalism offered a set of relatively clear criteria as to what the national interest was, the new order involved in this matter has become opaque (Harris, 1995:112-3). Therefore, Harris has suggested that, as external economic conditions change (e.g., international interest rates or commodity prices), governments are forced to attempt to adjust and readjust their domestic economies and public administration to the new external conditions. In this situation, governments appear to have the stark option of reform or collapse.

According to Harris, economic reforms are often precipitated by external shocks rather than adopted as considered choices (e.g., structural adjustment programmes). Furthermore, this situation disorients all policy-making based on the assumptions that governments have the power to control the destiny of their countries and that they are able to prevent a deterioration in economic growth and welfare of the population (*Ibid.*). Nonetheless, Stewart (1995:193) has asserted that, in the case of several developing countries, governments could have made choices during adjustment that may have resulted in offsetting any ill effects of adjustment on the poor. Similarly, Lustig (1992:6) has raised the question of whether the Mexican government could have implemented different policies to meet its balance-of-payments problems and to stem inflationary pressures without sacrificing so much in growth and in real wages.

Despite the consensus among scholars that an economic reform in developing countries was needed, because external circumstances made it almost impossible for them to continue with the previous inward-oriented economic model, Stewart (1998:40) has asserted that there are serious points in question as to who determines policies in the developing countries. Although apparently governments are free to adopt the policies of the Washington Consensus, as well as how far and how quickly they will go in certain aspects, the answer to the question of whether they are free to adopt alternative policy packages is no, unless they wish to become an international pariah.

5. ADJUSTMENT AND POVERTY

By the end of the 1980s, some studies showed a tendency for poverty to worsen under adjustment in developing countries which had received IMF and World Bank policy-based lending. Claims of such a worsening trend in developing countries were based on different factors: social expenditure cuts; the slowdown in progress on human indicators; a shrinking output; and mixed evidence concerning changes in income distribution. This situation fed a growing concern over the impact of adjustment on the poor. In popular opinion and among scholars in academic circles (for example, Cornia, *et al.*, 1987; Gahi, ed., 1991, and Stewart, 1995), macroeconomic policies have had a great responsibility in increasing poverty. In the case of Latin American countries, Stewart asserts that:

> [The] situation worsened markedly for the poor in Latin America during the 1980s, as a result of falling per capita incomes, deteriorating income distribution and reduced provision of social services. The cause of this deterioration was a deflationary macro-situation, which neither structural nor meso-policies did anything to offset. Indeed, both contributed to the situation, as the policies were associated with worsening income distribution, and the share of health and education in the budget and in GDP was reduced in most countries (Stewart, 1995:190).

It should be noted that although adjustment policies have been similar in essence, these programmes have not taken place in equal circumstances, nor are their effects on different countries the same.[10] The performance of developing countries that have adjusted their economies (whether with IMF/World Bank support or not) has been very different in terms of growth and poverty reduction. Countries that did not receive IMF/World Bank advice (because were not suffering debt problems) and that adjusted their economies in some degree were, among others, China, India, as well as several South and Southeast Asian countries. These countries were improving their historic growth rates, and some of them were succeeding in reducing poverty. In contrast, the economies of Sub-Saharan African countries and those of most Latin American countries were deteriorating (Mosley, *et al*, 1995:5). Moreover, Stewart (1995:167) has pointed out that the adverse effects on welfare that the last-mentioned countries suffered " ... occurred in both adjusting and non-adjusting countries."

Nonetheless, the effects of structural adjustment programmes may affect, regardless of income level, a wide cross-section of the population — national entrepreneurs, middle-class salaried employees, professionals in state-owned enterprises, public sector workers, students, and so on. The effects of adjustment may be positive or negative depending on where the different population groups were positioned in the economy before the adjustment.

In the adjustment process, part of the population may be exposed to declining incomes or increased unemployment, and, as external forces appear to force governments to reassess economic policies, the adjustment reforms are blamed for all manner of ills. As poverty appeared to increase during the adjustment period (particularly in Sub-Saharan African countries and in some Latin American countries) scholars, journalists, politicians, and popular opinion in debtor nations attributed significant responsibility for the observed increase in poverty to such programmes. The reduced or non-existent social support for the negative effects of such programmes prompted a reaction against internationalisation, and, therefore, to adjustment. This has been clearly illustrated by Walton and Seddon (1994:49-50):

> Crowds from Rio to Rabat crying "IMF, Get Out!" demanded a restoration of food and transportation subsidies, employment, and wages commensurate with inflation. Governments were blamed for sacrificing their own citizens in the interest of foreign banks.

According to the above-named scholars, this reaction may have been precipitated by the collapse of the patron-client arrangements that characterised the post-war period (particularly in Latin American countries). Walton and Seddon (1994:49) have asserted that "the debt crisis [and the subsequent implementation of structural adjustment] not only resulted in the elimination of artificially supported levels of domestic consumption (e.g. subsidies and overvalued exchange rates), but also in the abrogation of many of the customary guarantees such as housing, public employment, education, and health care." During the 1980s, restricted international financial credit and the decline of commodity prices forced many governments of developing countries to adjust their public budgets. This implied cuts in public investment and in current expenditures.[11]

Table 1.1. Latin America and the Caribbean: Selected social indicators, 1970-1990

Indicator	1970	1980	1990	1996
Illiterate population as percentage of population, aged fifteen and older	29.0	23.0	15.3	14[a]
Enrolment rates, aged six to eleven	71.0	82.3	87.3	91
Gross enrolment rates, secondary level	31.6	47.4	54.9	---
Population per physician	2 053	1 315	1 083	---
Percentage of the population with access to safe water	53.7	70.1	79.8	80.1[b]
Infant mortality rate	84.9	63.0	48.2	33.0
Life expectancy at birth	60.1	64.3	67.5	68.0[b]

Source: 1970-1990 ECLAC (1992: 35); 1994/6: World Bank (1996a) pp. xii and 226, and World Bank (1998b: 4.)
[a] 1995 data
[b] 1994 data

Existing evidence points to an increase of unemployment in Latin American countries and a decrease in minimum wages and in real wages in the formal sector (Stewart, 1995:177). Measured in terms of income, in most Latin American countries the net effect of "structural changes on the incidence of poverty in the 1980s was negative" (*Ibid.*:180).[12] The Economic Commission for Latin America and the Caribbean (ECLAC, 1995, table 10:145-6) has asserted that the percentage of poor households rose from 35 per cent in 1980 to 39 per cent in 1990. Stewart (1995:181) has suggested that the worsening poverty in most countries was due to stagnation with inequity. According to this author, in nine out of fourteen Latin American countries with available data, average per capita income fell and income distribution worsened.

Despite this evidence, some social indicators show an improvement in specific areas of welfare. For instance, life expectancy in Latin American countries grew by almost three years between 1980 and 1990, and infant mortality continued to decline at a fast pace (see table 1.1). However, these improvements had a slower pace of growth compared to that of previous decades.

Based on these figures, it is difficult to assess the precise influence of structural adjustment policies on poverty. It seems that there is a paradox regarding poverty. That is, at the same time that income declines other social indicators improve. Chapter 3 will discuss the economic conditions that have led to this apparent paradox and whether, during adjustment, poverty increased as measured by income and by other social indicators.

In the following section I will discuss the conceptual and methodological problems involved in determining whether or not an increase in poverty occurring in the course of the adoption of an adjustment policy is due to the programme or to other factors (Azam, 1995:101).

6. METHODOLOGICAL ISSUES OF THE RELATIONSHIP OF ADJUSTMENT AND POVERTY

Almost two decades after the introduction of structural adjustment policies, their appropriateness for overcoming the economic crises of developing countries remains as controversial as when these policies were first introduced. The transmission mechanisms by which structural adjustment policies might affect the welfare of the population are still in debate (Stewart, 1995; Thomas, 1993; Genberg, 1992; Bulmer-Thomas, 1996). According to Stewart (1995:210-1), over the adjustment period, stabilisation and adjustment policies were associated with worsening poverty as measured by income and also with a slowdown and some reversals in improvement in social indicators. By contrast, the World Bank (1995:85) has suggested that, over the past decade, adjusting countries have shown better growth records along with greater improvements in socio-economic indicators than those in non-adjusting countries.

Three methodological approaches have been developed in order to analyse the effects of adjustment on economic growth and on the living conditions of the population. The first, and most commonly used, is the "before and after" method. In this method, the performance of a set of economic indicators is compared before and after the introduction of the adjustment policies. The differences in the indicators are commonly attributed to the effects of the policy changes. The second is the "control group" approach. In this approach, the average performance of macroeconomic indicators of adjusting countries is compared with that of non-adjusting countries (i.e., "the control group"). The differences in the economic indicators are attributed to the adjustment programme. Basically, this method assumes that the macroeconomic behaviour of the non-adjusting countries ("the control group") reflects what would have happened in the absence of adjustment policies (Ajayi, 1995:61-62). Although both methods provide a useful description of what happened, it is difficult to determine whether changes in poverty or macroeconomic variables can be directly attributed to the implementation of the programme or to other exogenous factors.

The third method of measuring the impact of adjustment is based on the use of econometric models. In these models, an evaluation of the impact of structural adjustment policies on poverty is compared either with the impact of alternative trade policies or with the continuation of the previous economic regime. These counterfactual models project what might have happened to the economies of developing countries and labour markets had structural adjustment policies not been implemented (see Bourguignon and Morrison, 1992).

These methodologies have been challenged on several grounds. The criteria used in classifying "adjusting" and "non-adjusting" countries present serious difficulties. As a norm, the criterion to classify countries as "adjusting" or "non-adjusting" has been whether or not they have received World Bank support. However, the criterion does not include countries in which governments have carried out adjustment policies without WB support. As a result, the conclusions in the study of the effects of adjustment tend to be biased. Nelson (1992:225) has pointed out that during the 1980s private consumption in Asian countries that adjusted their economies without the intervention of the WB (dominated by the performance by China) grew more than 5 per cent a year. According to the above-mentioned author, since nearly half of the world's extremely poor live in South Asia, particularly noteworthy, among other examples, is India's considerable though undramatic economic growth during the 1980s.

Similar problems arise because the classification of countries based on whether the countries have accepted or received adjustment loans ignores the fact that there are substantial differences in the relative degrees and intensity to which structural adjustment has been carried out in each country. Some countries implemented a wide range of economic and political reforms, while others concentrated only on specific sectors of the economy. For instance, in the 1990 World Report on adjustment, Burkina Faso was classified as an "adjusting" country on the basis of a single fertiliser-sector loan in 1985 (Woodwar, 1992:204). As a result, countries that have implemented virtually no policy reform have been classified as "adjusting" countries.

In attempts that have been made to evaluate the outcome of adjustment, the criteria for the time period during which the evaluation should be undertaken is not apparent. This imposes difficulties in analysing the effects of adjustment, because the apparent failure or success of adjustment may depend on the time period of analysis. For example, the empirical analysis in the study of adjustment has been limited to the 1980s (e.g. Cornia, *et al.*, Stewart, 1995, Ghai, ed. 1991). However, the picture of economic growth and the alleviation of poverty is far less pessimistic if the data are extended into the 1990s. According to the World Bank (1996a: 129), while there seems to be an economic slowdown and an increase in poverty during the adjustment period,[13] policy changes have contributed to a resurgence of growth and have had a positive impact on poverty in the "post-adjustment" period. The Bank's report (World Bank, 1996a:54) on "adjusting" countries concludes that poverty declined in 23 out of 33 countries with available poverty data.

In the analysis of the effects of adjustment, the evidence relative to an increase in poverty has tended to be based on simple associations between broad measures of economic performance and social indicators, rather than on formal tests of particular transmission mechanisms. Some of these studies present time series through the 1980s of various components of the economic performance and of the welfare of low-income groups; however, the degree of reliability and accuracy of official data on which the conclusions are based poses serious problems. Moreover, few countries in the developing world have sufficiently detailed and timely data to provide empirical evidence to compare social indicators before and after structural adjustment. In some cases, data problems are extremely severe: for instance, Mosley (1995:73) has noted that no African country has a time series of even a headcount index of the number of people living in poverty for the 1980s. In the present case of Mexico, for instance, the nearest household income and expenditure survey conducted before the 1982 economic crisis is the 1977 survey, a year when the economy was undergoing an economic slowdown, prior to the oil boom (1978-1981).

In addition, studies of the impact of adjustment also encounter difficulties with regard to the quality of the data. There are some indicators of poverty alleviation that do not show up in production and growth figures, or which are not statistically enumerated. For instance, improvements in the supply or quality of the infrastructure, such as potable water, adequate nutrition, better shelter, and so on, are frequently poorly reported in national statistics (Whitehead, 1996:73). This may lead to an overestimation of the poverty level.

When analysing the experience of adjustment, it is difficult to differentiate the causes of increasing poverty, such as those arising from adjustment policies on the one hand and those arising from economic shocks (for example, falling commodity prices and rising interest rates), on the other. Therefore, it is difficult to know whether changes in the performance of macroeconomic variables can be directly attributed to the implementation of the programme or to another exogenous factor. Econometric models have been developed to estimate the impact of exogenous shocks, to take into account endogenous factors that affected the pre-programme performance of the economy of the country, and to adjust for the counterfactual policy approach that would have been followed in the absence of the programme (see World Bank 1990, and Elbadawi, *et al.*, 1992).

These models have been criticised in view of the fact that the outcome depends on the theoretical assumptions that underlie the simulation models, particularly when counterfactual effects are being assessed. It is difficult to assess what would have happened to the poor in the absence of adjustment programmes, even when the prevailing situation before the adjustment is known, given the changes in the non-programme determinants (World Bank, 1990:23). For example, in the 1990 World Bank report, the counterfactual model was based on the manner in which governments have responded to external shocks and to economic performance trends in the past. However, in this report, the period during which the policy equations were estimated is not specified. Even if the period were specified, it is impossible to analyse the policy responses of particular governments in each country, because the government in question may not have been in office long enough to provide the basis for modelling the policy equation. Moreover, government policy responses vary significantly according to political circumstances (Woodward, 1992:201). This approach has also been criticised because it is unable to assess the effects of a set of policies applied with different speeds, intensities and sequences (Thomas, 1993:9).

7. SUMMARY

In summation, after the debt crisis erupted, the approval of stabilisation and adjustment reforms by the IMF/World Bank became, and still is, a precondition for refinancing the debts of the developing countries. This, together with the increasing dependence on trade, financial support and investment resulting from the globalisation process, forced the governments of many developing countries to implement adjustment reforms. As a result, the governments of developing countries (as those of the developed countries had done so) began to dismantle trade and currency regulations as well as capital, finance, and, more recently, labour market regulations.

As poverty appeared to increase during the adjustment period, the issues of the social impact of structural adjustment have attracted a great deal of attention. Some scholars attribute significant responsibility to the stabilisation and adjustment programmes for the increase in poverty that has been observed in the last two decades. Claims have also been raised in terms of whether or not governments could have implemented different policy reforms that may have prevented a deterioration of the living conditions of the poor.

As noted before, governmental capacity to determine the shape of national economies has been undermined in the last three decades. As global integration develops, the supposedly autonomous national basis for production (upon which government policy seeks to act) tends to decline, and governments are increasingly required to respond to external signals. According to Stewart (1998:40) the policy reforms carried out in the 1980s (e.g. trade and financial liberalisation) made governments of developing countries increasingly dependent upon international trade, foreign investment, and loans. Therefore, at present, governments, which wish to continue to receive much-needed international investment and loans, have limited freedom to choose their economic policy. Nonetheless, as previously noted, there is a growing debate concerning the limited answers that the IMF/World Bank approach offers to different questions in development.[14]

Attempts have been made to consider the extent to which different social groups may be exposed to losses from adjustment. However, the idea that structural adjustment policies have increased poverty has been challenged on the grounds that there are several methodological difficulties in tracing the links between economic policies and changes in the welfare of the poor. In methodological terms, there has been a recognition of the problem of isolating the impact of structural adjustment from other factors (such as changes in the global economy, natural disasters, or social collapse of countries; e.g. draught, and civil wars). Moreover, there are several difficulties in defining the causal relationship between specific policy measures on particular income groups, individuals, and households. This is because, quite frequently, it is a combination of policy measures, rather than an isolated measure, which simultaneously affects both the economy and society.

The fact that most evidence shows a decline in income and an improvement in other social indicators (e.g. life expectancy and mortality) makes it difficult to draw any strong conclusion concerning the impact of policy reform. In chapter 2 I will present the main features of policy reform carried out in Mexico between 1982 and 1994. I will also attempt to explore the most likely effects of adjustment policy on poverty.

Notes

[1] The neighbourhood studied is called Xalpa. Naturally, it does not represent Mexico City but only represents itself. All conclusions should be referred only to the neighbourhood and do not necessarily apply to Mexico City as a whole or to the country. (For the methodology used in the Xalpa survey, see Damián, 1999, Methodological Appendix 1.)
[2] For the methodology used to measure poverty in Mexico City, see Methodological Appendix 1 (at the end of the book).
[3] ENEU (Encuesta Nacional de Empleo Urbano – National Survey of Urban Employment).
[4] However, in its origin import substitution was not a deliberate policy of industrialisation. Governments of Latin American countries were forced to adopt protectionist policies since the 1929-1933 Great Depression. This was because, as the US and European economies contracted, the demand for Latin American exports declined and capital inflows almost ceased. Most countries were obliged to cut imports

and to adopt measures to stimulate the production of consumer and intermediate goods internally (see Harris, 1990, chapter 1). In African countries protectionism was adopted in the aftermath of decolonisation, when most leaders believed that political independence could be consolidated only if they could preserve control over the economic forces (see Mosley, et al. 1995: chapter 1).

[5] These initiatives were later implemented by some countries, such as South Korea and Taiwan, and in Eastern Europe where, following the collapse of "socialist" states, democratic governments have also made economic reforms (*Ibid.*).

[6] For example, Brazil's cumulative debt increased from $12.6 billion in 1973 to $41 billion in 1978 (Harris, 1990:76).

[7] One of the main criticisms to the neoclassical approach to state intervention was pointed out by Harris (1990: 68), who asserts that "...[if] a neutral state is required to explain Hong Kong's growth (as the neoclassicists would have it), it does not explain the performance of [South Korea, Singapore and Taiwan], where there was consistent state intervention." He argues that the picture presented by the neoclassical school of the development of the "Gang of Four" omitted "... the decisive and discriminatory role of the state and the public sector, and placed all emphasis on changes in policy."

[8] For example, in the preparations for the 1994 presidential elections in Mexico, the government sustained the exchange rate in order to avoid a currency devaluation that might have damaged its position in the election results. As a result, the peso was overvalued, affecting the Mexican economy's terms of trade, a situation that contributed to the precipitation of the 1994 financial crisis.

[9] For instance, even when governments of the more developed countries tried to prevent the flotation of the dollar in 1971 they failed (*Ibid.*).

[10] Although adjustment policies have been blamed for the increase in poverty in Sub-Saharan African countries, the slowdown in their economies was felt before adjustment policies were introduced. Mosley, et al (1991:6, table, 1.2) shows that per capita GDP declined from 3.6 per cent between 1965 and 1973 to 0.3 per cent between 1973 and 1980.

[11] The Mexican government opted to make larger cuts in public investment than in current expenditure in order to avoid massive losses in employment (see table 2.6).

[12] Chapter 3 analyses the methodological problems of the measurement of poverty by means of income surveys.

[13] The adjustment period is dated from the beginning of the first loan to a year after the final disbursement (see World Bank 1996).

[14] For further discussion, refer to chapter 6 (Conclusions).

2 Adjustment Policies in Mexico

1. BACKGROUND TO THE 1982 ECONOMIC CRISIS

1.1. Evolution Before 1982

During the post-war economic boom, Mexico, like many other developing countries, was able to achieve high levels of economic growth. Between 1940 and 1970 economic growth in Mexico was impressive. Output grew at an annual rate of slightly more than 6 per cent during this period. On a per capita basis, this growth meant a rate of growth that exceeded 3 per cent (Hansen, 1971:41).[1]

In terms of welfare, the growth of the Mexican economy was almost equally impressive. Economic expansion led to improvements in the living conditions of the population as well as a reduction in the level of poverty. While at the beginning of the century the diet of the Mexican population was confined to corn, rice, and beans, by the 1960s it included considerable quantities of eggs, poultry, meat, fish, green vegetables and processed foods. The Mexican population increased their living standards by a substantial margin: shoes appeared on the feet of the urban poor and of the poor in the countryside, and bicycles became commonplace in rural areas where they had been a rarity (Vernon, 1963:93).

During the 1970s, while most of the world economies stagnated, expansionary policies in Mexico promoted an annual growth rate of more than 6 per cent between 1970 and 1976 (see table 2.1). In the first half of the 1970s, the government was concerned with what it perceived as high levels of unemployment.[2] As a result, the Echeverría administration (1970-1976) increased public expenditure and investment in order to sustain demand and to maintain employment. This caused the public sector deficit to raise from around 2 per cent of GDP in 1971 to 9.1 per cent in 1976.

The expenditure-led growth came to a halt in 1976, because of high levels of inflation and of large fiscal and current account deficits generated by expansionary policies. The anticipated currency devaluation led to capital outflow, and, in August 1976, after twenty-two years of total stability, the peso was devalued by 40 per cent against the dollar. In that year, GDP growth slowed to 2.1 per cent. According to some scholars, the serious economic and financial crisis of the mid-1970s evidenced the macro- and micro-economic costs of a growing government sector and of inward-directed industrialisation. Other scholars assert that during the 1970s the import substitution model was becoming exhausted. This was evidenced by the decline in the rate of industrial growth. The growth of industrial output decreased from an annual rate of 8.6 per cent between 1965 and 1970 to an annual rate of 5.9 per cent between 1970 and 1975 (Boltvinik and Hernández-Laos, 1981, table 2: 461). Other factors that were affecting the performance of the Mexican economy were the 1970s world-wide recession and the increase in oil prices in 1973-1974 (before Mexico's new huge oil reserves were found).

Table 2.1. Mexico: Selected macroeconomic indicators (1970-1981)

	1970-1976	1977	1978	1979	1980	1981
GDP growth rate (per cent)	6.5	3.4	8.3	9.2	8.3	8.0
Per capita GDP growth rate (per cent)	2.6	0.2	5.6	6.3	4.7	6.6
Public deficit as per cent GDP	-2.0	-6.9	-5.7	-6.8	-7.5	-14.1

Source: 1970-76, World Bank (1984), table 1:1; 1977-1981 own calculations based on World Bank (1987), table 2.1.5: 130.

Although these economic difficulties indicated that Mexico needed to adjust its economy, the discovery of huge oil reserves in the latter half of the 1970s postponed economic reform. Rather than implementing structural reforms, the government, expecting uninterrupted oil revenues (as did foreign banks), set in motion a massive fiscal expansion (Aspe, 1993:13). In 1978 the Mexican economy responded to the expansionary policies with an impressive economic growth of more than 8 per cent that year (see table 2.1). It should be pointed out that the economic growth experienced by the Mexican economy during the 1970s was accompanied by improvements in the living conditions of the population, which were reflected in a significant decline in the level of poverty. Income poverty declined from around 72.6 per cent in 1968 to less than 48.5 per cent in 1981 (Hernández Laos, 1992, table 3.2:108-9).[3]

1.2. The 1982 Debt Crisis

On the basis of its known oil reserves, Mexico accumulated a sizable external debt, borrowing at variable interest rates. The Mexican economy's external debt increase more than twofold, from US$ 29.3 billion in 1976 to US$ 78.2 billion in 1981 (World Bank, 1987, table 4:153). At the time, international financial organisations did not oppose large-scale commercial borrowing to sustain high economic growth. Even by 1981, it was widely held that oil and commodity prices would continue to rise. For instance, the World Bank projected high oil prices, stating that real oil prices were likely to increase in real terms by 3 per cent annually throughout the decade (World Bank, 1981:13).

The possibility of increasing financial resources from external borrowing lifted fiscal and foreign exchange constraints. Not bound by tight budgetary constraints, the government set the goal of spurring the growth of the Mexican economy by bolstering an active and dominant public sector. The López Portillo administration (1976-1982) devoted increasingly greater resources to purchasing private-sector firms, especially firms that were no longer economically viable. The extent of the expansionary policy is illustrated by the fact that parastatal firms in Mexico numbered less than 300 up to 1970; by 1982, however, their number had reached 1,155 (Aspe, 1993:181).

The Mexican government, by following such a strategy constructed a peculiarly rigid economic structure, one that was highly vulnerable to external shocks. On the one hand, dependency on oil exports increased sharply. Oil exports climbed steadily after 1976, reaching a high, as a percentage of the value of total Mexican exports, of 77.6 per cent in 1982. On the other hand, the expansion in oil exports facilitated an inflow of foreign exchange that led to maintaining an overvalued exchange rate, at the same time making non-oil exports almost impossible and imports cheap (Weintraub, 1996:44-45). The economic boom generated by oil exports also diverted manufactured goods to their consumption in the domestic market, causing the growth rate of exports of manufactured goods to plunge from 22.9 per cent in 1977 to 3.2 per cent in 1980 (see table 2.2).

Table 2.2. Mexico: Growth rate of imports and exports (per cent) (1970-1981)

	1970-1976*	1977	1978	1979	1980	1981
Exports growth rate	7.9	19.5	25.9	38.9	54.2	11.5
Oil exports	n.a.d.	84.2	79.5	113.2	163.2	39.6
Manufactured exports	n.a.d.	22.9	21.3	13.9	3.2	10.9
Imports growth rate	9.5	-13.0	34.3	47.7	53.8	31.1

Source: * World Bank (1984), table 1:1; 1977-1981 own calculations based on World Bank (1987), table 2.1.5:130.
n.a.d. No available data.

At the beginning of the 1980s, the unstable environment in the world economy and economic recession in developed countries led to rising international interest rates. Since Mexico's debt was mostly dollar dominated, with and an important percentage of it carrying a floating interest rate, the debt service doubled from US$6.1 billion in 1980 to US$11.1 billion in 1982 (World Bank, 1994b, table A4.1:29). This, coupled with a drop in oil prices between 1980 and 1982 (from US$ 33.2 a barrel to US$ 28), caused the public sector deficit to increase sharply. As tables 2.1 and 2.3 show, the public sector deficit rose from 7.5 per cent of GDP in 1980 to 14.1 per cent in 1981, further rising to 20 per cent in 1982. Of the total public sector deficit, interest payments accounted for 5.4 percentage points in 1982. All of these factors led to capital flight, owing to investors' fear of another balance-of-payments crisis and devaluation.[4]

During 1982, half of the public external debt required repayment or refinancing within twelve months; external creditors, however, refused to roll over Mexico's short term debt (World Bank, 1994a:16). The increased public sector deficit, combined with the reduction in earnings from oil, led to another liquidity crisis. In August 1982, the government announced a temporary suspension of payments on foreign debt service.

In an attempt to stabilise the economy, the Mexican government implemented a regime of full exchange-rate, thereby in effect regulating all foreign trade transactions. In addition, the government nationalized the Mexican banking system on the grounds that this measure was necessary to guarantee the repayment of the external debt of Mexican commercial banks. In 1982, inflation climbed to an annual rate of almost 100 per cent, external debt rose to US$ 86 billion (nearly 90 per cent of GDP), and real GDP declined by 0.6 per cent — in per capita terms, annual GDP growth declined by -2.6 per cent in that year. (See table 2.3.)

2. THE MEXICAN ECONOMIC REFORM 1982-1994

2.1. The Stabilisation Period (1982-1985)

The 1982 debt crisis forced the Mexican government to negotiate policy-based loans with the International Monetary Fund (IMF). On the basis of this credit, in that same year, the De la Madrid administration (1982-1988) set in motion the Immediate Programme for Economic Reordering (PIRE, for its Spanish acronym), designed to achieve a medium-term recovery. Since then and until 1985, there was a period where macroeconomic stabilisation seemed to have been the government's top priority.

During the stabilisation period (1982-1985), the government attempted to adjust the economic imbalance by reducing real public investment, cutting subsidies for basic foodstuffs, increasing energy prices, imposing controls on bank credit and on imports. During that period the peso was devalued several times.[5] The aim of these policies was to contain aggregate demand and the growth of imports (the impact of these policies on poverty will be discussed in section 3).

Despite the government's effort to restore economic growth, the performance of the Mexican economy during the period of stabilisation (1982-1985) was erratic. From 1982 to 1985, in response to government spending cuts (e.g., government investment decreased 16.4 per cent in 1982 and 14.0 per cent in 1983) and the adoption of a tight monetary policy, Mexico's annual rate of inflation was brought down from around 100 per cent to about 65 per cent. Despite the reduction in inflation, real GDP declined by –5.3 per cent in 1983, thereafter slightly recovering in 1984 and in 1985 (see table 2.3). Although GDP per capita recovered in the latter two years, it did not offset the losses observed between 1982 and 1983 (see table 2.3). In real terms, GDP per capita in 1985 was 4 per cent lower than the 1982 level.

The poor performance of the Mexican economy during the stabilisation period (1982-1985)[6] has been partially attributed to the huge growth in debt payments and to the suspension of the inflow of foreign investment. Aside from the policy-based loans received from the IMF, and later on from the World Bank, from 1983 to 1989 the government was unable to obtain any new, voluntary lending from commercial banks.[7] On the contrary, Mexico's debt burden represented, between 1982 and 1988, an annual net transfers abroad which totalled, on average, nearly 7 per cent of GDP. According to Pedro Aspe (1993:35), former secretary of finance (1988-1994), such transfers caused considerable problems for the macroeconomic management of the Mexican economy.

Table 2.3. Mexico: Selected macroeconomic indicators (1982-1988)

	1982	1983	1984	1985	1986	1987	1988
GDP growth rate (per cent)[a]	-0.6	-5.3	3.5	2.5	-3.6	1.8	1.3
GDP per capita growth rate (per cent)[a]	-2.6	-6.1	1.6	0.6	-5.7	-0.2	-0.8
GDP per capita (1982=100)	100	93.9	95.4	95.9	90.5	90.3	89.6
Public deficit as per cent GDP[b]	-19.9	-8.6	-8.5	-9.6	-16.0	-16.0	-12.5
Inflation[c]	98.9	80.8	59.2	63.2	105.7	159.2	51.7
Exports growth rate (per cent)[d]	-0.3	6.6	12.9	-7.0	-16.4	25.2	11.3
Oil exports	13.1	-2.8	3.6	-11.1	-57.3	36.8	-22.2
Manufactured exports	-10.2	51.9	22.1	-12.1	-7.3	34.6	18.0
Imports growth rate (per cent)[d]	-35.5	-29.0	29.7	12.9	8.2	9.6	42.8

Source: Own calculations based on: [a] Boltvinik (1998a), table 1:337, [b] World Bank (1994b), table A5.2:31; [c] INEGI, Statistical Database; [d] World Bank (1994b), table A3.1:21.

By 1985, the stabilisation policy reforms had clearly failed to restore economic growth. In that year, in order to reduce Mexico's dependency on oil, Mexican policymakers decided to adopt an outward-oriented strategy aimed at expanding and diversifying exports, in compliance with the recommendations advocated by the IMF and the World Bank.

2.2. The Structural Adjustment Period (1986-1994)

Officially, structural reform in Mexico began in 1985, the year when the De la Madrid administration announced that Mexico would initiate negotiations with a view to joining the General Agreement on Trade and Tariffs (GATT), in order to promote trade.[8] However, it was not until the collapse of oil prices in 1986[9] that manufactured exports began to increase. In that year, the Mexican government implemented economic measures directed at promoting exports (e.g. the adjustment of the real exchange rate). As a result, the share of oil in Mexico's total exports declined sharply, from 68.2 per cent of the total value of exports in 1985 to 39.3 per cent in 1986. In contrast, the value of exports of manufactured goods, which accounted for 29.7 per cent of total export value in 1985, climbed to 48.5 per cent in 1986 (Villarreal, 1997: table CV:554). The transformation in the composition of the value of exports was due to two main factors: on the one hand, currency devaluation increased non-oil exports from US$ 6.9 billion in 1985 to US$ 9.7 billion in 1986; on the other, the drop in oil prices led to a sharp reduction in the value of oil exports, from US$ 14.8 billion in 1985 to US$ 6.3 billion in 1986.

Despite the Mexican government's policy of promoting economic growth by shifting to an export-led development strategy, adverse internal and external conditions made it difficult to restore economic growth and to combat inflation. On the one hand, the government's objective to avoid balance-of-payments crises required successive nominal currency devaluations. This, in turn, affected the stability of domestic prices and fed inflation, so that, by 1986, annual inflation had increased to more than 100 per cent (see table 2.3). On the other hand, falling oil prices meant lower revenues for the government. This, coupled with the prevailing internal and external high interest rates, severely restricted private and public sector resources, affecting the level of investment (capital investment was 40 per cent lower in 1986 than in 1981).

Although trade liberalisation measures aimed at promoting exports were adopted starting in 1986, the structural adjustment policies failed to restore economic growth: in that year, GDP declined by 3.6 per cent. This situation was made worse by the collapse of the Mexican Stock Market in October 1987, which was affected by the fall of the New York Stock Exchange and other major international stock exchanges around the world. In 1987 GPD grew by 1.8 per cent; inflation, however, soared to nearly 160 per cent. These factors caused uncertainty, prompting intense capital flight. As a result, the government announced another major currency devaluation in November 1987.

In December 1987, the government and representatives of labour, peasant and business organisations signed the Pact for Economic Solidarity ("the Pacto"). This time, the government introduced a new "heterodox" stabilisation strategy, which combined public revenue policies with further trade liberalisation, exchange rate controls, and fiscal austerity. "The Pacto" contained radical measures aimed at modifying the role of the state in the economy and Mexico's economic interaction with the rest of the world.

In its earliest stage, the main objectives of "the Pacto" were to combat inflation[10] through price and wage controls,[11] to reduce the government's budget deficit through fiscal and macroeconomic adjustment,[12] and to restructure public debt payments. In later stages, the Pacto (since 1989 known as the Pact for Stability and Economic Growth) focused on deregulation and privatisation of state-owned enterprises,[13] and on trade and financial liberalisation.[14]

Table 2.4. Mexico: Total debt and interest payments (as per cent of GDP)

Year	Total debt	Interest payments
1987	82.1	6.2
1988	59.8	5.2
1989	46.9	4.7
1990	43.8	3.1
1991	40.4	2.9
1992	34.6	2.3
1993	33.2	2.0
1994	35.2	2.2

Source: World Bank, (1996, table-Mexico:314).

During the Salinas administration (1988-1994), the debt burden was reduced and the Mexican economy recovered gradually. Negotiations with international banks resulted in Mexico and its creditors agreeing to a financial package that reduced the level of net transfers abroad (the Brady

Plan). Debt service was gradually reduced: by 1994 it represented 2 per cent of GDP, compared to 6.2 per cent in 1987 (see table 2.4). Under the terms of this agreement, Mexico's external debt was decreased from 82.1 per cent of GDP in 1987 to 35 per cent in 1994.

Mexico's debt service was also reduced owing to the relaxation of the OECD countries of their monetary policies, which led to lower interest rates internationally. At the same time, private confidence increased in response to the government's commitment to policy reform (especially, the liberalisation of domestic markets, new legislation on foreign investment, and privatisation). The economy returned to a negative level of net transfers, receiving massive private capital inflows at an average annual amount of US$9 billion in the 1989-1990 period, and over US$20 billion per year in the 1991-1993 period (World Bank, 1994a:7).

Table 2.5. Mexico: Selected macroeconomic indicators (1989-1994)

	1989	1990	1991	1992	1993	1994
GDP growth rate (per cent)[a]	3.3	4.5	3.6	2.8	0.7	3.5
GDP per capita growth rate per cent)[b]	1.3	2.9	1.6	0.8	-1.3	1.4
GDP per capita (1982=100)	90.8	93.4	93.7	94.4	93.1	94.7
Public deficit as per cent GDP[c]	-5.6	-3.9	-1.6	0.6	-0.4	-0.1
Inflation[d]	19.7	29.9	18.8	11.9	8.0	7.1
Exports growth rate (per cent)[e]	15.2	15.0	5.6	7.6	12.3	17.3
Oil exports	17.4	28.3	-19.2	1.7	17.7	3.1
Manufactured exports	9.6	10.7	13.0	6.2	18.5	19.2
Imports growth rate[e]	24.3	21.5	17.4	21.7	5.2	21.4

Source: Own calculations based on: [a] World Bank (1994b), table A2.4:10; [b] Boltvinik (1998a), table 1:337; [c] World Bank (1994b), table A5.2:31; [d] INEGI, Statistical Database; [e] World Bank (1994b), table A3.1:21.

Having remained stagnant throughout the 1982-1988 period, output began to recover between 1989 and 1994 (see tables 2.3 and 2.4). However, despite the improvements in some macroeconomic variables during the period of 1988-1994, the overall balance of the adjustment period in terms of GDP appears to be negative. Although GDP in 1994 was, in real terms, 17.5 per cent higher than the 1982 level, GDP per capita was more than 5 per cent lower than the 1982 level (see table 2.5).

Moreover, the economic reforms implemented by the Mexican government were unable to prevent another financial crisis. In December 1994, the peso was devalued about 100 per cent and it was allowed to float freely against the dollar (Gould, 1996:29-32).[15] The inflow of foreign capital dropped from 7.8 per cent of GDP in 1994 to 0.2 per cent in 1995, with GDP declining by -6.5 per cent in that last year (Banco de Mexico, 1996:16-17).

In terms of real wages, stabilisation and adjustment also had a negative impact. According to official figures, between 1981 and 1994 there was a decline in the minimum wage of more than 60 per cent (see section 3.8 in this chapter). The decline in real wages, the increase in the price of public sector goods and services and the reduction of subsidies have been seen as factors, among other changes in the economic policy, which led to an increase in the level of poverty during stabilisation and adjustment. In the following section I will present some of the most common arguments concerning the impact of these particular economic reforms on poverty.

3. THE IMPACT OF ADJUSTMENT POLICIES ON POVERTY

In the latter half of the 1980s, adjustment reform came to be identified as the very source of the problems of poverty. While some scholars argue that structural adjustment policies harm the population in general and the poor in particular, neo-orthodox economists reject this view, since they believe that the correction of economic problems is crucial to the welfare of the poor.

These conflicting views cannot be resolved by merely looking at the facts. Available data documented that the effect of adjustment policies has depended on the particular features of national economies. A recent book that analyses the impact of policy reforms on income distribution and poverty in Latin America found that the effect of policy reform seems to be diverse across Latin American countries (see Bulmer-Thomas, 1996). FitzGerald (1996:50) gives examples of how poverty had a different performance in some Latin American countries that undertook policy reform. For example, in Mexico, despite a radical trade liberalisation, poverty increased. By contrast, in Colombia poverty declined though through a slower and more recent implementation of trade liberalisation. In

Brazil, which also experienced a slow implementation of this type of policy reform, there was a modest increase in poverty. According to FitzGerald, the impact of adjustment policy on poverty depends, to a considerable degree, on differences in the initial structure of a given economy, on export performance, and on macroeconomic management (FitzGerald, 1996:50).

As noted previously, the transmission mechanisms between adjustment policies and poverty are extremely complex and difficult to observe in practice. For instance, trade liberalisation policy may affect the poor variously as a result of changes in the relative prices of tradeables and non-tradeables, and depending on whether the poor consume and/or produce tradeable or non-tradeable goods. FitzGerald (1996:33) has suggested that export growth may raise the level of employment in the trade sector, and thus, in turn, in the non-trade sector. This author has pointed out that even if this policy led to lower real wages and higher employment, the net effect on poverty would be ambiguous, since, in the process, there may be some winners as well as some losers.

There are other policies that may have affected the poor. For instance, it has been argued that currency devaluation increased prices, with a resulting decline in real wages (Lustig, 1992:62). However, the possible impact of currency devaluation on the poor may depend on the nature of the consumption patterns of the poor. To the extent to which the poorest members of society consume imports (or to the extent in which imports are inputs to domestic production consumed by the poor), the consumption effect is likely to worsen the position of the poor. In what follows I will discuss how some of the stabilisation and structural reform may have affected the poor in Mexico.

3.1. Debt Renegotiations and Social Spending

Early stages of the adjustment package have been criticised because they gave priority to financing external debt service. According to Stewart (1995:173), the debt burden in Latin American countries restrained development by pre-empting resources that might have gone to the social sector, with a negative impact on the poor.[16] It should be pointed out that the poor may or may not be affected by social spending cuts depending on the characteristics of the reduction in expenditure. Genberg (1992:55) has suggested that if the cutback in public expenditure is concentrated on current spending, there might be a reduction in the supply of public services, affecting those who benefit from them. This may negatively affect the poor to the extent in which they have access to the supply of social services. Conversely, in reducing mainly capital expenditure, current services can be maintained, but to the detriment of future capacity.

It has been claimed that the enormous amount of resources devoted to debt service payments, particularly between 1983 and 1988, jeopardised social expenditures that protect the welfare of the poor in Mexico. Lustig, (1992:79) has argued that "[social] spending, comprising primarily expenditures on education and on health, contracted by 33.1 per cent between 1983 and 1988 ... [as a result] ... spending on education declined by 29.6 per cent, and spending on health by 23.3 per cent."

Table 2.6. Mexico: Social spending using different deflationary indices, 1982-1996 (thousands of pesos of 1980)

Year	Total social spending			Per capita social spending		
	Average public consumption index in education and in heath	National consumer price indices	GDP implicit indices	Average public consumption index in education and in heath	National consumer price indices	GDP implicit indices
1982	430.7	440.6	441.0	6.125	6.265	6.271
1983	415.5	289.9	308.2	5.768	4.025	4.279
1984	433.7	290.6	321.3	5.881	3.940	4.357
1985	463.6	307.1	341.7	6.143	4.069	4.528
1986	455.6	264.2	315.1	5.904	3.423	4.083
1987	435.7	259.3	299.3	5.526	3.289	3.796
1988	438.7	236.6	296.8	5.449	2.940	3.686
1989	470.7	263.5	311.5	5.728	3.207	3.791
1990	514.0	295.0	341.1	6.132	3.520	4.069
1991	575.0	361.2	421.3	6.727	4.227	4.929
1992	595.3	410.8	486.0	6.834	4.715	5.578
1993	602.6	452.6	536.7	6.790	5.100	6.046
1994	627.8	550.5	595.5	6.946	5.593	6.588

Source: Boltvinik (1999), table 7: 52.

Boltvinik (1999:49-52) has challenged these claims. This author suggests that the claims concerning a decline in social spending during stabilisation and adjustment are mistaken. The author has pointed out that this confusion arises from the use of an incorrect price index to adjust public spending figures. Boltvinik explains that the social spending budget has been deflated using the consumer price index or the implicit GDP deflator, instead of using a deflator covering the goods and services paid by the government to provide social services (e.g., wages). Using the correct price index, Boltvinik shows that after the 1982 economic crisis social spending did not decline as sharply as many experts have believed, and that, as table 2.6 shows, by 1984 it had recovered. In per capita terms, social spending declined during the 1980s; however, the decline was not as impressive. By using the average public consumption index in education and in health, per capita social spending declined by only 5.8 per cent in 1983; in contrast, by using other indexes the decline is higher than 30 per cent. In fact, by 1990 per capita social spending had recovered: indeed, by 1994, it was 13.4 per cent higher than in 1982 (see table 2.6). In this sense, total social spending increased 45.7 per cent between 1982 and 1994, whereas population grew 28.5 per cent in the same period. It follows that social spending per capita also grew.

Social expenditure was relatively protected during stabilisation and adjustment. Its proportion of GDP increased from around an average annual percentage of 6.8 per cent between 1982-1988, to 9.5 per cent in 1993. Moreover, the percentage of the public budget devoted to social expenditure also increased from 30.9 per cent in 1982 to 53.6 per cent in 1993 (Córdoba 1994:267). As we will see in the following section, the increase in social expenditure made it possible to sustain and in some areas improve the supply of governmental services.

3.1.1. Social Spending on Education

There is some evidence that supports the idea that there was no deterioration in the supply of this public service. For instance, between 1981 and 1996, the student-per-teacher ratio declined from 37.5 to 28.7, and the student-per-school ratio in primary schools from 196.4 to 157 (see table 2.7). It seems that improvements in the supply of educational services were a result not only of an increase in social expenditure in education, but also of a change in the demand for these services. According to Friedmann, *et al.* (1995:349) the improvements in the supply of educational services were due to a reduction in the birth rate experienced in Mexico since the mid-1970s. The lower birth rate has led to a reduced demand for some social services, such as primary education and pre- and postnatal care.

Table 2.7. Educational resources, total and primary school, Mexico, 1977-1978 to 1994-1995

	Total		Primary School		
Year	Students per teacher	Students per school	Students per teacher	Students per school	Free textbooks per students
1981-82	27.7	201.5	37.5	196.4	4.9
1982-83	27.1	194.9	36.6	195.4	5.2
1983-84	26.6	190.2	35.9	194.9	5.4
1984-85	25.6	188.5	34.8	199.8	5.4
1985-86	24.8	183.0	33.6	197.2	5.4
1986-87	24.2	172.0	32.8	187.3	4.9
1987-88	23.9	170.5	31.9	185.3	5.0
1988-89	23.3	165.3	31.3	180.2	4.8
1989-90	22.9	163.7	31.1	179.7	5.0
1990-91	22.5	156.9	30.5	175.0	5.1
1991-92	22.3	151.4	30.0	170.2	5.2
1992-93	22.0	149.6	29.5	169.2	5.0
1993-94	21.7	146.1	29.1	165.8	5.7
1994-95	21.3	140.8	28.7	158.7	9.0

Source: 1981-82 to 1984-85 Salinas de Gortari (1991:345, 346, 349), in Friedmann, et al., (1995), table 9.12:360; 1985-86 to 1994-95 Zedillo (1995:125 and 127).

Another indicator of improvements in the supply of education is reflected in an increase in the average years of schooling of the population aged 15 years and above. The number of years of schooling rose from 5.4 to 6.4 years between 1980 and 1990, increasing to 7.2 years in 1995.[17] The number of years of schooling increased at a slower pace between 1980 and 1990 than between 1990 and 1995. The improvements in the number of years of schooling may have had a positive impact on living conditions, since a better education is highly correlated with improvements in wage levels and in nutrition.

3.1.2. Social Spending on Health

During the stabilisation and adjustment periods, social spending on health in Mexico was protected. Towards the mid-1990s, particularly in 1994, public spending on health as a proportion of GDP surpassed the levels recorded prior to the economic crisis of the 1980s. Measured as a proportion of the government budget, in 1990 spending on health recorded its highest level compared with the previous twenty years (Langer and Lozano, 1996:335).

Table 2.8 shows that human and physical resources in health care services rose during stabilisation and adjustment. For instance, the number of doctors, nurses and the stock of medical equipment increased between 1981 and 1994. Although social spending on health was protected during stabilisation and adjustment, in some cases health resources per capita declined, mainly because the population covered by health care agencies grew faster than some health resources between 1981 and 1994. In table 2.8, it can be seen that the total population covered by health services grew annually by 3.7 per cent between 1981 and 1994; in contrast, the number of hospital beds grew by only 1.7 per cent annually, and the number of doctors by 3.2 per cent during the same period.

Table 2.8. Mexico: Human and physical resources in public health care services. Rates of growth, 1981-1994

	1981-1988	1988-1994	1981-1994
Health service coverage*	4.0	3.3	3.7
Doctors	2.9	3.5	3.2
Nurses	6.6	3.3	5.1
Hospital beds	1.3	2.2	1.7
X-rays rooms	6.3	3.2	4.9
Clinical test laboratories	1.5	4.1	2.7
Operating theatres	2.1	4.0	2.9

Source: Own calculations based on Boltvinik (1998a), tables 13.1, 13.2 and 13.3:374-9.
* Refers to the total population that may receive health care services by health agencies covering persons who either contribute or do not contribute to the social security system.

Between 1988 and 1991 some social groups (e.g., students and taxi drivers) were incorporated into the social security system. Such social groups may have improved their health conditions during the 1990s. Moreover, despite the decline in some of the indices of health resources per covered population, the growth in human and physical resources during stabilisation and adjustment increased the capacity of the health service system to cover a greater proportion of the population (see chapter 3). The increase in health resources may have had a positive impact on the living conditions of the population, inasmuch as some health indicators, such as infant mortality, fell, and life expectancy improved during adjustment (see chapter 3).

3.2. Reduction of Subsidies

The IMF/WB adjustment programmes entailed a reduction in public spending. Therefore, an important element of the policy on public finances in Mexico was the emphasis given to reducing expenditure. The government attempted to achieve fiscal balance through the realignment of prices of public sector goods (according to international prices), the reduction of subsidies (for example, on food, on transport, on piped water and on electricity), the privatisation of many state-run enterprises, and the introduction of changes in the tax structure.

The public sector deficit as a percentage of GDP was nearly 20 per cent in 1982; but, between 1983 and 1985, it fell to less than 10 per cent. However, the collapse of oil prices in 1986 caused the public sector deficit to rise to 16 per cent of GDP. It was not until 1989 that the public sector deficit substantially declined to 5.6 per cent of GDP; by 1994 it represented only 0.1 per cent. The sharp decline in the public sector deficit during the 1990s was due, on the one hand, to the fall in international interest rates and to the reduction of the debt burden as percentage of GDP, and, on the other, to the government's structural reform of public finances.[18]

With regard to poverty, the impact of the reduction in the budget deficit may be very different depending on whether social services and subsidies to the poor are cut or on whether indirect taxes are increased. In the following section I will analyse some of the most controversial policy reforms adopted during stabilisation, i.e. the reduction in subsidies and the increase in the prices and tariffs of public sector goods and services.

3.2.1. The Reduction of Subsidies

The elimination of subsidies as part of the government's new public finance policy had adverse inflationary consequences between 1985 and

1987, primarily because, as a result of efforts made to reduce public spending, subsidies were sharply cut, thereby increasing basic foodstuff prices considerably. In 1985 the government reduced subsidies by more than half (from $226.2 billions of Mexican pesos in 1984 to $94.5 billions of Mexican pesos in 1985). In 1986 the amount of subsidies on foodstuff products reached its lowest level — $33.5 billions of Mexican pesos (see table 2.9). Meanwhile, inflation soared from 63.2 per cent in 1985 to 105.7 per cent in 1986.

Table 2.9. Mexico: Amount of subsidies on foodstuff products, 1983-1989 (billions of pesos of 1983)

Subsidised products	1983	1984	1985	1986	1987	1988	1989
Maize	75.7	72.9	54.4	19.6	23.1	36.8	57.7
Sorghum	70.2	48.3	5.8	6.4	2.4	6.1	2.8
Beans	7.7	9.1	8.7	3.0	7.6	5.6	8.8
Wheat	30.0	38.2	25.6	0.0	1.6	7.1	18.2
Rice	0.0	0.0	0.0	0.9	6.7	3.5	2.7
Oil products	30.5	56.7	0.0	0.0	0.0	0.0	14.0
Milk powder	4.7	1.0	0.0	3.6	3.7	15.0	33.5
Total	218.8	226.2	94.5	33.5	45.1	74.1	137.7

Source: Martín del Campo and Calderón Tinoco (1993), table 12:112.

After the amount of subsidies on foodstuff was reduced to its lowest level in 1986, the government initiated a targeted subsidy tortilla programme. Moreover, subsidies were increased for other basic foodstuff products (e.g. beans, rice, and milk powder). As a result of this, the amount of subsidies devoted to foodstuffs began to increase in 1987 (see table 2.9). Nonetheless, the inflationary pressures continued: in that year, inflation reached nearly 160 per cent.

In 1988, a new stage of the Pacto was initiated. As part of the new Pacto strategy, in order to curb inflation, the government froze a set of key prices subject to price controls. Accordingly, the government saw the need to increase the amount of subsidies on some basic foodstuff products (maize, beans, milk, wheat, rice, and milk powder). According to Martín del Campo and Calderón (1993: 117-118), through the increase in subsidies, the government secured the supply of basic foodstuffs, and the poor did not suffer from the increases in basic food prices (only in the years that followed 1988). These authors argue that this strategy helped bring the level of inflation down from 160 per cent in 1987 to less than 20 per cent in 1989.

The reduction or elimination of subsidies may affect the poor to the extent to which they consume subsidised products (e.g. maize, beans, and rice). As table 2.9 shows, maize and sorghum concentrated a major proportion of total subsidies in 1983. If, on the one hand, the elimination of the subsidy on maize may negatively affect the poor (because the consumption of maize is clearly related to the consumption patterns of the poor in Mexico), on the other, the elimination of the subsidy on sorghum appears less clear in terms of its likely effect on the poor. However, it should be noted that the subsidy on sorghum prevents the increase of meat prices, and, therefore, the poor may benefit from subsidies on sorghum, allowing them to consume meat. In 1985 and 1986, subsidies on other products consumed by the poor were reduced (beans and wheat) and, in some cases, they were eliminated (wheat and oil products). This may have negatively affected the consumption of the poor. However, the effect of the changes in food subsidies on consumption and nutritional levels in Mexico has not been estimated.

The precise impact of the policy of reducing or eliminating subsidies on the living conditions of the poor, particularly with regard to nutrition, is difficult to assess. This is because changes in consumption patterns may be affected not only by food price variations, but also by other factors, for example, education. However, there is some indication that nutritional-related infant and child mortality increased during the stabilisation and adjustment periods (see chapter 3).[19] Moreover, it has been claimed that as the reduction in food subsidies came to be reflected in consumer prices, this affected the quantity and quality of food consumption in poor households (Lustig, 1992:87).

In a study on the impact of adjustment in Mexico City, the changes in food spending patterns of low-income families (see Instituto Nacional del Consumidor, 1989) were analysed.[20] Despite that this study did not intend to compare the consumption of traditionally subsidised products before and after the subsidies were reduced, data on family expenditure suggest that, between 1985 and 1988, there was an increase in family expenditure devoted to buy traditionally subsidised foodstuffs (e.g. maize tortilla, bread, beans, etc.). According to this study, as non-subsidised foodstuff prices increased (e.g. meat, chicken, eggs, milk, etc.), the amount of traditionally subsidised foodstuffs consumed by low-income families increased. Therefore, as the amount of subsidies on foodstuffs was reduced during adjustment, it seems that both the reduction in subsidies and the increase in other foodstuff prices negatively affected poor families. Apart from this study on Mexico City, there is no systematic study on whether the reduction in the amount of subsidies in Mexico was reflected in changes in the consumption patterns of the poor.

The reduction or elimination of general subsidies has been criticised on several grounds. As noted previously, the Mexican government redefined the subsidy policy going from a generalised subsidy scheme to a targeted one, on the grounds that a substantial portion of general food subsidies "leaked" to or benefited the non-poor. One of the main criticisms of the elimination of general price subsidies is that they were not replaced by targeted subsidies on a one-to-one basis, and, therefore, transfers received by poor families in the form of food subsidies may have declined (Lustig, 1992:87). Based on this proposition, it has been argued that the elimination of general subsidies may have had negative effects on welfare, particularly in the area of nutrition. As noted above, there is some indication that nutritional-related infant and child mortality increased during adjustment (see chapter 3).

There are other more general criticisms concerning targeted programmes. For example, Sen (1995) has criticised targeted programmes on the grounds of the various costs associated with targeting, including:

1) Informational manipulation, that is, "if the subsidy is aimed at the poor who are identified by some specific criterion of being counted as poor, those who would not satisfy that criterion could nevertheless pretend that they do by providing inaccurate information" (*Ibid.*:12).
2) Incentive distortion, that is, "targeted subsidies can also affect people's behaviour. For example, the prospect of losing the subsidy if one were to earn too much can be a deterrent to economic activities" (*Ibid.*:13).
3) Disutility and stigma, that is, "any system of subsidy that requires people to be identified as poor and that is seen as a special benefaction for those who cannot fend for themselves would tend to have some effects on their self-respect as well as on the respect accorded them by others ... there are also direct costs and losses involved in feeling –and in being– stigmatised" (*Ibid.*:13).

4) Administrative and invasive losses, "any system of targeting – except targeting through self-selection– involves discriminating awards in which some people (typically government officials) judge the applications made by the would-be recipients. The procedure can involve substantial administrative costs, ... No less important, losses of individual privacy and autonomy can be involved in the need for extensive disclosures" (*Ibid.*:13-14).

Stewart (1998:56), based on the evidence for many countries that implemented the IMF/World Bank targeting programmes, argues that targeted programmes have had the following shortcomings:

1) Discrimination against some of the poor because either they do not fulfil all the requirements to receive food subsidies or they do not approach the agencies responsible for giving economic support, although they have the characteristics of the target population.
2) Targeted programmes reduce the per capita social resources benefit.
3) Targeted programmes do not have political support since they exclude an important proportion of the population.

According to Stewart (1998:56), although people whose income is above the poverty line are benefited by general subsidies, this type of subsidies have a more progressive distribution than income distribution, and, at the same time, poor people obtain real benefits from them. According to Stewart (1998:56), despite that general subsidies may leak benefits to the "better off", the benefits received by the non-poor from general subsidies might be recovered by progressive taxation.

3.2.1.1. Targeted subsidies: the case of the tortilla programme. Between 1983 and 1987 the tortilla subsidy was reduced sharply, from $66.6 billions of pesos to $9.95 billions of pesos (see table 2.9). Martín del Campo and Calderón (1993:128) have argued that the reduction in the tortilla subsidy responded to efficient principles. These authors claim that, in terms of the main objective of subsidies — that is, to transfer income to poor households — general subsidies in Mexico were a very inefficient mechanism.

Based on an official study on general subsidies on tortilla, the above-name authors argue that, to the extent that general subsidies on tortilla benefited directly the production, rather than the consumption, of tortillas, there were three main efficiency problems: 1) a major proportion of the subsidy was concentrated on a few producers of maize flour; 2) part of the subsidised maize was distributed without knowing its final destiny; and 3) the subsidised tortillas were distributed by market mechanisms, rather than according to the particular needs of the poor. According to Martín del Campo and Calderón (1993:121), as a result of these problems, the number of benefited families (1.7 million) were only half the number that should have been benefited by this subsidy, taking into consideration the amount of money devoted to the subsidy on tortilla (*Ibid*.: 121).

However, as the Household Income and Expenditure survey shows, the proportion of family income spent by the population on maize tortilla, the most important subsidised product, exemplifies the relevance of subsidies for the poor in Mexico compared to the "better off". In 1994, the poorest 20 per cent of the population spent on tortilla 10 per cent of their total budget devoted to buy food, compared to 2.3 per cent spent by the richest 10 per cent of the population (own calculations based on INEGI, 1995). It should have become clear that the amount of money spent on tortilla by the poorest strata of the population in Mexico is relatively much higher than that spent by the "better off". Therefore, the subsidy on tortillas for the poorest is much more important than it is for the "better off". In the following section, I will present the Mexican experience of targeted subsidies on tortillas.

With the idea that general subsidies were leaking to (or benefiting) the "better off", the government began to replace a general subsidy to the production of tortilla with a targeted tortilla subsidy, in order to benefit directly the consumption of this product. After several failed attempts to implement a targeted subsidy programme on tortilla, the government implemented a programme in which the targeted population was reached through labour unions and government popular stores (CONASUPO)[21] located in poor urban areas. Through this programme, the number of benefited families increased 4.9 times between 1985 and 1989; however, the percentage of families benefited by this programme was relatively low. It has been estimated that in 1989 of the total number of targeted families (families whose income is up to 2.5 times the minimum wage) 40 per cent enjoyed this subsidy (Martín del Campo and Calderón Tinoco, 1993:124-126).

In an attempt to evaluate if the targeted subsidy on tortilla was a more efficient mechanism to reach the poor, Cornia and Stewart (1995: 82-84) have compared the efficiency of the general tortilla subsidy with the targeted one in Mexico. These authors measure two types of mistakes to which any intervention may be subject. The F-mistake refers to the programme's failing to reach the targeted population,[22] and the E-mistake refers to the mistake made when the intervention reaches the non-targeted population[23] (Ibid.:82-83).

Table 2.10. Mexico: E- and F-mistakes in targeted tortilla programme (per cent)

	Urban	Rural	Total
General subsidies on maize			
F-mistake	Very low	100	54
E-mistake (top three deciles)	39	0	----
Targeted subsidy on tortilla			
F-poor families*	73	100	88
F-poor pregnant/lactating women; children 0-12	75	100	90
E-mistake "better off"	40	0	----

Source: Stewart (1995), table 4.8:92.
* Families with incomes below 1.5 times the minimum wage.

As table 2.10 shows, both types of subsidy programmes (general and targeted ones) failed to cover the rural poor who account for an important proportion of the poor in the country. Therefore, the F-mistake in these areas is very high. In the same table, it can be seen that the switch to the targeted tortilla programme did not reduce the E-mistake, as the government had intended. In both cases, the percentage of the non-targeted population who received the subsidy was around 40 per cent. Moreover, the F-mistake in the targeted subsidy on tortilla was higher than it was when there was a general subsidy on maize. Through the targeted subsidy programme on tortilla 88 per cent of the targeted population did not receive the subsidy, as compared to 54 per cent of failure to reach the targeted population through general subsidies (see table 2.10). The increase in the F-mistake was due to the fact that the targeted tortilla programme failed to reach 73 per cent of the urban poor, while the general subsidy on maize covered the large majority of the urban poor.

Taking the above figures into consideration, it can be said that the urban poor were negatively affected by the progressive replacement of general subsidies on maize and maize flour with targeted subsidies on tortillas.

3.3. Prices of Public Sector Goods and Services

In addition to the reduction in foodstuff subsidies, there was an increase in the price of goods and services provided by the government, such as piped water, electricity, and public transport. There are no empirical studies in Mexico that give an account of how the increase in the price and tariffs of public sector goods and services affected the income of poor households during adjustment.

It has been suggested, that in some cases, the poor had, in any event, a limited degree of access to this type of goods and services before adjustment. For example, it has been said that piped-water subsidies in Mexico City mainly benefited businesses and the middle- and upper-classes, since poor households account for a lower share of water consumption. Moreover, in many instances, due to an insufficient or limited provision of infrastructure, the poor have to buy water from private vendors at much higher prices than those paid by the more affluent. For example, in 1991, in the richest neighbourhoods of Mexico City, water consumption averaged 600 litres per capita a day, whereas in the poorest, water consumption averaged 20 litres. Similarly, in urban areas where there was no piped water, people bought less than 500 litres for the same price paid for 50 cubic meters in urban areas supplied with adequate infrastructure (Damián, 1992:34-35).

Another example of an increase in prices and tariffs of public sector services during adjustment was the price of the ticket of the underground system (the Metro) in Mexico City. The price of a ticket for the underground system covered only one-third of its cost before adjustment, but during adjustment it was increased, according to Samaniego, in order to cover more adequately its cost. It is believed that the poor had limited access to the Metro, because this mode of public transport did not extend to the poorest areas of the city; consequently, the poor did not necessarily benefit from the subsidy of this public transport (Samaniego, 1996:61). Furthermore, because the poor generally live at a fair distance from the underground system, they have to use a more expensive transport system, together with the Metro. Therefore, the poor were negatively affected by the increases in the price ticket of the Metro. Additionally, as a result of increases in the price of gasoline, the price of using other modes of public transport also rose during adjustment, thereby also negatively affecting the poor.

3.4. Tax Reform

Another measure that allowed the government to reduce the public sector deficit was tax reform. In 1989, the tax system was simplified, and tax rates were reduced. The corporate tax rate was brought down from 42 per cent to 35 per cent, and the highest personal income tax rate was reduced from 50 per cent to 35 per cent (Gould, 1996:27). Tax revenues were also increased through improved administration in tax collection. In consequence, from 1988 to 1993, the number of registered taxpayer firms increased from 1.8 million to 5.6 million, and the number of registered taxpayer employees from 11.1 million to 14 million in the same period.[24] In the early 1990s, tax revenues increased nearly 30 per cent, principally as a result of the government's widening of the tax base in Mexico (Aspe, 1993:108).[25] Since the poor usually do not pay income taxes, this particular policy may not have had a direct impact on poverty. Nonetheless, it should be noted that, in 1992, the government decreased the Value Added Tax (IVA) from 15 per cent to 10 per cent, benefiting consumers in all strata.

  One tax reform that may have had a direct impact on the living conditions of the poorest strata of the population, which has not been analysed, is the implementation of a "negative" tax. As part of the tax reform, in 1993 the government instituted a progressive tax scheme, which benefited workers in the lowest wage brackets. Workers earning up to 3.1 times the minimum wage thus received an income transfer of around 10 per cent, instead of paying taxes (Boltvinik, 1998a:272). This policy benefited around eight to nine millions workers. However, it benefited only workers in the so-called "formal" sector.

3.5. Poverty Alleviation Programmes

As political reaction against adjustment increased, the World Bank promoted poverty alleviation programmes, making funds available through Emergency Social and Investment Funds. In 1988, the Mexican government set in motion a poverty alleviation programme known as the "National Solidarity Programme". The main objectives of this programme were: 1) to provide poor communities with basic infrastructure; 2) to provide assistance to small enterprises, and 3) to finance development projects in different regions of Mexico. The National Solidarity Programme encompassed most social programmes that already existed in Mexico, and it covered housing, health, education, nutrition, and infrastructure, among other areas. The National Solidarity Programme accounted for only a small proportion of social spending (6.4 per cent in 1990); however, in principle, this programme was based on a targeted scheme, instead of being a generalised programme (Trejo and Jones, coords., 1992:184-87).

There are some difficulties in evaluating the effectiveness of the National Solidarity Programme. For instance, although there is some information by state on the amount of money received from this programme, no data exists about the type of communities that received such funds, and whether or not the poor benefited from this programme. Moreover, the relevance of some projects financed by the National Solidarity Programme in terms of poverty alleviation is also in doubt. For example, Solidarity funded the construction of two highway infrastructure roads (in the states of Aguascalientes and Zacatecas) and a Mexico-U.S. border bridge (in the northern state of Nuevo León), allocated money to enlarge an airport (the Nueva Laguna Programme), and also provided resources for housing loans and for scholarships awarded to news reporters and their children (*Ibid.*).

In general, the effectiveness of poverty reduction programmes has been criticised on the grounds that the programmes are unable to change the economic conditions that affect the level of poverty. The National Solidarity Programme does not escape this criticism. Pánuco-Laguette and Székely (1996:209) have found that although this programme favoured the poorest states in Mexico (including Chiapas, Oaxaca and Guerrero), these poor states were the ones in which the most dramatic rise in poverty took place between 1989 and 1992. On the contrary, although a small share of the National Solidarity Programme was devoted to the Northeastern region of Mexico, there was a reduction of poverty in this area during the same period. This shows the narrow limitations of targeted poverty alleviation programmes in modifying the social and economic conditions that lead to the impoverishment of the population.

It can be said that income-distribution measures and poverty-reduction programmes may also be affected by competition for political office. The National Solidarity Programme has also been criticised on the grounds that the government used the programme to gain political support (see Molinar and Weldon, 1994).

3.6. Wage Controls

Wage controls have been the most controversial part of adjustment policies. As part of the strategy to curb inflation, the Mexican government adopted a policy of wage and price controls. The wage control policy included programmes that limited minimum and contractual wage increases.[26] Minimum and contractual wage increases were set according to the "expected" level of inflation for the following year. Nonetheless, as the inflation rate generally turned out to be higher than expected, wages set by this mechanism declined in real terms. According to Pedro Aspe (1993:18), finance minister during the Salinas administration (1988-1994), the aim of this policy was "... to avoid the massive company shutdowns and the uncontrollable growth of unemployment."

However, some authors have suggested that this policy placed an unnecessary burden on wage earners. For instance, Gould (1996:27) has argued that fiscal and monetary austerity is sufficient to stop inflation, whereupon wage controls are unnecessary.

To assess the impact of income policy on poverty, some authors have analysed changes in the level of the minimum wage. During the 1980s and 1990s the minimum wage declined. In 1994 the minimum wage had declined by more than 60 per cent, as compared with the minimum wage of 1981 (see table 2.11).[27]

There are some doubts about evaluating the exact cost of a revenues policy that uses minimum and contractual wage trends as a proxy for overall changes in real wages. This is because, on the one hand, data on contractual wages only take into consideration wages paid in the "formal" sector, omitting an important percentage of the labour force found in the "informal" sector, and because, on the other hand, the minimum wage is a legal category that represents neither the amount of money that workers receive, nor labour scarcity, and, therefore, this category does not account for actual changes in real wages. This can be exemplified by comparing the performance of the minimum wage with average earnings in the recorded sector (average earnings refers to all payments received by salaried workers).[28] Between 1982 and 1988 the minimum wage and average earnings declined; from 1989 onwards, however, average earnings increased and the minimum wage continued to decline (see table 2.11). Moreover, the minimum wage is not a reliable indicator of wage performance, since it may change for political purposes and, consequently, it may move in an opposite direction to labour scarcity.

Table 2.11. Mexico: Minimum wage, average earnings and private consumption, 1981-1994 (1981=100)

Year	Minimum wage[a]	Average earnings[b]	Per capita private consumption
1981	100.0	100.0	100.0
1982	97.7	94.0	95.7
1983	75.8	76.6	88.7
1984	71.0	75.7	89.8
1985	70.0	76.1	90.9
1986	64.1	74.0	86.8
1987	59.9	69.6	84.9
1988	52.7	66.4	84.8
1989	49.1	68.8	88.7
1990	44.1	69.1	92.7
1991	42.2	72.1	94.1
1992	40.1	77.2	95.4
1993	39.1	80.7	95.8
1994	39.2	n.a.d.	95.6

Source: Boltvinik (1998a), table 1:337, table 3:342 and table 4:348.
[a] Minimum wage for the Federal District.
[b] Total earnings divided by number of salaried occupations (see endnote 28).
n.a.d.: No available data.

In addition to the previously noted difficulties in considering the minimum wage for the evaluation of overall trends in real wages, it is important to note that the percentages of workers earning the minimum wage declined during the adjustment period. In 1980, of the total employed population, 34.4 per cent received up to one minimum wage, whereas this percentage dropped to 19 per cent in 1995. In urban areas, this percentage declined even further: in 1987, 30.6 per cent of the employed population in urban areas received up to one minimum wage; in 1994, however, this percentage had declined to 8.8 per cent (INEGI, 1997a:37-38).

With regard to the extent to which average earnings declined during adjustment, it can be seen that, although they did not decline as much as the minimum wage, average earnings in 1988 represented 66.4 per cent of the 1981 level. From 1989 on, despite that average earnings recovered, at the end of the adjustment period (1993) they were 20 per cent below the 1981 level (see table 2.11).

In order to exemplify the decline in average earnings, Boltvinik (1998a: 272-273) has compared the number of workers needed to buy the Standard Basket of Essential Satisfiers (SBES) for an average household (4.9 persons in 1982) in 1982 and in 1993.[29] In 1982, 1.75 household workers earning the average income were necessary in order to buy the SBES; in 1993, however, this number had increased to 2.2 workers. Moreover, it is important to note that while in 1982 the average household in Mexico comprised very nearly the number of workers needed to buy the SBES (1.5 workers per household, according to the 1984 ENIGH),[30] in 1993 this number was well bellow that number. According to the 1994 ENIGH, there were, on average, 1.7 workers per household, when 2.2 workers were needed in order to buy the SBES.

But consumption did not decline quite as much as wages. The decline in per capita private consumption was considerably less than the decline in average earnings. That is, consumption per capita dropped by 15.2 per cent between 1981 and 1988, whereas average earnings declined 33.6 per cent in the same period. From 1988 onwards, both began to recover, so that, by 1993, consumption per capita was 4.2 per cent below the 1981 level, whereas average earnings were 9.3 per cent below that level (see table 2.11). Despite that consumption did not decline as much as wages, it is important to note that this might be a result of changes in Mexico's income distribution structure, since the evidence suggests that income distribution worsened during stabilisation and adjustment Consequently, consumption for the poorest strata of the population may have dropped more than average per capita consumption. Table 2.12 shows that, although income distribution had improved between 1977 and 1984 (the Gini index went down from 0.526 to 0.477), by 1989 it worsened, nearly reaching the 1977 Gini level. Income distribution continued to deteriorate: by 1994 the Gini index had increased to 0.538 (see table 2.12).

Table 2.12. Mexico: Gini index of monetary and total income, 1977-1994

	1977	1984	1989	1992	1994
Per capita monetary income[a]	0.526	0.477	0.518	0.532	0.538
Monetary income[a]	0.496	0.456	0.490	0.509	0.514
Total income[b]	n.a.d.	0.429	0.469	0.475	0.477

Source: [a] Cortés (1997) table 2.12:52; and [b] Boltvinik (1998a) table 6:353.
n.a.d.: No available data.

There is some controversial evidence on employment trends that seems to contradict the idea of a decline in real wages, from the point of view of economic theory. Employment surveys indicate that during the 1980s the decline in real wages was accompanied by an increase in the level of employment, a proposition not normally accepted by economic theory. Most scholars have postulated that the increase in the level of employment took place because, as wages declined during the stabilisation and adjustment period, a greater number of household members were forced to participate in the labour market in order to offset income loses. However, as we will see in chapter 4, the evidence can be disputed on several grounds.

4. SUMMARY

During the 1940-1970 period, import substitution promoted economic growth in Mexico and, at the same time, living conditions improved. This occurred in a phase of development in which the state was able to propel economic growth. However, during the 1970s, in addition to the worldwide recession that had a negative impact on some developing countries, the import substitution model was showing signs of exhaustion. By the 1980s, the Mexican economy became highly dependent on oil exports and the rest of the economy was not internationally competitive. The decline in oil prices, combined with the increase in international interest rates and the subsequent debt crisis, forced the government to implement stabilisation and structural reforms.

One of the results of these stabilisation and structural reforms has been a radical economic transformation in which the state redefined its role and the economy became more open to international trade. Nonetheless, it took longer than expected for the economy to recover. During the period 1982-1988, internal and external circumstances were unfavourable to achieving economic recovery. The macroeconomic variables experienced a slow improvement, and, at times, their performance was negative.

It is difficult to determine whether any decline in economic growth was due to policy reform or to other factors, such as external shocks. For instance, in 1986 the reduction in the demand for oil from the industrialised countries and the subsequent fall in oil prices reduced public revenues in Mexico by an amount equivalent to the total value of agricultural production (Aspe, 1993:16).[31]

It was not until the period 1989-1994 that the Mexican economy experienced sustained economic growth. Nonetheless, it seems that GDP per capita did not recover the losses it had suffered during the 1980s. Moreover, at the end of 1994 the Mexican economy experienced another financial crisis.

There are some economic policies which are closely related to the welfare of the population — for instance, public spending. It has been argued that public spending was reduced, thereby negatively affecting the amount and quality of government social services. However, public spending on health and on education was protected during stabilisation and adjustment. Therefore, some social indicators (e.g. the number of years of schooling and life expectancy) improved.

By contrast, in an attempt to reduce the public sector deficit, the Mexican government implemented some economic policy measures which may have had a negative impact on the population: for example, the reduction of general subsidies and/or their replacement by targeted subsidies. The government's argument for reducing subsidies was that general subsidies were economically inefficient because, on the one hand, they did not reach the poorest sector of the population and, on the other, they leaked benefits to the "better off". Nonetheless, it has been found that, in the case of the tortilla subsidy, the replacement of the general subsidy by a targeted one not only did not improve the economic efficiency of the subsidy, but also increased the failure to reach the targeted population as compared with the general tortilla subsidy. This affected the urban poor in Mexico negatively.

In response to the growing criticism of the social costs of adjustment, poverty alleviation programmes began to be implemented in several adjusting countries. In Mexico the National Solidarity Programme aimed to compensate some of the losses suffered by the poor during the process of adjustment. However, there are some difficulties in evaluating its real impact since no available data exist at the level of communities in order to assess whether the poor benefited from this programme.

One of the most controversial economic policies followed by the Mexican government, wage controls, seems to have had a negative impact on the welfare of the population. Most of the evidence points toward a decline in real wages. However, no evidence exists on wages in the so-called informal sector, whereupon the general trend on wages is difficult to assess. Moreover, from the point of view of economic theory, as employment seems to have expanded during the 1980s and 1990s (see chapter 4), one would expected it to be associated with an improvement on wages, not the opposite. Nonetheless, if wages declined one would expect poverty to increase. Chapter 3 analyses the evidence on changes in the level of poverty. Chapter 4 will discuss whether employment has increased despite a decline in wages.

Notes

[1] For a detailed analysis of the Mexican economic performance during the period of import substitution, see Vernon, 1963; and Hansen, 1971.
[2] See Gregory, 1986.
[3] In the next chapter, the methodological difficulties of measuring poverty will be discussed.
[4] Capital flight out of the country reached US $11.6 billion in 1981 (Lustig, 1992:24).
[5] As noted in the Introductory chapter, the appropriateness of these policies to overcome developing countries' economic problems has been challenged (see Stewart, 1995 and 1998, and Stiglitz, 1998). For further discussion, refer to the Concluding chapter.
[6] Throughout the book I will refer to the stabilisation period, which covers the years from the end of 1982 to 1985.
[7] In August 1982, the government reached an agreement with the IMF, the US Treasury, and commercial banks to reschedule US$ 23.1 billion in pre-existing payments and to receive additional new funds of nearly US$ 13 billion (Gurría, 1996:97).
[8] This process was expanded through the North American Free Trade Agreement (NAFTA) with the United States and Canada in 1993. By then, the share of imports covered by import permits had fallen to less than 2 per cent, compared to 100 per cent in 1983 (Banco de México, 1993).
[9] The oil price in 1986 fell to US$10 dollars, against a budget figure of US$22 dollars.
[10] The effects of the "Pacto" on the level of inflation were felt since it was first introduced. While in 1987 inflation reached almost 160 per cent, in 1988 it had gone down to 51.7

per cent. At the end of the Salinas administration (1994) the inflation level was only 7 per cent (see table 2.3).

[11] The likely effect of wage controls on poverty will be discussed in section 3.8 of this chapter.

[12] The public sector decreased from more than 12 per cent of GDP in 1988 to 0.1 per cent in 1994 (see tables 2.3 and 2.4). The reduction of the public sector deficit was helped by the privatisation of state-owned enterprises.

[13] During the De la Madrid administration privatisation was concentrated in small enterprises; during the Salinas administration large public enterprises were privatised (including, eighteen commercial banks, airlines, the public telephone company, iron and steel works, sugar mills, and a substantial proportion of CONASUPO –stapler distributor (Aspe, 1993: 214-216).

[14] Trade liberalisation, coupled with currency devaluations, contributed to reducing Mexico's reliance on oil exports. The proportion of oil revenue in total export revenue was reduced from 77.6 per cent in 1982 to less than 20 per cent in 1994 (World Bank, 1994b, table A3.1:21).

[15] In the early 1990s the revaluation of the peso stimulated the use of imported inputs, which led to a large current account deficit. Moreover, during 1994 rising interest rates in the United States began to drain Mexican foreign reserves. The government changed the peso debt into dollars, with a higher interest rate than the prevailing one in the US. By the end of 1994 the debt in dollars was almost entirely short term and higher than foreign reserves (Boltvinik and Puyana, 1996:16). These events took place in a very uncertain political atmosphere. On December 20, 1994 under pressure from the foreign exchange market and dwindling foreign exchange reserves, Mexico abandoned its exchange rate band.

[16] Net transfers (i.e. net lending minus interest payments) to developing countries became negative, undermining the already fragile economic conditions of these countries. In spite of attempts to reduce the debt burden, developing countries had a negative transfer of US$ 24 billion in 1986, compared with a positive transfer of US$ 29 billion in 1980. Latin American countries were the most affected by the reduction of the inflow of resources, with a decline of US$ 20 billion in that year, compared to US$ 4 billion in Africa (Stewart, 1995:5). Latin American transfer of resources abroad represented almost 4 per cent of GDP during the period 1983-1985.

[17] For 1980 and 1990 National Population Censuses; for 1995 INEGI, 1997.

[18] An important element of the public deficit reduction was the privatisation of state-owned enterprises, particularly in the first half of the 1990s. For instance, revenues from privatisation represented 3.83 per cent of GDP in 1991 (Aspe, 1993, table 4.7:219).

[19] It should be noted that, although nutritional problems for children appeared to increase, it is difficult to assess whether or not this has resulted from changes in the classification of causes of death.

[20] The INCO (Instituto Nacional del Consumidor –National Consumer Institute, 1989) study is based on a non-representative survey of low-income families (low-income families were defined as those whose income was below 3.5 the minimum wage). Therefore, the result should be taken with care. (For further discussion on the representativeness problems of this survey, refer to chapter 3).

[21] National Popular Subsistence Corporation – Compañía Nacional de Subsistencia Populares.

[22] F-mistake measures the proportion of the targeted population, who does not receive the subsidy.

23 E-mistake estimates, in this case, the money cost of the excess coverage, as proportion of the total money value of the subsidy (Cornia and Stewart, 1995:83-84).
24 It is not clear in which proportion firms and employees registered in the tax system between 1988 and 1993 were new registered taxpayers or had for some years been evading tax payments.
25 According to Valdés-Ugalde (1996), fiscal adjustment increased tax revenues by 217 per cent in the period between 1988 and 1993.
26 Contractual wages are those which are agreed to by employers and unions, and which have official approval.
27 Contractual wages also shrunk by more than 50 per cent between 1982 and 1991 (Aspe, 1993, table 1 6:19).
28 Average earnings refer to total earnings received by salaried workers divided by the number of salaried employment registered in National Accounts. Total earnings include all payments in money and in kind (e.g. foodstuff, housing, etc.) received by salaried workers, as well as all economic contribution to the social security system effected by employers (INEGI, 1997a:10). However, average earnings do not include some of the self-employed workers, and therefore, a considerable proportion of workers are not included. According to Boltvinik (1998a:262) another difficulty of these figures is that they include lay-off severance and compensations, and, therefore, as more firms closed down, there may have been an apparent improvement in average earnings between 1990 and 1994.
29 The SBES is a normative basket of goods and services (satisfiers) required to meet all basic needs. The SBES was defined for average households size (4.9 persons) for Mexico in 1982 (see Boltvinik, 1988a:305-327). For a general description of the SBES see COPLAMAR (1983), Annex 2. See also Methodological Appendix 1.
30 Household Income and Expenditure National Survey (Encuesta Nacional de Ingreso y Gasto de los Hogares –ENIGH).
31 According to Lustig (1993:36), in addition to the drop in oil prices, other factors that affected the economic growth of the Mexican economy in 1986 were the relaxation of the public sector deficit (which reached 16 per cent of GDP in that year), the suspension of financial support by the IMF in the mid-1985, and the earthquake in that same year.

3 Poverty and Household Living Standards

1. INTRODUCTION

Many scholars have stated that the 1982 economic crisis and the stabilisation and structural adjustment policies implemented by the Mexican government led to an impoverishment of the Mexican population. For instance, Lustig (1993:236) has argued that the adjustment may have left Mexico with an increasing number of poor households, and the poor worse off than before (see also Boltvinik, 1994c; and Cortés and Rubalcava, 1991).

Two perspectives with regard to the study of the impact of structural adjustment on poverty in Mexico can be distinguished. The first is a sociological/ anthropological approach, which focuses on gender and household survival strategies during adjustment (Benería, 1992; Tuirán, 1992; González de la Rocha, 1993; Chant, 1994). These studies give particular attention to changes in certain characteristics of the poor (e.g. labour force participation, housing, reproduction, etc.), which they attribute to policy reform (these studies will be discussed in the next Chapter).

The second perspective on poverty attempts to provide measurements of poverty at the national level, using different measuring methods and internationally accepted poverty indices.

In the previous Chapter I considered the impact of adjustment policies on those economic variables which might have an impact on living conditions of the population. In this Chapter I will discuss whether there is enough evidence to conclude that there was an increase in poverty *during* the period of stabilisation and adjustment policies. For this purpose, I start by considering the problems of the national household income and expenditure surveys (ENIGHs), the main source for poverty measurement, and the possible implications this might have in the results (section 2). Section 3 describes the concepts and methodologies applied in defining and measuring poverty in Mexico. Section 4 looks critically at what might be considered the three most important poverty measurement studies carried out in Mexico. The empirical evidence at the national level will then be analysed in order to assess changes in poverty. Section 5 looks at available studies, which are mainly income poverty studies, while section 6 looks at the evidence on the satisfaction of some basic needs (health, education, housing). Section 7 deals with the evolution of poverty in Mexico City. It starts reviewing social micro-studies. It then presents the results of a poverty measurement exercise that was carried out for this book, in which the Integrated Poverty Measurement Method (IPMM) is applied to the data for Mexico City in three national household income and expenditure surveys. The chapter ends by presenting evidence on changes in household living conditions during the periods of stabilisation and adjustment in Xalpa, a working class neighbourhood of Mexico City.

2. PROBLEMS OF DATA SOURCES USED TO MEASURE POVERTY

There is no consensus among scholars about the trends in poverty during the 1980s and 1990s. Disagreements have emerged on three main issues: 1) the most appropriate measurement method; 2) the definition of the poverty threshold(s); and 3) the procedures used to adjust household income/consumption data from the surveys to attain consistency with National Accounts (NA).

Most of the poverty studies have based their analysis on the National Household Income and Expenditure Surveys (Encuestas Nacionales de Ingresos y Gastos de los Hogares-ENIGHs). These surveys, and similar ones which preceded them, have been carried out at irregular intervals of between two and seven years since the mid-1950s. The nearest ENIGH conducted before the economic crisis of 1982 is the 1977 ENIGH, and the nearest one after that is the 1984 ENIGH. During the period of structural adjustment covered by this book, three additional surveys were carried out: in 1989, 1992, and in 1994. These surveys have been used to measure the impact of the economic crisis on household income and consumption and, to a lesser degree, on household members' participation in the labour market.

Comparability problems between some ENIGHs arise due to changes in the definition of rural and urban populations (see table 3.1). This problem affects not only the urban and rural poverty results but also the national results in studies which make use of significantly different poverty thresholds for the rural and urban population (e.g. INEGI-CEPAL). The 1984 ENIGH considered high density *municipalities* (identified sometimes as urban) to be municipalities which had *at least one* of the following features: 1) one or more localities of 15 000 inhabitants or more, 2) a total population of more than 100 000 inhabitants; 3) a state capital; and 4) were part of a metropolitan area. The municipalities that did not have any of these characteristics were considered to be low-density areas (identified sometimes as rural). After classifying municipalities by rural/urban areas, the household sample was selected.

Table 3.1. Operational definitions of rural/urban for sample design in 1984, 1989, 1992, 1994 and 1996 ENIGHs

Concept	ENIGH 1984[a]	ENIGH 1989[a]	ENIGH 1992, 1994 and 1996[b]
High density or urban	**Municipalities with:** Metropolitan area or State capital, or locality of 15,000 or more inhabitants, or total population of 100,000 inhabitants or more.	**Housing Units in:** Metropolitan areas or State capitals, or in locality of 2,500 or more inhabitants, or in *municipality with a total population of 100,000 inhabitants or more.*	**Housing units in:** Localities of 2,500 inhabitants and more.
Low density or rural	**Municipalities** not fulfilling any of the above requirements.	**Housing units** not fulfilling any of the above requirements	**Housing units in** localities with less than 2,500 inhabitants.

Source: Own elaboration based on ENIGH publications, INEGI [a](1992c) and [b](1993a).

In the 1989 ENIGH there is a contradiction. The results of the 1989 ENIGH are presented by high and low density, defined in the glossary of terms in the publication providing such results (INEGI, 1992a) *almost identically* as in the 1984 ENIGH. However, the definitions are not identical. The publication notes the following exception of housing units that were classified as low density in the 1989 ENIGH: '[housing units in] the rural portion of 19 municipalities that are high density [a total population of 100,000 or more], but comply with the criteria of having only localities of less than 2,500 inhabitants and/or the land is used for agricultural purposes, or areas are in their natural forms' (p. 287). Chapter II in the methodological document of the same survey (INEGI, 1992b:28-29) repeats exactly the 1984 definition without the exception noted above. Nevertheless, chapter III, which deals with the sample design, presents a table (table 3:83) the sample design of both surveys. Table 3.1 summarises this comparison and also presents the definitions adopted in the 1992, 1994 and 1996 surveys.

As can be seen, the main contrast between the 1984 survey and the subsequent ones is that the 1984 survey sampled municipalities and the 1989 and later surveys sampled housing units. Additionally, in 1984 localities with 15,000 inhabitants or more were defined as urban, and in 1989 all localities with 2,500 inhabitants or more. Such changes in definitions clearly affected the distribution of the urban-rural population. Moreover, while the surveys of the nineties made a clear-cut distinction between housing units located in localities above and below the 2,500 threshold, the 1989 ENIGH adopted an ambiguous position, retaining one characteristic of the municipality (which has been highlighted in italics): its *total population*. Otherwise, the definition in the 1989 ENIGH, by including housing units in part of a state capital or of a Metropolitan Area, comes close to the definition of the nineties, which totally includes such sub-sets of housing units in the 2,500 or more set.

These definitional changes, combined with the problem of the obsolescence of the sample frame derived from population censuses, which is examined immediately, give rise to the absurd evolution of urban and rural population in Mexico depicted in table 3.2. As can be seen, and as was predictable, neither the rural/urban evolution during the 1984-1989 period nor that during the 1989-1992 period are coherent. In the 1984-1989 period the entire increase in population is classified as low density/rural. This is derived from the fact that in 1989, as opposed to 1984, not all of the population in municipalities classified as high density was classified as such, but only population living in localities that were larger than 2,500. This underestimates high-density population. But the real definition in 1989 must be far away from that adopted in 1992 and applied afterwards. Otherwise the contrast wouldn't be as sharp as it is. Between 1989 and 1992 the increase in "urban" population is 12.4 million, while the decrease in rural population is more than 7 million. The changes will bias completely the evolution of poverty for any procedure that defines significantly different thresholds between both areas. Although the 1992-1994 evolution looks as expected, with a small increase in the proportion of urban population, again the 1994-1996 evolution looks odd as this proportion decreases.

Table 3.2. Evolution of rural and urban population according to ENIGHs
(Millions of inhabitants and percentage of total population)

Year	National population	Urban / high density*	Rural/ low density*
1984	76.22	48.28 (63.3%)	27.95 (36.7%)
1989	79.14	48.92 (61.8%)	30.22 (38.2%)
1992	84.34	61.30 (72.7%)	23.04 (27.3%)
1994	89.81	65.61 (73.1%)	24.20 (26.9%)
1996	92.98	67.65 (72.8%)	25.32 (27.2%)

Source: INEGI, 1989a, 1992a, 1993a, 1995 and 1998.
* Percentages calculated based on data sources.

A second problem is the diminished usefulness of the sample frame as one gets away from a population census year (e.g. as one moves from 1984 to 1989), and this sample frame become old. A problem shared with all other surveys.

A third problem of the ENIGHs, which it shares with the employment surveys and with almost all surveys national in scope, is that their sample depends on the reliability of the Population Censuses, which has been challenged, particularly the 1980 National Population & Housing Census (see next chapter).

The data derived from the ENIGHs have an additional problem, whose nature is independent from the above-mentioned problems of urban/rural definition, of the obsolescence of sample frame and of the reliability of the National Population and Housing Censuses. This is the fact that total household income derived from the ENIGHs seems to underestimate, in great measure, real household income. According to Cortés (1997: table 4.21:135) this underestimation was 46.7 per cent in

1984, 42.7 per cent in 1989 and 38.7 per cent in 1992. In other words, total household income in ENIGH was 53.3 per cent, 57.3 per cent and 61.3 per cent of total estimated household income in National Accounts. There are at least three general sources for this underestimation. First, there is what can be called the demographic underestimation. To the extent that ENIGH underestimates the total number of households, and hence the total population, total household income would be underestimated. Second, the exclusion of the very rich households in the ENIGHs has been pointed out by Cortés (1997:133-142). This results from a double problem. On one hand, the real difficulty to interview very rich people, who tend to refuse to answer any survey but especially one dealing with their income and expenditures. On the other hand, there is a sample design problem. Households selected in the ENIGHs are taken to represent many other households with similar income/expenditures characteristics. The thing with the very rich is that they do not represent anybody, nor can they be represented by someone else. They are really unique. If this is correct, then the very rich should be selected with probability equal to 1. Third and last, interviewed people seem to underreport their income and their expenditure as well. This underreporting seems to be specially acute in a country like Mexico, where a very high proportion of the population evades taxes and is afraid of any relation the survey might have with the tax authority.

As a consequence, in the study of poverty, not only in Mexico but also in all Latin American countries, the issue of adjusting the survey data so that they become congruent with NA becomes a central one. In order to make the ENIGH figures more reliable and comparable between years, as the degree of underestimation is not fixed, most experts and institutions adjust the ENIGH household income figures to estimated National Accounts income figures (e.g. Hernández Laos, 1992; Boltvinik, 1994a; Friedmann, et al. 1995; INEGI-CEPAL, 1993; World Bank, 1993; Lustig and Székely, 1997).

Mexican National Accounts do not estimate household income. The variable most closely related to household income in National Accounts is private consumption. In order to estimate household income starting with private consumption, consumption by non-profit organisations must be subtracted (as they are included in private consumption figures), and then household savings have to be estimated and added to private consumption.

Naturally, adjusting income figures to NA is a procedure that implicitly assumes the reliability of NA data. This overlooks various problems of NA, amongst them the very likely fact that NA cannot identify some informal activities, thereby tending to underestimate household income as well. To the extent that this underestimation is present, evolution over time might be distorted also; in such cases, it might be possible that, as the unrecorded sector (or more precisely, those activities that NA does not capture) increases its share in economic activity, GDP and employment have been increasingly underestimated. This underestimation of production by the informal sector would have its counterpart in the underestimation of consumption by households. If we buy prepared food from a lady that knocks at my door, both her activity and part of my consumption (the value added by her activity) might not be recorded by National Accounts.

Another problem when adjusting income figures to NA is related to the coefficients used to adjust income data. For example, since self-employed income is registered as profits, the coefficient to adjust their income is the same used for entrepreneur income, and, therefore, self-employed income may be overestimated, thus underestimating the level of poverty (see Methodological Appendix 1).

The uneven underestimation of household income in the ENIGHs explains why evolution of household income looks different depending on whether income figures are adjusted or not to NA figures. While the NA record a decline in income per capita of 5.4 per cent between 1984 and 1989, the ENIGHs report an income increase of 20 per cent in the same period (Lustig and Székely, 1997:47). Therefore, measuring poverty with the ENIGH original raw data would result in a decline of poverty between 1984 and 1989, a proposition not normally accepted by most scholars and international organisations, as these were years of economic recession in Mexico.

Nevertheless, there are some scholars who do not adjust the ENIGHs income figures to National Accounts (e.g. Cortés, 1997; Pánuco-Laguette and Székely, 1996).[1] If ENIGH figures are not adjusted for under-reporting of income, it follows that poverty will be overestimated. This is because even the 1990 population census, which asked only one income question, reported 4 per cent more aggregated household monetary income than the expanded 1989 ENIGH (Cortés and Rubalcava, 1994:6). According to Pánuco-Laguette and Székely, (1996:192) the main discrepancies between the ENIGH and National Accounts are registered in entrepreneurial incomes and imputed rents, which appear to have increased disproportionately in the former. However, according to these authors, 'it is not possible to determine if the discrepancy is due to inaccuracies in the National Accounts or in the ENIGHs'. This is a very doubtful statement. If the discrepancies were small, one might doubt where the inaccuracies are, but, as table 3.3 shows, the ENIGHs provide a functional distribution of income that is a complete reversal from that provided by National Accounts. While in National Accounts wages and salaries represent around 30 per cent of current income, they represent around 60 per cent in the ENIGHs.

Table 3.3. Functional distribution of income in ENIGH surveys and in National Accounts (per cent)

Year/ Concept	1984 ENIGH	NA	1989 ENIGH	NA	1992 ENIGH	NA
Wages and salaries	61.4	30.0	58.6	28.2	60.5	30.4
Profits	24.9	51.0	24.1	56.1	22.3	54.5
Rental income	13.7	19.0	17.3	15.7	17.2	15.1
Total	100.0	100.0	100.0	100.0	100.0	100.0

Source: Cortés, 1997, table 4.24:139.

On the contrary, profits (which are called entrepreneurial rent in the ENIGH) represent more than 50 per cent of current income in National Accounts, while representing less than 25 per cent in the ENIGHs. But, on the other hand, wages and salaries in both sources give a similar total estimate (see Methodological Appendix 1). Thus, if there were to be inaccuracies in National Accounts with regard to profits, these would imply that National Accounts overestimate profits, something nobody has ever imagined being possible. Therefore, the conclusion Cortés (1997:139) arrives at is the correct one: 'the relative participation of income generated by independent activities, as entrepreneurs or as self-employed, are clearly underestimated in the ENIGHs'.

3. METHODS USED IN MEXICO TO MEASURE POVERTY

The methods generally used in Latin America to measure poverty are the Poverty Line (PL) and the Unsatisfied Basic Needs (UBN) methods. The mainstream approach in terms of the identification of poverty in Mexico bases its analysis on the PL method (see World Bank, 1993; CEPAL-PNUD, 1992; INEGI-CEPAL, 1993; Lustig and Székely, 1997). This approach is commonly known as the indirect method, which compares household income with a poverty line. The poor are considered to be households whose income per capita falls below the poverty line.

The main limitations of the PL method are the following: on the one hand, it assumes that the satisfaction of basic needs depends only on current private income or on current household consumption; and, on the other, it does not take into consideration other welfare sources such as dwelling assets, access to public services, and so on. The Unsatisfied Basic Needs method determines a group of specific needs (e.g. housing, access to public services, etc.) and classifies as poor such households in which one or more of these basic needs are unsatisfied. In this method, the selection of a household's basic needs usually depends on the available information provided by population censuses and household surveys. In practice, the indicators used are those referring to overcrowding, inadequate dwelling (in terms of building materials), inadequate water supply, lack of or inadequate sewage disposal system, non-attendance of minors at primary school, and, also, an indirect indicator of a household's economic capacity (normally this is built associating the educational level of the head of a household with the economic dependency rate) (Boltvinik, 1996:246). The variants of the UBN method which have been mostly applied in Mexico are those where the unit of observation is the municipality and not the household, and which results in the ranking of municipalities rather than in the identification of poverty (see CEPAL-PNUD, 1992, and CONAPO, 1993).

One of the main limitations of the usual applications of the UBN method in Latin America is that it selects indicators of need satisfaction that basically depend on the ownership of basic assets (e.g. dwelling) or on a household's access to public services (e.g. piped water), while implicitly failing to take into account other sources of welfare (current income, household savings or borrowing capacity, educational levels and available free time). One of the problems in applying the UBN method is that the number of poor people identified is not independent of the number of categories of the selected basic needs (Boltvinik, 1996:246). The UBN method shares with all normative poverty measurement methods the requirement that a threshold must be defined; in this case, however, the thresholds are multiple and complex.

4. THE MEASUREMENT OF POVERTY IN MEXICO

4.1. The INEGI-CEPAL Study

Some studies such as the INEGI-CEPAL (1993) define the poverty line through a Standard Food Basket (SFB) method (see also CEPAL-PNUD, 1992). The poverty line defined by this method is based, among other indicators, on observed diets; on household income and expenditure surveys; on recommended nutritional requirements in terms of age, weight, height, sex and type of activity; and, on a minimum income level (the cost of the standard food basket) required to acquire the quantities of foodstuffs that fulfil the recommended nutritional requirements. More specifically, the cost of the food basket is interpreted as the extreme poverty line (EPL). The extreme poor are considered to be households whose income falls below the cost of the EPL.

The biological approach, with which one is tempted to identify the INEGI-CEPAL and the UNDP-CEPAL studies,[2] has been criticised because it poses a number of problems. For example, when the minimum nutritional requirements are translated into minimum food consumption requirements, it is usually assumed that people's food habits, together with the relative prices and availability of goods, are the same for the whole population of a country or, at most, a distinction is sometimes drawn between the urban and rural areas.[3] As Sen (1984:12) has pointed out, the difficulties in the use of this method come from variations among countries in physical characteristics, in climatic conditions and in work habits, so that the "drawing" of a line somewhere and the setting of "minimum nutritional requirement" have 'an inherent arbitrariness that goes well beyond variations between groups and regions.' Furthermore, as Sen (1984:13) has also noted, the identification exercise under the nutritional approach does not need to go through the intermediary of income at all. Rather than undertaking an examination of a social group's income level, one can examine whether people are in fact meeting their nutritional requirements, thereby making it clear that the direct approach of measurement is always an alternative to the indirect one. However, in Mexico (as in most Latin American countries) the required nutritional data are scarce and not very reliable. (See below, section 6 in this chapter.)

The definition of the extreme poverty line can be criticised on the grounds of not taking into consideration other food-preparation and consumption expenditures (e.g. fuel, or kitchen utensils), neglecting completely non-food requirements. 'This is because food cannot be consumed without being prepared, for which at least fuel and a few kitchen utensils are required; because food is not consumed with one's hands straight from a saucepan, at least a few utensils are required to consume it; because nudity in public places is a punishable offence in all countries; and because without paying for transport it is impossible to get to work, to mention only the most obvious contradictions.' (Boltvinik, 1996:249).

With regard to the calculation of the poverty line, in these types of studies the social stratum that purchases a quantify of food that covers just above the minimum nutritional requirements is selected from a household income survey. The average income of this social stratum is taken as the extreme poverty line. In order to calculate the poverty line, the extreme poverty line is divided by the Engel's coefficient, that is, the proportion of household income spent on foodstuff, by this social group.[4]

This approach has been criticised on the grounds that, although it calculates in great detail the food basket cost, other consumption items (basic satisfiers) appear as a big black box (there is not even a list of the general categories to be included). There is an implicit assumption that households above the minimum nutritional requirement also fulfil the minimum thresholds for other basic needs, a proposition that, according to Boltvinik (1996:247), does not hold true. Several studies on poverty in Latin America have demonstrated that many households, while not poor in terms of nutritional needs, are indeed poor with respect to other basic needs measured by the UBN method (such as housing, public services, etc.) and vice-versa.

Furthermore, the INEGI-CEPAL (1993) report has been challenged on the grounds that on very *ad hoc* bases two different food baskets were used to measure poverty, one for 1984 and another one for 1989 and 1992. Although the same specifications for the calories and proteins requirements for the Mexican population were the point of departure, in defining the poverty line the composition of the food basket was modified for 1989 and 1992 (for instance, adding more cereals, including less meat). As a result of this, the cost of the food basket was cheaper in 1989 and 1992 than in 1984. In spite of the reduction in the cost of the basic food basket, the INEGI-CEPAL study reports an increase in poverty between 1984 and 1989. Boltvinik (1995a:18, and 33-35) maintains that the increase in the level of poverty was more dramatic than that reported by the INEGI-CEPAL study.

The INEGI-CEPAL study was confronted with the consequences of the changes of definition of urban/rural population (high/low density) applied in the ENIGHs to classify household data, as I have analysed above. As the INEGI-CEPAL methodology implies an urban (high density) poverty line which is much higher (in a proportion of 100 to 67) than the corresponding rural one, the resulting abrupt change in the composition of urban and rural population in 1992 — a larger urban population than that which would otherwise have resulted — would have implied an abrupt increase in the incidence of poverty. So a correction had to be made. But the one implemented by INEGI-CEPAL implies that the percentage of urban population in Mexico goes down from 61.8 per cent in 1989 to 59.2 per cent in 1992. This contradicts the urbanisation trends observed in Mexico in the last 15 years. According to President's Zedillo 1998 Report to the Congress (Zedillo, 1998, Annex, table on page 248), urban population (considered as those living in localities with 2,500 and more inhabitants) increased from 66.3 per cent in 1980, to 71.3 per cent in 1990 and to 73.5 per cent in 1995. As a result of the correction implemented by INEGI-CEPAL, the effect is the opposite: the reduction in the proportion of the urban population (i.e. the population whose income is affected by a higher poverty line) implies the reduction of poverty, given the lower poverty line used to classify a significant proportion of the formerly "urban" households as poor or non poor.

The INEGI-CEPAL study concluded that there had been a decrease in poverty, particularly in extreme poverty from 18.8 per cent to 16.1 per cent between 1989 and 1992. However, Boltvinik (1995a) argues that the decrease in poverty claimed by the government in the INEGI-CEPAL report resulted from the reclassification of the urban/rural population, which I have shown in the preceding paragraph, rather than from improvements in household income.

Another drawback of the INEGI-CEPAL study is the methodology followed to deflate income. In the ENIGHs, total income is composed of monetary income (i.e. salaries, profits) and non-monetary income (e.g. imputed rent for those who are owner-occupiers, gifts, etc.). According to Boltvinik (1995a:28), the INEGI-CEPAL report used a general consumer price index to deflate monetary income and non-monetary income. However, as the housing price index increased faster than the general consumer price index, the use of the latter index overestimates improvements in a household's real income, especially for the Mexican poor who are generally owner-occupiers. Therefore, the value of the imputed income from property rental, which is the most important component of non-monetary income, should be deflated by using the housing price index and not the general consumer price index (*Ibid.*).

Finally, another source of biased results in the INEGI-CEPAL report was a double accounting of gifts. This is because the ENIGH reported gifts received by households (as part of non-monetary income), but income spent on gifts given was not subtracted by INEGI-CEPAL. Therefore, the value of the gifts was counted twice, overestimating the household income levels (*Ibid.*).

4.2. The COPLAMAR Study[5]

Other studies on poverty in Mexico carried out during the 1980s and 1990s have based their analysis on the COPLAMAR study. Examples of studies that have based their analysis on the poverty line as defined by the COPLAMAR study are Hernández Laos, 1992; Boltvinik, 1994; Levy, 1994 and Pánuco-Laguette and Székely, 1996,[6] among others.

The COPLAMAR study is one of the very few carried out in Mexico before the 1982 economic crisis. This study is also one of the first studies to make use of both poverty measurement methods (the PL and UBN methods). A feature of the COPLAMAR study that specially distinguishes it from other studies on poverty in Mexico (e.g. ECLAC, 1992; World Bank, 1993; INEGI-CEPAL, 1993; Lustig and Székely, 1997) is the methodology it uses to calculate the poverty line. As mentioned above, unlike the majority of poverty studies (which calculate the poverty line based on a Standard Food Basket, SFB, and then apply the Engel's coefficient), the COPLAMAR study took into account not only a food basket but also non-food commodities classified into the following groups: 1) articles required for the preparation and consumption of food; 2) equivalent rent of housing and other housing expenses, including furniture; 3) health and hygiene; 4) education; 5) recreation and culture; 6) transport and communications; 7) clothing and shoes; and 8) personal care and other needs (For a detailed explanation of the COPLAMAR procedure for obtaining the poverty line, see Methodological Appendix 1.)

In the COPLAMAR study (Volume 1, *Food*, 1982b) a set of alternative normative food baskets were constructed, all of them providing minimum nutritional requirements. The publication compares the results using some of them. The differences between the baskets are derived on the basis of the group habits from which the diets are built. The central estimate is based on the habits of the fifth national decile. Some other estimates were built on the base of urban deciles or on rural ones. The poverty line was calculated using as its main entry on food consumption the normative basket defined for the fifth national decile. The habits were observed on the bases of a survey conducted in 1975 by CENIET (1977) for which quantities consumed by households for each food item were available.

The selection of the food basket of the fifth decile as the demarcation point of the extreme poverty line has been criticised on the grounds that it does not provide the "cheapest" possible alternative to fulfil the "minimum" nutritional requirements. According to Levy (1994: table 7:48), using the same recommended calorific intake level, but with a cheaper food basket, extreme poverty calculated for 1984 declined from 19.5 per cent to 10.1 per cent. The relevance of such a "minimum cost diet" has been challenged by Sen (1984:12) who argues that 'choosing a minimum cost diet for meeting specified nutritional requirements from food items sold at specified costs ...turns out to be very low-cost indeed, ... and people's food habits are not in fact determined by such a cost minimisation exercise.'

In the COPLAMAR study the poverty line was established by taking into account, on one hand, the "universally" recognised norms, defined as the "basic needs" acknowledged in human rights declarations, as well as in the country's legislation (COPLAMAR, 1983). On the other hand, the study took into consideration 'Mexico's reality as reflected in the lists of goods and services frequently consumed by households.' (See Boltvinik, 1998b:2.48.)

From the consumption pattern of the seventh decile, a list of "socially generalised consumption goods and services" was elaborated. This list was subjected to various processes of elimination, among others, luxury goods. From the final list, the quantities of each item were determined normatively.[7] From the goods and services selected in this study, the poverty line was defined by satisfiers that have to be met through private consumption (i.e., satisfiers whose cost must be paid or produced by households). (See Boltvinik, 1998b.) The satisfiers to be met by public expenditure were: primary and secondary education (nine years of schooling), health services, and the infrastructure for piped water and sewerage.

The difficulties in selecting a reference group for the definition of a poverty line have already been pointed out by Sen (1984:16). This author affirms that one of the most difficult aspects of the concept of relative poverty is the choice of a reference group. According to him, the process involves political aspects related to people's expectations as well as views of what is fair and who has the right to enjoy what. In the case of the COPLAMAR study, some authors have challenged the selection of seventh decile as the demarcation point of poverty. For instance, Escobar (1996:543) points out that the COPLAMAR poverty line includes certain items (e.g. washing and drying machines)[8] which have not been evaluated in terms of the welfare they provide to achieve "basic needs". Therefore, the deprivation of households is compared neither in neither absolute nor in relative terms, 'except in comparison with the unquestionably well off.' (*Ibid.*)

In addition, the COPLAMAR study has also been criticised on the grounds that, by using the seventh decile as the poverty line's point of demarcation, around 80 per cent of the population is automatically considered to be poor (e.g., Levy, 1994:50). Nonetheless, it should be noted that this criticism does not hold true; although socially generalised consumption goods and services listed in the COPLAMAR study are based on the consumption pattern of the seventh decile, the final list does not correspond to quantities bought or consumed by the seventh decile, but to normative quantities.[9] This can be seen by the fact that in the COPLAMAR study around 55 per cent of the population was considered to be poor in 1977 (COPLAMAR, 1982a), and not 80 per cent as stated by Levy.[10]

It should be clear from the previous discussion that, in general, the definition of the poverty line depends on the set of items considered as the "minimum" or "generally acceptable" needs to be met by income (e.g. diet, clothing, housing, household facilities, etc.). The percentage of the population living in poverty as well as the poverty gap varies according to the definition of the poverty line; this definition then becomes a central activity for the measurement of poverty. To illustrate the difficulties in defining poverty in Mexico — for instance, in 1984 — the range of the estimated percentage of households whose income was below the poverty line varied between 40.2 per cent and 69.8 per cent depending on the definition of the poverty line (see table 3.4) and on whether or not the particular study in question had adjusted ENIGHs income data to National Accounts.

4.3. The Integrated Poverty Measurement Method (IPMM)

In recent years an alternative approach to measuring poverty has been developed (Boltvinik, 1994a, 1994b). This approach — the Integrated Poverty Measurement Method (IPMM) — combines the Poverty Line (PL) method with the Unsatisfied Basic Needs (UBN) method. The PL method measures poverty taking into account current household income, while the UBN method estimates the satisfaction of certain "basic needs", such as access to government services, housing, or education. The IPMM method differs from that used in the COPLAMAR study in that while the latter made use of both methods but without integrating both measurements, the IPMM approach allows one to assess each household simultaneously from the point of view of the PL method and the UBN method.

According to Boltvinik (1994a), the "basic needs" for which satisfaction should be checked by the Poverty Line method are the following: food, fuel, personal and home care, clothing and footwear, public transport, basic communication (post, telegraphs and cargo), leisure and culture, payment for housing services, and expenses related to school-attendance- and health-care related expenses. In particular, the Unsatisfied Basic Needs (UBN) method considers: dwelling characteristics; furniture and household appliances; access to some services (water supply, electricity and sewerage); educational level; and availability of time for education, recreation and domestic work. Boltvinik (1994a) explains that certain needs, such as health, can be measured either by the PL method or by the UBN method, depending on whether the specific household meets them through private or public services. (For a detailed explanation of IPMM see Methodological Appendix 1.)

The IPMM builds a global index for each household that synthesises the particular indices calculated in each item. The global index is a weighted average of the individual items. The weights are the percentage share of each item in overall costs. Accordingly, the IPMM classifies as poor households whose global index falls below the normative level which, in turn, has also been built by a weighted average of the normative levels of individual items. (See Boltvinik, 1994a: chapters 5-8.)

The IPMM method attempts to provide a more accurate measurement of poverty in comparison to that provided by previous studies on poverty, which were exclusively based on income. The IPMM approach overcomes some of the criticism which has already been pointed out in connection with other methodologies used to measure poverty. For example, because the measurement of need satisfaction is based on a multi-dimensional index which allows for compensation between unsatisfied and over-satisfied needs, the measurement of satisfaction of basic needs based on the UBN method does not depend on the number of items selected as basic needs. Nonetheless, the UBN method, as applied in several research studies, has its own weaknesses. For instance, the standards established in 1981 for the overall basket have not been thoroughly modified, despite their obvious obsolescence in some respects.

Another problem shared by most of the studies of poverty in Mexico, as elsewhere in other countries, is that the household is considered as a unit in which all members pursue common welfare objectives. In other words, such studies assume that all household income-earning members contribute all of their income to a "common fund" in order to satisfy equally the needs of all household members. Therefore, there is an idea of altruism in household relations. As highlighted by Kabeer (1991:12), 'all members are not equally empowered to pursue the full array of objectives encompassed within the household collectively: the membership is internally differentiated by material constraints which may strongly influence *which* objectives, and more importantly, *whose* objectives are actually realised.'

In my own survey in Xalpa I found that female and male household members contribute, on average, 60 per cent of their income to the household budget. I also found that male and female household heads both contribute the same percentage (74 per cent), while wives contribute more (85 per cent) and daughters and sons much less (42 per cent and 35 per cent, respectively).

5. TRENDS IN POVERTY IN MEXICO AFTER THE 1982 ECONOMIC CRISIS

Before looking at the results of some studies which provide poverty calculations after the 1982 crisis, I will describe succinctly the main characteristics of their methodology to make it easier to connect this section with the previous one and thus be better prepared to assess the results of the studies.

All studies quoted in this section, except for Boltvinik's IPMM (1998b), are poverty line studies. None of them solves adequately the problem of urban-rural classification analysed in section 2. Two of them, INEGI-CEPAL and Lustig-Székely, correct the 1992 figures to avoid the drastic drop in the low density (rural) proportion of the population, producing instead an overestimation of that proportion. The rest of the studies do not correct this population classification problem. This problem affects calculations to the extent that poverty thresholds are very different in both areas.

Hernández-Laos (1992)-Boltvinik (1998a) use the COPLAMAR poverty line which was described in some detail in sub-section 4.2.[11] Boltvinik-Hernández-Laos adjust household income to NA following the procedure developed by CEPAL-PNUD (1992), which determines specific correction coefficients for each source of income (e.g. one coefficient for wages, another for entrepreneurial rent, etc.). These authors use the poverty lines for the rural and the urban areas (in which the poverty lines for the two areas have a very small difference of 3.4 per cent in the original estimate) unaltered throughout their study. They do not correct for the urban-rural classification problem.

INEGI-CEPAL's methodology, which belongs to the food basket variant of the PL methodology, was described and criticised in some detail in section 4.1. This study also uses the CEPAL-PNUD adjustment procedure to NA based on specific corrections by income source. They overcorrect the urban-rural classification problem. Two additional particularities of this study must be highlighted. First, they use very different poverty lines for the urban and rural areas (a 53.9 per cent difference calculated on the lowest rural poverty line in 1992). Second, the poverty lines used in 1989 and 1992 are lower than the ones used in 1984.

Lustig and Székely (1997: 45, 48, 55) use INEGI-CEPAL's poverty lines, so that their study can also be classified as belonging to the food basket poverty line methodology. The only difference between their estimates and those of the INEGI-CEPAL study is the way they adjust income figures to NA. Their adjustment procedure uses, instead of a correction coefficient by income source, a correction coefficient by branch of activity (e.g. agriculture, industry, services, etc.). This way of correcting misses the main source of underestimation: the underestimation of entrepreneurial rents (see section 3 of Methodological Appendix 1 for a detailed exposition of this topic). Naturally, their poverty lines also have the same two features present in the INEGI-CEPAL studies; namely, the large differences between urban and rural poverty lines and the lower poverty lines for 1989 and 1992. They also borrowed the overcorrection of the urban-rural problem implemented by INEGI-CEPAL.

As for Pánuco and Székely (1996:218), they use a poverty and an extreme poverty line drawn from COPLAMAR, arbitrarily including sections of the normative basket, thus converting the COPLAMAR extreme poverty line (which only includes food, housing, health and education) into their moderate poverty line, and the food portion of COPLAMAR into their extreme poverty line. These authors do not adjust their figures to National Accounts nor do they correct the rural-urban problem. They use the same poverty line for both geographical areas and keep them throughout the period.

Concerning Boltvinik (IPMM), he uses, in the corresponding poverty line dimension of IPMM, COPLAMAR's poverty lines with some minor adjustments, but conserving the small difference between rural and urban areas and establishing specific poverty lines for metropolitan areas, which are also very similar to the other poverty lines. This author adjusts to National Accounts using the methodology developed recently by Cortés (1997). He does not correct the urban-rural classification problem.

Most of the analyses of poverty in Mexico, despite their huge methodological differences, agree that the 1982 economic crisis and the economic policies implemented by the state to counteract the crisis, resulted in an increase in the level of poverty in Mexico. Hernández-Laos (1992:110-111) argues that the 1982 economic crisis made the level of poverty rise. According to this expert, during the oil boom period there was a significant drop in the level of poverty (from 58.0 per cent in 1977 to 48.5 per cent in 1981).[12] Two years after the 1982 economic crisis poverty increased to 58.5 per cent, a level almost identical to the one prevailing in 1977 (see table 3.4).

Although the ENIGHs reported a decline in average monetary income per capita between 1977 and 1984,[13] Cortés's (1996) figures suggest that the poorest 60 per cent of the population saw their monetary income per capita increase during this period (see table 4.7, chapter 4 of this book), thereby implying a decrease in poverty incidence. The difference in terms of poverty trends between these two experts stems from the fact that Hernández-Laos adjusted the ENIGH income data to National Accounts, while Cortés did not adjust them.[14]

As noted above, official estimations (INEGI-CEPAL, 1993) point to an increase in the incidence of poverty from 42.5 per cent in 1984 to 47.7 per cent in 1989 (see table 3.4). Other studies on poverty agree that between 1984 and 1989 poverty increased (e.g. World Bank 1993; Boltvinik, 1998; Lustig-Mitchell, 1994). According to the Psacharopoulos, *et al.* (1997), poverty incidence increased in Mexico from 16.6 per cent in

1984 to 17 7 per cent in 1989, and extreme poverty increased almost twofold from 2.5 per cent in 1984 to 4.5 per cent in 1989. The calculations by Lustig and Mitchell set the corresponding figures at 38.1 per cent and 50.6 per cent for poverty, and 15.7 per cent and 27.1 per cent for extreme poverty. All these studies adjusted the ENIGHs income figures to NA. When this is not done, as is the case of Pánuco-Laguette and Székely (1996: 198), the findings are different and mostly opposite. They found that although the percentage of extremely poor increased from 10.3 per cent to 10.7 per cent during the period 1984-1989, moderate poverty decreased slightly, from 29.9 per cent in 1984 to 28.3 per cent in 1989.[15] Nonetheless, according to these authors, although moderate poverty declined, households who were moderately poor were poorer in 1989 than in 1984 (table 3.4).

Table 3.4. Mexico: Different poverty estimates
(per cent of total population)

	1977		1984		1989		1992		1994	
	P	EP	P	EP	P	EP	P	EP	P	EP
Hz-Laos-Boltvinik[a]	58.0	34.0	58.5	29.9	64.0	---	66.0	---	66.0	---
INEGI-CEPAL[e]	---	---	42.5	15.4	47.8	18.8	44.1	16.1	---	---
Lustig & Székely[b]	---	---	42.4	13.9	49.6	17.1	47.4	16.1	47.3	15.5
Pánuco & Székely[c]	---	---	40.2	10.3	39.0	10.7	38.6	10.8	---	---
Boltvinik (IPMM)[d]	---	---	68.4	38.0	73.3	46.0	74.2	49.0	---	---

Source: [a]Boltvinik, 1998b, table 3.1:3.12; [b]Lustig and Székely, 1997, table 19; [c]Pánuco and Székely 1996, table 8:198; and [d]Boltvinik, 1998b:7.5.
Key: P = Poverty
      EP = Extreme poverty

The almost complete consensus with respect to the direction of the evolution of poverty is lost in the 1989-1992 period. According to the INEGI-CEPAL report, the level of poverty declined, from 47.7 per cent to 44.0 per cent, and extreme poverty was reduced from 18.8 per cent to 16.1 per cent. Naturally, Lustig-Székely obtained the same trend as INEGI-CEPAL, as their calculations are so similar. Pánuco-Laguette and Székely (1996:199) also found that during the structural adjustment policies period there was a relative improvement of the poor. According to them, although the proportion of extremely poor remained almost constant (10.7 per cent-

10.8 per cent), the extremely poor were better off in 1992 than in 1989 when their condition is measured by the poverty gap and the Foster Greer and Thorbecke squared gap.[16] Moreover, both moderate poverty incidence and these two poverty indices also declined, although slightly. The percentage of moderately poor went down from 28.3 per cent in 1989 to 27.8 per cent in 1992.[17] Taking extreme and moderate poverty together, the incidence of poverty changes almost imperceptibly from 39 per cent to 38.6 per cent in this sub-period (table 3.4). It is important to remember that these authors did not adjust their figures to National Accounts.

The period 1989-1992 has been considered as one of recovery in macroeconomic terms. National Accounts calculations show an improvement in income between 1989 and 1992 as a result of a general improvement in the economy. For example, between 1989 and 1992 GDP per capita grew at a 1.3 per cent rate annually, while private consumption per capita increased 2.6 per cent annually during the same period. Additionally, average real wages per worker (or rather the average cost for entrepreneurs) as captured by NA increased 3.9 per cent annually in the same years.

In opposition to the above-quoted results for the 1989-1992 period, which point to a reduction in poverty, Boltvinik (1998b: 3.9) argues that there was a slight increase in poverty as measured by the PL method, rising from 64 per cent to 66 per cent, respectively. According to this author, although GDP grew faster than total population, the increase in income per capita was small and was concentrated in the highest decile in the income distribution scale. Boltvinik shows that distribution of income deteriorated in those years (the Gini coefficient of total income went up from 0.4694 in 1989 to 0.4749 in 1992, while the Gini of monetary income increased much more: from 0.4889 to 0.5086). Thus, according to Boltvinik's calculations, poverty increased. Measuring poverty through the Integrated Poverty Measurement Method, the level of poverty incidence goes up from 73.3 per cent to 74.2 per cent between 1989 and 1992 (table 3.4) and this is explained by an important increase in the poverty line dimension of poverty (see section 7 below for a detailed analysis).

Therefore, the controversy is practically reduced to the 1989-1992 period. As we have seen (section 4.1), the INEGI-CEPAL calculations have a serious problem with urban-rural composition. The problem of urban-rural composition, given the huge differences between the poverty lines in both areas, explains by itself the downward shift of poverty incidence. The Lustig-Székely study, in so far as it follows INEGI-CEPAL in this aspect, has the same problem. So the result of these studies for the 1989-1992 period cannot seriously be defended. The other study quoted gives an almost constancy of poverty incidence in both years without adjusting income figures to NA. This study is unaffected by the urban-rural classification problem as it uses the same poverty lines in both areas. It shows that income in the critical deciles (the second for extreme poverty and the fourth for overall poverty) remained almost constant. But if unadjusted income remained almost constant — and, according to Cortés (1997, table 4.21:135), the underestimation between both surveys was reduced from 42.7 per cent to 38.7 per cent — there would be a strong argument, at this level of the poverty lines, in support of a slight increase in poverty in these two years. This is what Boltvinik found, at a different level of the poverty lines, which made him conclude on the direction of change. Nonetheless, if informal activities are underreported in NA, the conclusion becomes obscure.

Between 1992 and 1994 there is a consensus among scholars that poverty did not increase. According to Lustig and Székely (1997:16), although private consumption and the share of wage income increased in National Accounts between 1992 and 1994, the level of poverty did not decrease. Boltvinik (1998a, table 3.1:312) also estimates that in 1994 income poverty remained at the same level as in 1992 (66 per cent).

In sum, several measurements of poverty in Mexico have been made that cover the period that followed the 1982 economic crisis. Although most of these studies argue that poverty reached its highest level in 1989 (see table 3.4), thereafter recording a slight decrease between 1989 and 1992, their case is not sufficiently strong given the errors found in their procedures. But even if the opposite evidence (the one held almost in solitary by Boltvinik) is not considered strong enough, the consensus is (from all those studies that adjust their figures to NA) that the losses suffered by the poor between 1984 and 1989 were strong enough to result in an increase in the level of poverty in the 1984-1994 period as a whole (see table 3.4). Thus, while in the INEGI-CEPAL study poverty increased from 42.5 per cent in 1984 to 44 per cent in 1992, Lustig and Székely's figures go from 42.4 per cent to 47.4 per cent. Other studies hold that, although the Mexican economy recovered staring in 1989, income distribution worsened, and therefore the level of poverty in actual fact never went down. For instance, according to the figures of Hernández-Laos-Boltvinik, the level of 'poverty rose from 58.5 per cent to 66.0 per cent (see table 3.4).

Although income poverty (henceforth, referred to as income poverty) seems to have increased, there is some strong evidence that some social indicators in Mexico improved during the eighties. As a result of this, the incidence of poverty as measured by the Unsatisfied Basic Needs method, shows a systematic downtrend. This paradox will be analysed below (in section 6.4 and in sections 7.2 and 7.3, which present a comparison of the evolution of poverty in Mexico City and at the national level). In the following section we will analyse some wellbeing indicators at the national level.

6. IMPROVEMENT IN SOME WELLBEING INDICATORS

6.1. Health Related Indices

It has been argued that stabilisation and adjustment policies have affected the nutritional status of the Mexican population. As there is evidence that income declined, it follows that families saw a reduction in their ability to meet their food needs. However, the data on nutrition for Mexico are rather scarce and unreliable, and therefore it is difficult to draw any conclusion with regard to this indicator.

Nonetheless, some authors have used the available evidence to show that, despite the decrease in income, there was an improvement in food consumption *in certain areas* of Mexico. For instance, Friedmann, *et al.* (1995:368) point out that in deprived rural areas the proportion of malnutrition declined from 31 per cent in 1986 to 21 per cent in 1990 and to 16.2 per cent in 1991 (the first semester).[18] These authors also suggest that during the period of stabilisation and adjustment policies in Mexico, the rural poor continued to improve their nutritional status. In rural areas, where an important proportion of the extremely poor of Mexico live, average estimated consumption of calories per capita remained almost at the same level (a 1.7 per cent decrease), while that of proteins increased almost 14 per cent between 1978 and 1989.[19]

For these data Friedmann, *et al.* quote a document published by the "Comisión Nacional de Alimentación" (National Food Commission), a coordinating body to conduct policies. When one goes directly into the documents which report the results of the national nutritional rural surveys conducted by the National Institute of Nutrition, one finds that in these reports the only instruments used for the measurement of nutritional status are weight and height for age as well as (in some of the surveys) the arm perimeter, all of them for children of one to five years. The comparative results in the last four national rural surveys, as reported in the 1996 national publication (INNSZ 1997, Vol.1: 61-63,) are the following. In the first place, it is established that the same indicators were not available in the four surveys. So, a regression analysis had to be performed in the 1989 survey in order to determine the relation between the indicators available in the 1974 and 1979 surveys *vis à vis* those available in 1989 and 1996. Once this was done the results are as follows. The proportion of undernourished children one to five years of age were: 50.7 per cent in 1974, 50.2 per cent in 1979, 47.3 per cent in 1989, and 47.8 per cent in 1996. As can be seen, it looks almost like a trajectory without trend. The slight decrease cannot be taken as more than fluctuations within the errors that any survey has, and might be due to the indirect procedure with which the 1974 and 1979 data were made comparable. It looks as if the rural population was scarcely affected by the ups and downs of the Mexican economy.

Table 3.5. Mexico: Selected wellbeing indicators, 1970-1994

	1970	1980	1990	1994/5
Infant mortality (per 1000 births)	79.0	53.0	36.6	31.1
Life expectancy (years)	62.1	68.1	70.0	71.0
Illiteracy (per cent)*	24.7	16.6	12.4	10.4
Schooling (years)*	3.7	5.4	6.3	7.2

Source: Lustig and Székely, 1997, table 5:n.p.
* 1995 data, INEGI, 1997b, Education tables 5B: 403, and 6:407.

With regard to infant mortality, table 3.5 shows that it declined from 53.0 per 1000 births in 1980 to 31.1 in 1994, and life expectancy rose from 68.1 years to 71 years between 1980 and 1994. This evidence, assuming infant mortality and life expectancy were determined by income, would contradict the evidence of a significant decline in income, a paradox that will be discussed in some detail at end of this section and in section 7 of this chapter. Nonetheless, it is important to note that these improvements were not as impressive as they were between 1970 and 1980, as can be seen in table 3.5. On the other hand, Boltvinik and Echarri

(1997) have shown that from 1985 to 1990 the downward trend in infant mortality came to a virtual stop, when it scarcely moved, going from 29.4 to 28.9 per thousand births; however, from 1990 onwards, infant mortality resumed its rapid downward trend. The authors also show that this stagnation is equally present in pre-school age mortality rates, where it lasts from 1982 to 1990, and in school age mortality, where it can be observed during the period 1983-1990. Boltvinik (1998b) attributes these processes of stagnation to income deterioration during the eighties.

Moreover, although infant mortality declined, there is some indication that nutritional-deficiency-related infant mortality duplicated from 1985 to 1990, from 57.8 per 100,000 infants to 115.9, and then began to decrease from 1990 onwards (see Boltvinik and Echarri, 1997, table 8:n.p.).

Very few studies have been conducted in Mexico City aimed at measuring the impact of the economic crisis and adjustment on the nutritional status of the population. Two of them provide data on anthropometric indices to assess the nutritional status of pre-school children in 1988 and 1995.[20] However, they are not comparable because one survey refers only to the Federal District, while the other covers the whole Metropolitan Area of Mexico City (MAMC). Nonetheless, the findings of these surveys are worth mentioning. While the 1988 survey reports that 10 per cent of pre-school children in the Federal District were severely undernourished, the 1995 reports that this percentage was 17.5 per cent for the MAMC. It may be possible that this steep increase resulted from the different geographical coverage of the surveys. Nonetheless, this increase raises the question of whether some of the change may be explained by a real deterioration in children's nutritional status. Unfortunately, there is no available data to allow us to attempt to answer this question.

Finally, there is another study on the impact of the economic crisis and adjustment for the capital city. However, this does not attempt to measure the nutritional status of the population, but rather the changes in the consumption patterns of the population. The National Institute of the Consumer (Instituto Nacional del Consumidor –INCO), carried out a follow-up survey of families in Mexico City between 1985 and 1988. In this survey, questions related to food consumption were asked. According to the INCO (1989) study, in four out of five household groups there was a reduction in protein- and calory-spending per capita between June 1985 and February 1988 (see table 3.6).[21]

Table 3.6. Mexico City: Consumption of proteins and calories per capita, June 1985 and February 1988

Social strata*	Consumption of protein per capita (Grams)		Consumption of calories per capita (Kilocalories)	
	June 1985	February 1988	June 1985	February 1988
Formal				
Low income	66.3	62.8	1934.8	1819.2
Low-middle income	61.6	59.3	1686.3	1605.8
Middle income	74.7	71.4	1956.9	1877.0
Informal				
Low income	54.6	52.5	1659.7	1547.1
Middle income	61.7	61.7	1782.0	1823.1

Source: INCO, 1989, table 5:56 and table 6:57
* Families classified according to income level and characteristics of the head of the household job (for further discussion please refer to endnote 40, chapter 4).

Up to this point the conclusion seems to be as follows. Despite the decrease in overall infant mortality, Infant mortality related to nutritional problems seems to have increased,. This means that infant mortality related to other diseases significantly declined during adjustment. This, together with the improvements in life expectancy, raises the question of how these indicators improved despite increases in income poverty.

6.1.1. Health Care Coverage

One element that may have contributed to improvements in some of the welfare indices is the increase in the health care system's coverage. The percentage of the population with social security registration, and thus entitled to health-care and income-transfer benefits (pensions and income maintenance when sick or unable to work), rose from 48 per cent in 1982 to almost 60 per cent in 1990; nonetheless it went down to 52.5 per cent in 1994 (Boltvinik, 1998a: table 13:372).

The above figure is a "nominal" coverage of health care services through the social security system and is calculated by taking into account the number of workers that receive this service because they either work in "formal" jobs or are pensioners, including the number of family members that by law are entitled to this service (e.g. husband, wife and economically dependent children). The decline in the percentage of the population with access to social security in the early nineties may have resulted from two factors. On the one hand, the proportion of pensioners increased between 1990 and 1995. This population group has a lower proportion of family members who are entitled to receive public health services. On the other hand, Boltvinik (1998a:308) presents data to show that, despite the economic growth observed between 1990 and 1994, the number of "formal" jobs did not increase.

In the Mexican health care system a majority of the population without access to social security receive health services from social assistance health services provided by the public sector, especially but not exclusively, by the Secretaría de Salud (Health Ministry). In order to calculate the real coverage of health services it is necessary to analyse the resources mobilised by the whole set of public health institutions (including social security institutions) in order to estimate their capability (expressed in number of people) to provide services of standard quality.[22] This was done by COPLAMAR (1982, vol.3, *Health*) for 1978 and by Boltvinik (1998a: table 13.1, 374) for the period 1980-1994.

The public sector as a whole (including social security institutions) had the resources to provide medical attention to 41.1 per cent of the national population in 1978. The public sector's capacity to provide health services grew very quickly to reach 51.3 per cent in 1982, and, despite some stagnation between 1982 and 1984, reached 56.7 per cent in 1986, and 63 per cent in 1994. This growth in capacity was a result of the combined growth in social security and social assistance resources. The potential health-care coverage of social security increased very slowly from 33.7 per cent of national population in 1982 to 34.6 per cent in 1986, but then recovered some momentum and reached 37.3 per cent in 1994. Meanwhile, potential social assistance coverage increased from 17.6 per cent in 1982 to 22.1 per cent in 1986, growing more rapidly than social security's potential coverage in this period, reaching 25.7 per cent in 1994 (Boltvinik, 1998[a], table 13.1:374).

Thus, despite the economic crisis, potential access to health services continued growing, although at a much slower pace than in the 1978-1982 period. Nevertheless, it should be noted that from 1989 onwards (exactly when the economy started growing), coverage became almost stagnated, slightly rising from 60.1 per cent in 1989 to 63 per cent in 1994.

As can be seen, before the 1982 economic crisis, the public sector health-care system was able to provide health services to around 50 per cent of the population, and, by the end of the adjustment period (1994), this capacity had increased to more than 60 per cent. Therefore, welfare indicators may have improved, given that a greater proportion of the population had access to health services. This may partially explain improvement in infant mortality and life expectancy despite a deterioration in income.

6.2. Education

Some studies have shown a general increase in the level of education for the Mexican population during the 1980s and in the first half of the 1990s. In 1980, almost 17 per cent of the population aged 14 and over was illiterate. This figure went down to a level of 12.4 per cent in 1990, and by 1995 this percentage was below 10 per cent (see table 3.5). Moreover, the percentage of the population with primary school education and higher rose from 51.7 per cent in 1980 to 63.1 per cent in 1990 (Boltvinik, 1998a; table 9:358). However, this increase was at a slower pace than the one observed between 1970 and 1980, when the percentage of population with primary school education and higher went up from 29.5 per cent to 51.7 per cent.

The proportion of children between the ages of six and fourteen who attended primary school continued to rise. It is also significant that the primary school dropout rate fell from 6.9 per cent in the academic year 1981-1982 to 5.0 per cent in 1991-1992 (Friedmann, et al., 1995, table 9-14:367). According to Boltvinik (1998a:296), despite this relative decline, the number of dropouts continues to be high. The number of dropouts went down from around one million of children in the academic year 1981-1982 to around 460 thousand in 1993-1994 (*Ibid.*: 365).

Between 1980 and 1994 the average number of years of schooling did not increase at the same pace as during the period 1970-1980 (see table 3.5). While between 1970 and 1980 the number of years of schooling rose from 3.7 to 5.4, between 1980 and 1990 it only increased to 6.3. Between 1990 and 1995, when the Mexican economy recovered, the number of years of schooling increased almost one year, rising from 6.3 to 7.2 years.

In contrast, in higher education there was a severe deceleration. The national adult population (aged 15 years and over) having at least higher education (i.e. having complete higher education and/or postgraduate studies) was 1.1 per cent of the total adult population in 1970 (282 thousand) and showed a very impressive increase in the seventies reaching 2.7 per cent (one million of adults) in 1980. But in the eighties the growth of this population was much slower, reaching 2.9 per cent of the population (1.4 million adults) in 1990 (Boltvinik, 1998a:290-291). According to data published in the Third Report to the Nation by President Salinas (Carlos Salinas, 1991), the percentage of graduates from the preparatory level (high school) which entered university-level studies dropped sharply from a peak of 90 per cent in 1979-80 to 57.7 per cent in 1988-1989. These two pieces of evidence would show a possible area of negative impact of the crisis on education. What is not clear is what proportion of the analysed phenomena is explained by restrictions in the supply of higher education and what proportion by restrictions in the demand for higher education.

It can be said that despite the crisis, there were improvements in the educational level of the Mexican population, though at a slower pace than that observed in the 1970s. These improvements may have resulted both from a secular trend, which expresses itself in the goal, internalised by almost all urban families, of providing every child with at least primary school and from increases in public spending devoted to education (see sub-section 3.3.1, chapter 2). As education has tended to improve, this may have had a positive impact on some other welfare indices, such as life expectancy and infant mortality.

6.3. Housing

There were some improvements in the quality of shelter during the 1980s. The percentage of people living in overcrowded dwellings[23] went down from 61.0 per cent in 1980 to 52.9 per cent in 1990. Similarly, the percentage of dwellings with walls made of durable materials increased from 56.1 per cent to 69.5 per cent in the same period (Boltvinik, 1998a; tables 10:366-7 and 12:370). Moreover, the number of dwellings supplied with the three basic public services (water supply, sewerage and electricity) went up from 39.7 per cent in 1980 to 44.6 per cent in 1990 (*Ibid.*; table 11:368-9). These figures demonstrate that there were significant improvements in the material characteristics of dwellings, which may have also positively affected life expectancy and infant mortality.

6.4. The Paradox: Income Poverty Increases and UBN Poverty Decreases

Some scholars argue that the economic crisis and adjustment have not had a negative impact on social indicators, because, on one hand, the improvements in certain social indicators, such as infant mortality or life expectancy, resulted from past investments. For example, Friedmann, *et al.* (1995:369) argue that improvements in Mexican population health indices resulted from previous investment in physical and human capital, such as hospitals and doctors. On the other hand, Boltvinik (1998a:323) points out that in the case of Mexico, despite the crisis, the government did not reduce public social expenditure. On the contrary, investment in public infrastructure was not interrupted and more employment was created in public services. Therefore, the provision of public services continued to grow, although public service workers saw their real salary decline (see sections 3.3.1 and 3.3.2, chapter 2).

It can be said that poverty as measured by the Unsatisfied Basic Needs method declined in Mexico during the stabilisation and adjustment periods. This is because the satisfaction of certain needs such as health, water, sewerage, education, and so on, is not necessarily income-related.

The relationship of these needs with the measurement of poverty by means of the Poverty Line is more opaque. Although most of the studies on poverty affirm that income poverty increased between 1984 and 1994, at the same time other social indicators (such as housing and the ability to continue studying) were also improving. The evidence suggests that the Mexican population was able to afford improvements in their dwellings. People were in general living in less overcrowded homes, using better construction materials, and their educational levels also showed improvements.

This paradox has to be explained. The interesting fact one has to start with is that this apparent paradox is present not only in Mexico but also in many Latin American countries. The UNDP Regional Project to Overcome Poverty (Beccaria, *et al.*, 1992, table 1: 381) estimated poverty in Latin America by PL, UBN and by an initial version of the IPMM. Calculations were made for 1986 and 1990. During that period, income poverty increased from 44 per cent to 47 per cent of population, while

UBN poverty decreased from 50 per cent to 48 per cent for Latin America as a whole. IPMM increased slightly from 61.5 per cent to 61.8 per cent. The inverse movements of UBN and PL are repeated in various countries; for instance, in Venezuela, where UBN poverty went down from 46.2 per cent to 41 per cent during approximately the same period when income poverty increased from 22 per cent to 26.6 per cent (*Ibid.*, tables 2 and 3). But perhaps the better known case is that of Chile. When the campaigns of both the pro-Pinochet group and the anti-Pinochet group were at their height in 1989, the pro-Pinochet group argued that during his government poverty had gone down, using for that purpose two UBN studies which in effect showed an important decrease in poverty from 1970 to 1988. Contrariwise, the opposition, comparing CEPAL's PL calculations for 1970 with calculations made with the same procedure for a survey carried out in 1988, showed not only that in Chile there had been a very steep increase in poverty incidence during the period (from 17 per cent to 44 per cent), but also that this increase had been the largest for all Latin American countries (see Ortega and Tironi, 1990).

The Regional Project to Overcome Poverty explained the paradox by simply regarding UBN poverty as the structural aspects and PL as the contingent aspects of poverty (Beccaria, *et al.*, 1992:381).

Boltvinik (1998a:323) has explained this paradox on the basis of the three following factors:

1) The stock-variable character of most UBN indicators *vis à vis* the flow-variable character of income. Whereas flow variables can change their values easily, that is not the case with stock variables which might experience only marginal changes. Thus, in stock variables the level observed today is determined mostly by the level observed yesterday.
2) UBN indicators are almost universally referred to a normative standard which is left unchanged over time, generating a downward trend in the absolute dimension of poverty (e.g. illiteracy). In contrast, many PL studies (e.g. those by CEPAL) change their normative base (the food basket) frequently to reflect the changes in diets.
3) Many UBN indicators are determined by factors other than current private income, i.e. by other welfare sources, which might move in a different direction than private income during recessions. This can be explained by the non-commodity character of many goods and services (e.g. education, health care, water, and sewerage

supply). Even indicators of housing (size and quality), which are partially determined by income, have other non-income determinants, such as access to legal possession of land, which is largely determined, for the poor, by policy in Latin American cities.

In the next section I will present the results on poverty in Mexico City as measured by means of the IPMM in an attempt to clarify this paradox.

7. POVERTY AND LIVING CONDITIONS IN MEXICO CITY

Mexico City has historically concentrated the largest share of economic activity and population in Mexico. Despite the relevance of the city in economic terms, prior to the calculations on the evolution of poverty presented below (in sub-section 7.2) there were only some calculations for specific years, but no available time series on poverty evolution.

Although based on micro-social studies or samples with non-representative data, some authors have concluded that the 1982 economic crisis and structural adjustment policies had a negative effect on the economy of Mexico City, and this in turn has resulted in a deterioration in the living conditions of the population, particularly of the poor (INCO, 1987; INCO, 1989, Benería, 1992; Tuirán, 1992). In this section I will first describe the results and conclusions of some of these studies and then present my own evidence, based on the National Household Income and Expenditure surveys of 1984, 1989 and 1992 to confirm, reject or modify such findings.

7.1. Evidence from Partial Surveys or Micro-Social Studies

Based on a National Consumers Institute (Instituto Nacional de Consumidor-INCO) survey,[24] Tuirán (1992:183) analyses the changes in the household head's real income and income per capita. This author asserts that in four out of five income household groups[25] the real income of household heads declined (between −5 per cent and −33 per cent depending on the group). According to him, middle-income families were the most affected by this decline. In three of the five family groups per capita income declined; in one of them per capita income remained almost at the same level (decreasing only one per cent); and in another one it increased 9 per cent. Overall, households suffered a decline in per capita income of 10 per cent (*Ibid.* 188).

Benería (1992:90), in another follow-up study in Mexico City,[26] found that between 1982 and 1988 the great majority of poor and lower-middle-class households were experiencing "great difficulties" in making ends meet and therefore households had to adjust their budget and consumption habits. As unemployment and debt were causing "some difficulties", households in all income categories experienced a certain degree of "belt-tightening".

Despite the fact that these studies point to a deterioration in household income in Mexico City, other social indicators improved during adjustment (as they did at the national level). For example, the number of persons per dwelling declined from 5.4 in 1980 to 4.8 in 1990 (Coulomb, 1992, table 1:160). It has been suggested that, although the reduction in the number of persons per dwelling may indicate an improvement in living conditions, this decline resulted from the demographic changes observed in Mexico City during the 1980s. In other words, there was a larger proportion of "adults" in 1990 as compared to 1980 and, therefore, "new" households were established, reducing the average household size and hence the number of persons per dwelling (Coulomb, 1992:159). However, the fact that more dwellings were built during the 1980s challenges the idea of a generalised deterioration in income levels during that period, inasmuch as there would be serious difficulties to finance the building of new houses in a context of generalised household income losses.

Probably one of the most striking phenomena observed in Mexico City during adjustment was the rise in the percentage of owner-occupancy, which went up from 54 per cent in 1980 to nearly 70 per cent in 1990 (*Ibid.* table 1: 160). That is, an important proportion of the population of Mexico City was building their own dwelling or buying new homes during the period of stabilisation and structural adjustment policies. Similarly, the number of dwellings with only one room decreased from 23.8 per cent in 1980 to 21.5 per cent in 1990.

Moreover, according to the 1980 and 1990 Population Censuses the provision of other public services continued to rise, that is, the number of dwellings with sewerage increased from 80 per cent in 1980 to 88.2 per cent in 1990, and those with electricity from 97 per cent to 98.5 per cent in the same period.

It can be said that, in spite of the 1982 economic crisis and of the changes in public policies during the 1980s, certain groups of the population continued to finance dwelling improvements as well as to invest in new houses during the 1980s. This evidence also seems to contradict the idea of a generalised impoverishment of the population in Mexico City during the period of stabilisation and adjustment (particularly of low-income and middle-income groups). Thus, we arrive at the paradox of apparently decreasing income accompanied by a simultaneous improvement in some social indicators, particularly in the housing sector, which look contradictory with declining income. This is the same paradox we found at the national level.

7.2. Evidence from Representative Household and Expenditure Surveys

In order to go beyond these partial, scattered and problematic pieces of evidence, I decided to calculate poverty by the Integrated Poverty Measurement Method, IPMM (which was explained in section 4 of this chapter). The calculations were based on the micro-data of households located in the Metropolitan Area of Mexico City (henceforth, referred to as Mexico City) in three National Household Income and Expenditure surveys (ENIGHs), those of 1984, 1989 and 1992. In order for these calculations to be comparable with national data, I followed exactly the procedure applied by Boltvinik (1998b) in his IPMM calculations at the national level.[27] The methodological issues involved are explained in Methodological Appendix 1. The reason for choosing the IPMM to analyse poverty in Mexico City is that it includes the measurement of both income poverty as well as poverty in other living conditions (measured by the Unsatisfied Basic Needs Methodology, UBN), a property allowing one, so to speak, to internalise the above-referred paradox into the measurement procedure and thus try to understand it.

Table 3.7 presents poverty incidence (percentage of poor people in the population) in Mexico City in 1984, 1989 and 1992 (left-hand side of the table) and compares these results with the national results[28] (right-hand side of the table). The table is divided into four horizontal sections. In the upper section the integrated results are presented; going down, poverty incidence is presented by UBN, by PL (income) and by a combination of income- and time-deprivation. In Mexico City, IPMM poverty incidence, denoted as "H" in the literature on poverty measurement, increased by more than ten percentage points, from 53.8 per cent in 1984 to 62.6 per cent in 1989, thereafter decreasing slightly (0.4 percentage points) to 62.2

per cent in 1992. For the 1984-1992 period as a whole, which covers most of the stabilisation and adjustment periods, poverty increased from 53.8 per cent to 62.2 per cent, in relative terms a 15.6 per cent increase in eight years. In absolute terms, this represented an increase of around 2.1 million poor people.

When the evolution of poverty incidence for Mexico City is compared with the national evolution, what stands out the most is that the relative increase in IPMM poverty in the 1984-1989 period was less acute at the national level (from 68.4 per cent to 73.3 per cent) than in Mexico City. As a consequence, the distance separating poverty incidence (H) in Mexico from that in Mexico City was significantly reduced from 1984 to 1989. While in 1984 H was almost 15 percentage points higher at the national level than in Mexico City, in 1989 the distance narrowed to less than 11 percentage points, slightly rising to 12 percentage points in 1992. The increase in this distance during the 1989-1992 period is explained by the fact that poverty incidence at the national level increased slightly (to comprise almost three quarters of the population), in contrast to the change in Mexico City, also slight, which moved in the opposite direction. In the overall period analysed in table 3.7, poverty incidence at the national level increased from 68.4 per cent to 74.2 per cent, a relative increase of 8.5 per cent, much lower than the increase observed in Mexico City.

It should also be noted that the structure of poverty incidence (the relative importance of indigents, very poor and moderately poor)[29] changed for the worse both at the national and at the metropolitan level. Indigents, who represented 10.1 per cent of Mexico City's population in 1984, almost doubled their share of the population, accounting for 17.7 per cent in 1992. The same change was experimented by indigents at the national level, though at a much slower pace, increasing their share from 25.5 per cent in 1984 to 34.6 per cent in 1992. The very poor also increased their share in population in both of the areas of study, and again the change was swifter in Mexico City (from 9.9 per cent in 1984 to 15.8 per cent in 1992, with a higher peak in 1989) than at the national level (from 12.5 per cent to 14.4 per cent during the same period).

Thus, when contrasting only two strata, the extremely poor[30] and the moderately poor, it can be seen that at the same time that the proportion of the extremely poor in the population grows, the proportion of the moderately poor diminishes, at both the national and the metropolitan levels. As a consequence, the proportion of the extremely poor within the sum total of all the poor in the city changed from 37.1 per cent in 1984 to 53.9 per cent in 1992. This implies a qualitative change in extreme poverty (which was a minority problem in 1984 in Mexico City), which by 1989 had become the dominant type of poverty and remained as such up to 1992 (representing in both years around 53-54 per cent of the sum total of all the poor).

At the national level, extreme poverty was already the dominant type of poverty in 1984, representing 55.6 per cent of all the poor. During my period of analysis, that trend accentuated, with extreme poverty accounting for two thirds of all the poor, or 66.0 per cent, in 1992. This, of course, is reflected in the widening poverty gap or poverty intensity. Looking at the same table, let us now consider the evolution of the two main dimensions included in the IPMM: the UBN and the income-time $(YT)^{31}$ dimensions (second and fourth sections of table 3.7). The composite indexes of each of these dimensions for each household are combined (weighted average in which UBN receives a 0.37 and income–time a 0.63 weight) to obtain the aggregate index of IPMM for each household (this index varies from 1 to −1). It follows that it is the evolution of the above-mentioned two main dimensions which determine the evolution of IPMM poverty.

UBN poverty incidence *decreased* from 1984 to 1989 both at the metropolitan level (from 59.1 per cent to 56.3 per cent) and at the national level (from 74.0 per cent to 70.1 per cent). From 1989 to 1992 it remained stable in Mexico City, showing a very slight upward movement at the national level (reaching 70.7 per cent). In sharp contrast, income-time poverty (YT) *increased steeply* from 1984 to 1989 for both areas of analysis, especially for Mexico City (from 37.9 per cent to 55.7 per cent). During the period 1989-1992 income-time poverty showed a slight decrease for Mexico City (down to 55.9 per cent) and continued to grow at the national level (comprising almost two thirds of the population).

From the foregoing discussion, two things stand out. First, the paradox of rising poverty in one dimension and decreasing poverty in the other one is present in the 1984-1989 period and in the whole period 1984-1992, at both the national and the metropolitan levels, despite the fact that that paradox cannot be observed in the 1989-1992 period. Second, it turns out that income-time poverty is the dimension that explains the increase of IPMM poverty both in the 1984-1989 period and in the 1984-1992 period as a whole, with the decrease in UBN poverty incidence acting as a moderating factor. Thus the IPMM shows a moderate increase as compared with the much steeper increase in income-time poverty.

Table 3.7. Poverty incidence in Mexico and in Mexico City. Integrated Poverty Measurement Method (IPMM), 1984, 1989 and 1992

	Mexico City			Mexico		
	1984	1989	1992	1984	1989	1992
IPMM strata						
Indigents	10.1	17.3	17.7	25.5	32.2	34.6
Very poor	9.9	16.8	15.8	12.5	13.8	14.4
*Extremely poor**	*20.0*	*33.1*	*33.5*	*38.0*	*46.0*	*49.0*
Moderately poor	33.8	29.5	28.7	30.4	27.3	25.2
Sum: all poor	**53.8**	**62.6**	**62.2**	**68.4**	**73.3**	**74.2**
Non poor	46.2	37.4	37.8	31.6	26.7	25.8
Total population	100.0	100.0	100.0	100.0	100.0	100.0
Unsatisfied Basic Needs						
Indigents	12.7	11.1	12.1	34.1	28.9	31.3
Very poor	10.2	11.4	13.5	15.1	15.5	16.1
*Extremely poor**	*22.9*	*22.5*	*25.6*	*49.1*	*44.4*	*47.4*
Moderately poor	36.2	33.8	30.3	25.9	25.7	23.3
Sum: all poor	**59.1**	**56.3**	**55.9**	**74.0**	**70.1**	**70.7**
Non poor	40.9	43.7	44.1	26.0	29.9	29.3
Total population	100.0	100.0	100.0	100.0	100.0	100.0
Income Poverty						
Indigents	9.8	18.0	16.0	16.4	26.6	28.0
Very poor	7.0	12.3	13.7	8.6	12.4	12.7
*Extremely poor**	*16.8*	*30.3*	*29.7*	*25.0*	*39.0*	*40.7*
Moderately poor	15.1	18.6	18.3	16.3	16.0	17.1
Sum: all poor	**31.9**	**48.9**	**48.0**	**41.3**	**57.0**	**57.8**
Non poor	68.1	51.1	52.0	58.7	43.0	42.2
Total population	100.0	100.0	100.0	100.0	100.0	100.0
Income-Time Poverty						
Indigents	13.1	24.9	24.2	24.5	35.7	38.5
Very poor	7.7	13.7	13.1	9.8	12.1	11.2
*Extremely poor**	*20.8*	*38.6*	*37.3*	*34.4*	*47.8*	*49.7*
Moderately poor	17.1	17.1	16.6	16.4	14.9	15.2
Sum: all poor	**37.9**	**55.7**	**53.9**	**50.8**	**62.7**	**64.9**
Non poor	62.1	44.3	46.1	49.2	37.3	35.1
Total population	100.0	100.0	100.0	100.0	100.0	100.0

Source: For Mexico City own calculations based on ENIGH databases, INEGI, 1984, 1989 and 1992; for national results, Boltvinik, 1998b, table 7.1: 7.5 and table 7.2: 7.8.
* Sum of indigents and very poor.

7.2.1. Mexico City: IPMM Poverty Decomposition

Table 3.8 decomposes the IPMM poverty gaps for Mexico City into its components in order to allow for an analysis of the role of each component in IPMM change.[32] This table has the particularity that all the data refer to average gaps for the IPMM poor as a whole. As noted earlier, IPMM poverty incidence in Mexico City grew from 1984 to 1989 by almost ten percentage points, from 53.8 per cent to 62.6 per cent, thereafter, from 1989 to 1992, slightly decreasing by less than one percentage point to 62.2 per cent. The IPMM poverty gap[33] also increased quickly during the 1984-1989 period (from 0.2832 to 0.3535), thereafter continuing to grow, but at a slower pace, reaching 0.3586 in 1992. This is a synthetic view of what was previously expressed as the relative growth of the poorest groups and the relative decline of the moderately poor.

Table 3.8. IPMM poverty decomposition. Mexico City, 1984, 1989, 1992. Average deprivation gaps

	1984	1989	1992
IPMM poverty gap (I)	0.2832	0.3535	0.3586
Income-time gap (YT)	0.2591	0.3988	0.3942
Excess working time (EWT)	0.1604	0.1501	0.2114
Income poverty gap (Y)	0.1735	0.3100	0.3010
Global UBN gap (UBN)	0.3236	0.2778	0.2990
Housing (space and quality)	0.4738	0.3704	0.3732
Sanitary services	0.2032	0.1215	0.1689
Electricity and telephone	0.4402	0.4329	0.3978
Basic durable goods	0.1291	0.0248	0.0374
Educational gap	0.2354	0.1442	0.1681
Health care & social security	0.2568	0.3139	0.3742

Source: Own calculations based on ENIGHs databases, INEGI, 1984, 1989, and 1992.

Throughout the period, the poor by IPMM saw their mean income-time poverty gap increase very substantially from 0.2591 to 0.3988, subsequently declining slightly to 0.3942. The UBN poverty gap, on the contrary, is smaller in 1992 than in 1984, despite a rise from 1989 to 1992. Thus, the paradox of some living conditions improving and others deteriorating is present within the IPMM procedure. Because the deterioration in income-time is larger than the improvement in the living conditions depicted under UBN and because the income-time dimension of poverty carries a larger weight, the combined outcome of these inverse evolutions is the overall deterioration of living conditions, i.e. the increase in poverty.

The two components of income-time deprivation deteriorated during the period of analysis, but income deterioration was much larger than time deterioration. While excess working time gap increased from 0.16 to 0.21, a 31 per cent increase, the income gap grew by 76.4 per cent. This implies that for the IPMM poor one does not find the picture described by the authors quoted in chapter 4, whereby deterioration in income was prevented to a large extent by incorporating extra work. The picture, which might be derived from the previous figures, is that income deterioration was very large and that time deterioration was a less significant phenomenon. This would mean that an additional effort was made by a minority of households, but one that was very far away from preventing the drop in real income. Additionally, the increase in the time deprivation index occurred mostly in the 1989-1992 period, when the economy was again growing; during the years of the crisis (1984-1989), however, that index declined. Therefore, the counter-cyclical role of added work is called into question (see Escobar, 1996: 549). The relationship between income decline and extra domestic work effort of households will be discussed in chapter 4 (section 7).

As mentioned above, UBN had a different behaviour. For the period as a whole, all but one component of UBN saw their gap reduced. Nevertheless, the one exception, health care and social security, is not a pure UBN or direct deprivation indicator but a mixed one (i.e. it is calculated by direct observation for part of the population and indirect, through income, for the rest) as can be seen in Methodological Appendix 1. Thus, all five pure UBN component indicators were improving (i.e. the gap was being reduced). These improvements were observed for the population sets that were classified as IPMM poor in both years. This implies that the same families were experiencing the paradox within themselves. At the same time as their income was deteriorating, their housing, sanitary services, other services (electricity and telephone), their basic durable goods, and their educational levels were improving.

Is this possible? Or, can the evidence on UBN be interpreted as proof of the unreliability of income data? Our answer to the first question is yes, it is possible. Our answer to the second question is negative. Even if one were to dismiss all of the Latin American evidence, where income information might be considered as problematic as it is in Mexico, the fact would remain that an influential school of thought in Anglo Saxon literature, especially British and Irish, is pointing in the same direction.

Nolan and Whelan (1996) have summed up the critical points in this discussion quite clearly. In the first place, they point out their surprise on the fact that:

> greater interest in exploring the relationships between income and deprivation has not been sparked off by the results of the limited number of poverty studies which have included both income and direct measures of deprivation −notably Townsend's pioneering British work, followed up by Mack and Lansley and Townsend and Gordon, and that of Mayer and Jencks in the USA. While taking quite different stances on the way poverty should be measured, *these all show an income-deprivation relationship that is rather looser than commonly supposed* (*Ibid.*: 3, emphasis added).

In the empirical analysis conducted with data collected in Ireland, Nolan and Whelan found quite low correlation coefficients between income and deprivation, both on specific deprivation items and on aggregated scores. The correlation coefficients between the enforced lack of each item and the current disposable household income are all negative and lie in the range of -0.05 to −0.18. The average correlation across the 20 items is −0.13 (pages 80-81).

> These correlations are similar to those...reported by previous studies such as Townsend, Mack and Lansley and Mayer and Jencks. While Townsend emphasised the fact that his deprivation indicators are indeed correlated with income (and other measures of resources), some other authors (for example Mayer and Jencks) have focused on the fact that the correlation is so far below 1 — in their case, how little of the variation in scores on a deprivation index is explained by equivalent income (*Ibid.*: 82).

This evidence from developed countries, where the measurement of household income is more reliable, shows the very weak relation prevailing between income and deprivation (or UBN poverty). Thus, my empirical findings, which reveal the paradox of income poverty increasing at the same time that some living conditions captured by direct deprivation indicators are improving, cannot be dismissed on the grounds of unreliability of the income indicator.

8. CHANGES IN HOUSEHOLD LIVING CONDITIONS IN XALPA, MEXICO CITY

Xalpa, the neighbourhood selected to carry out my fieldwork, is an outlying settlement located within the Iztapalapa borough (*delegación*), on the east side of Mexico City. Xalpa[34] was settled on "ejidal" land[35] at the beginning of the 1970s. The majority of the owner-occupiers bought or acquired their plots through illegal transactions,[36] and did not obtain legal ownership documentation until 1993-1994. Legal documentation is the definite step towards obtaining possession certainty, but it is not a necessary condition; indeed, certainty can be achieved without legal documentation. As will be argued later, the introduction of public services to the settlement can be interpreted as a recognition by public authorities of the legitimacy of land tenure and thus can bring about the kind of certainty necessary for people to invest in their dwellings.

Table 3.9. Xalpa: Household socio-economic characteristics by income strata

Income strata*	Household size	Dependency ratio (equivalent adults per worker)	Household expenditure per equivalent adult
1	6.9	4.6	128
2	6.1	3.0	213
3	5.0	3.1	300
4	4.3	2.6	441

Source: Own household survey.
* Income strata refer to the amount of money per equivalent adult per month. The strata are as follows: 1) from $62 to $190 pesos; 2) from $192 to $236 pesos; 3) $237 to $344 pesos; 4) from $345 to $847 pesos.

Before presenting the evolution of the living conditions of my sample in the period 1982-1994, I will analyse the main household demographic characteristics in order to present one of the factors that has been associated with the level of poverty (a household's demographic cycle). At the time the survey was carried out, the average household expenditure per capita in Xalpa[37] was $269 Mexican pesos.[38] The sample data suggest that the poorest households have a higher proportion of dependent children compared with other household groups. The poorest households in the sample (which were classified in the lowest stratum, the first, out of a total of four income strata) had a per equivalent adult (EA)[39] household expenditure of $128 Mexican pesos per month, an average household size of almost seven persons, and a dependency ratio[40] of 4.6 EA per household worker. By contrast, the "better off" in my sample had a per EA expenditure of more than $440 Mexican pesos per month, an average household size of 4.3 persons, and a dependency ratio of 2.6 equivalent adults per worker (see table 3.9). The second and third strata have a similar dependency ratio; nonetheless, they have different levels of expenditure per equivalent adult (see table 3.9).

The data also show that a household's standard of living is highly correlated with the household's ability to supply labour. This ability is in turn also correlated with a household's domestic cycle. The poorest stratum in my sample had the lowest labour force participation rate[41] and the highest number of children up to 15 years of age (see table 3.10). It is important to note that the second lowest income-strata household group had the highest level of labour force participation rate, although their expenditure per equivalent adult is below the average for the entire household sample. This shows that household living conditions depend not only on the number of household members engaged in paid activities, but also on other socio-economic factors, such as a worker's position at work, education, skills, and so on (an aspect that will be discussed in chapters 4 and 5).

With regard to the main concern of this chapter, that is, whether or not there were changes in household living conditions during stabilisation and adjustment, I will discuss some of the difficulties in collecting retrospective household data. In order to obtain data on changes in a household's living conditions I made use of the recall-memory technique (see Damián, 1999, Methodological Appendix 1). However, since it is extremely difficult and highly unreliable to collect data on wages and income by means of this technique, I collected data on only some needs which seemed to be income (e.g. dwelling improvements, household appliances, some recreational expenditures, etc.), income needs being one element in the process of assessing the impact of stabilisation and adjustment on living conditions.

Table 3.10. Household demographic characteristics

Income Strata	Household labour force participation rate	Number of children of 5 years of age and below	Number of children of 15 years old and below	Number of people per room
1	0.47	0.65	2.78	2.3
2	0.59	0.23	1.66	1.7
3	0.54	0.32	1.64	1.5
4	0.54	0.52	1.31	1.3

Source: Own household survey

8.1. Public Services and Dwelling Improvements

Public services in Xalpa began to be provided at the end of the 1970s and beginning of the 1980s. Since then, and throughout the years of economic crisis, the neighbourhood has undergone improvements and upgrading by public authorities. This is a very important fact to keep in mind in interpreting the empirical findings that follow. Consolidation of the neighbourhood is associated with the introduction of public services. This fact implies recognition by public authorities of the legitimacy of people's land tenure and thus implies private tenure certainty. This will then be associated with more investment in improving the dwelling. However, at the time of the fieldwork in the neighbourhood there were still some sections of the neighbourhood where roads were not paved, and where dwellings had neither piped water supply nor sewerage. In my sample, households had almost all public services supplied and only around 10 per cent of them had no paved roads.

The majority of households in my sample (81.3 per cent) were owner-occupiers; another proportion (12.1 per cent) built their houses in a shared plot or was living on borrowed properties; and a small proportion of them was renting (6.6 per cent). Most of the owner-occupiers acquired their plots before the 1982 economic crisis. Those who were living in shared plots were generally sons or daughters who, after getting married, built their homes in the same plots as their parent's homes. This means that they were unable to buy another plot or house. Nonetheless, they were able to afford building their own houses.

In my sample, more than 50 per cent of the households was able to afford paying labour in order to build their homes. Of the total number of dwellings included in my sample, more than 21 per cent were built by construction workers, 30.5 per cent by family members with the participation of construction workers, and the remaining percentage were built completely through "self help". Household members participated in the "self-help" process as a result of two factors: 1) a trade-off between expenditures on housing and expenditures on other necessities; and 2) the involvement of one of the household members in the building industry (e.g. bricklayer).

With regard to the impact of adjustment on a household's living conditions, it has been suggested that the ability of the working class to improve their material conditions was postponed, if not cancelled, during the adjustment period. As Benería (1992:94) has stated: 'Unpainted wall, unpainted floors, leaking roofs, and broken tables and chairs were a common sight not just in the poorest homes but in other that had regularly taken care of these tasks.'[42] However, my data show that, in spite of the crisis and adjustment, some households made improvements in some of these material conditions after 1982.

The material conditions of the majority of housing units in Xalpa improved since the 1970s. When households first entered the neighbourhood,[43] some were living in provisional rooms (12 per cent), others in one room dwellings (24.2 per cent),[44] and the majority of households were living in two rooms dwellings (44 per cent). Only a small proportion of households was living in dwellings with more than two rooms (20 per cent).

The majority of households (80 per cent) built at least one additional room since settling in the neighbourhood; of this percentage, 20.9 per cent of them did so before the 1982 economic crisis and half of the latter (11 per cent) also built another room after 1982. The percentage of households that built another room between 1983 and 1985 was 11.9 per cent. This percentage increased to 25.2 per cent between 1986 and 1990, and to 27.8 per cent between 1991 and 1994 (see table 3.11). As a result of these improvements, the average size of a dwelling increased from around two rooms in 1982 to four rooms in 1995. It can be seen that, although households in Xalpa were able to afford to buy construction materials and other expenditures associated to enlarge their homes throughout my period of analysis, this capacity was at its lowest level during the 1983-85 period, thereby reflecting severe income restrictions.

Table 3.11. Period at which dwelling improvements were carried out (per cent of all dwellings)

Period/Type of improvement	At least another room	Walls	Roofs	Floors
Between 1970 and 1982	9.9	----	1.1	----
Before and after 1982	11.0	1.1	1.1	1.1
Between 1983 and 1985	11.9*	5.5	4.4	3.3
Between 1986 and 1990	25.2*	4.4	5.5	3.3
Between 1991 and 1994	27.8*	12.1	12.1	9.9
Not specified	2.2	----	----	----
Per cent of dwelling improved	80.0	23.1	24.2	17.6

Source: Own household survey
* Includes pro-rata of 11 per cent of before and after 1982. These improvements are then counted twice.

Besides building at least another room, households were able to finance other types of dwelling improvements. Before 1982 these improvements were negligible, apparently as a consequence of the prevalence of land tenure uncertainty before that date. After 1982, when public services were already installed, walls were repaired or renovated in 23 per cent of the dwellings. Some of the improvements on walls (5.5 per cent) were made between 1982 and 1985, or between 1986 and 1990 (4.4 per cent), a period during which the effects of the economic crisis were most felt in the city's economy. Most of the improvements of walls, however, were made between 1991 and 1994 (12.1 per cent, or more than half of all the improvements recorded), a period characterized by recovery in the economy.

Households in Xalpa undertook other dwelling improvements. In more than 24 per cent of the dwellings, roofs were converted from temporary materials into concrete. As in the case of walls, there was a fewer percentage of roof improvements after the economic crisis than during the period when the Mexican economy recovered. In this sense, most roof improvements were carried out between 1991 and 1994. Moreover, floors in 17.6 per cent of the houses were improved or renovated after the 1982 economic crisis, and again the majority of the floors were improved between 1991 and 1994 (see table 3.11).

It can be seen that my data suggest that in Xalpa the quality of housing improved, though in a lesser degree during the period immediately following the economic crisis of 1982 than during the adjustment period. This can be considered indirect evidence that during the period 1982-1990 household income (at least in Xalpa) was at a lower level than during the period 1991-1994. As in many illegal settlements in Mexico City, improvements in Xalpa's dwellings may have resulted from a process of consolidation of the neighbourhood that began in the 1970s. I found that the process of dwelling improvement was associated with, on one hand, the length of time that households had been settled in the neighbourhood, and, on the other, with the economic capacity of households that varied over time. This capacity was, in turn, associated with the availability of jobs and the level of salary/income that different household members received. These findings are similar to those I have already highlighted above with regard to improvements in housing conditions in Mexico and Mexico City.

8.2. Household Appliances

At the time of interviewing, the majority of dwellings had "basic" appliances and furniture (tables, chairs, beds, stoves, radios and T.V. sets). However, the "worst off" households lacked some electric appliances and furniture. For example, 30 per cent of households had no refrigerator, and 37 per cent had no sofas.

In another study of the impact of adjustment on household living conditions in Mexico City, it was found that in several households there were a variety of broken households items that the households did not repair because they were unable to afford the repairs (Benería, 1992:94). Although my questionnaire was not designed to verify whether or not households were unable to repair their household appliances when broken, I nevertheless identified if households were able to afford buying, despite the economic crisis, some household appliances.

Of the total number of households interviewed, around 40 per cent had bought their furniture (tables, chair, beds, and sofas) before 1982. The data show, after the 1982 economic crisis, a reduction in the frequency of households who bought some furniture as well as household and electrical appliances, and, in some cases, a reduction to less than half the level of the previous period (see table 3.12). By 1982, in terms of basic household furniture (beds, chairs, tables, and sofas), 41.5 per cent of the households had at least one of these appliances. As for households that bought their household furniture after the 1982 economic crisis, a lower percentage of them did so between 1983 and 1985 than between 1986 and 1990 (13.7 per cent and 17.8 per cent, respectively). This percentage recovered to 25.0 per cent during the period 1991-1994 (see table 3.12)

Table 3.12. Period at which furniture and household appliances were bought

Period	Furniture	Household appliances	Electrical appliances
Before 1970	13.5	11.1	5.6
Between 1970 and 1982	28.0	25.5	15.2
Between 1983 and 1985	13.7	16.2	6.8
Between 1986 and 1990	17.8	10.0	20.8
Between 1991 and 1994	25.0	35.0	48.2
Not specified	2.0	2.2	3.4
Total	100.0	100.0	100.0

Source: Own household survey

With regard to basic household appliances (e.g. stoves, refrigerators and washing machines), before the 1982 crisis 36.6 per cent of my sample had bought at least one basic household appliance. As table 3.12 shows, this percentage declined during the period 1983-1990. This may suggest that households postponed buying this type of household appliances even longer than furniture or other electrical appliances (see table 3.12). In this case, household capacity to buy household appliances seems also to have improved during the period 1991-1994, when 35 per cent of the households in my sample bought at least one of these appliances.

Before 1982, 20.8 per cent of households bought at least one electrical appliance (e.g. radios, T.V. sets). The majority of households (48 per cent) acquired at least one electrical appliance between 1991 and 1994 (see table 3.12). Moreover, 50 per cent of the dwellings had telephones, which, in most cases (53 per cent), were acquired between 1991 and 1994.

The data collected on this item —basic household consumer durables— in my fieldwork suggests that, despite the crisis and adjustment, most of the poorest households were able to buy some furniture, household or electrical appliances; however, the capability to do this was at its lowest in the eighties and saw a recovery in the nineties (as reflected in table 3.12) when the economy recovered. There were some households which, although unable to buy some of these household items, saw their living condition improved since they received some furniture and household appliances as gifts. More than 20 per cent of households received furniture as a gift.

A commentary is called for with respect to this indicator of durable goods. As can be seen in table 3.8, which was analysed in the previous section, the basic durable goods indicator is, among all indicators of UBN, the one with the lowest gap in Mexico City. In fact, in 1992 the average gap of durable goods for all IPMM poor in Mexico City was almost negligible: 0.0259, which is more than six times smaller than the second smallest UBN gap (the educational one). Apparently what happened was that relative prices of domestic appliances, included as normative in measuring this indicator, have been dropping. In the case of Mexico there is a double process which explains this tendency. On one hand, the international tendency for these prices to go down. On the other, the opening of the economy meant the elimination of the protectionist barriers, which translated into lower prices for these goods. In this sense, the very sharp drop experienced by the basic durable goods gap in Mexico City between 1984 and 1989, as the economy was opened in 1986, is not surprising.

It is also important to note that many of the improvements analysed for Xalpa reflect a consolidation process of household living conditions, since a major proportion of them were in an early stage of the domestic cycle when they settled in the neighbourhood (during the 1970s). If, on one hand, the most striking thing is that some of these households were able to afford buying some furniture or households appliances even during the worse period of the economic crisis (e.g. 8 per cent of households bought furniture between 1983 and 1985), on the other hand, it is very clear that the eighties saw the greatest restrictions in households capabilities to improve their homes.

8.3. Social Life

It has been suggested that during stabilisation and adjustment, as a result of an increase in poverty, households in Mexico City had to reduce or eliminate expenses associated with social activities (Benería, 1992:97). However, some households included in my sample were able to continue celebrating traditional parties (e.g. first communion, weddings, and baptism), even during stabilisation. For instance, 33 per cent of the sample celebrated baptisms, and 24.2 per cent celebrated a first communion, though the majority of such festive celebrations (60 per cent) took place between 1990 and 1994. This evidence clearly points out that during the eighties many celebrations of this type were postponed or took place without a party.

It has also been suggested that households were forced to reduce or eliminate expenses associated with visits to relatives or with being able to go on a holiday after the 1982 economic crisis. Benería (1992:96) affirms that households decreased or eliminated annual or biannual trips to other parts of Mexico associated with Christmas, religious holidays, vacations and other family gatherings. I found that the number of households being able to perform these activities increased after 1985. Around 1985 almost 40 per cent of my sample went on trips to other parts of Mexico, and after 1985 this percentage increased to 66 per cent. Nonetheless, I found that around 1985 in almost 70 per cent of cases all household members used to go on trips together; however, after 1985 this percentage was reduced to less than 50 per cent, with a resulting increase in the number of trips done by one or few household members. In both cases the majority of households went on trips to visit their families (around 60 per cent) and less than 30 per cent went on holidays.

This is the evidence from my survey in Xalpa. This is reinforced by the evidence taken from published data on national urban household income and expenditure surveys (see table 3.13). If we were to postulate the null hypothesis that households were not subject to a decrease in real income in the eighties, we would have to reject that hypothesis on the evidence provided by table 3.13. For the hypothesis to be true there would have to be no significant difference between the 1977 data (before the

1982 crisis) and the 1984 data (during the crisis). Furthermore, the 1992 figures would show no significant difference with the 1984 figures. But there are very notable differences: 1984 indicators are in general below both those in 1977 and in those in 1992. This is true both of percent of households reporting the expenditure and of the percent the expenditure represents of all expenditures. The percent of all urban households reporting expenditures on clothing and shoes in 1984 is five or more percentage points below the 1977 and 1992 figures. The percentage of total expenditure devoted to clothing and shoes goes down very significantly from 1977 to 1984 (from 10.5 per cent to 7.4 per cent) and then, in 1992, shows a slight recovery but remains much below the 1977 figure (7.8 per cent).

Table 3.13. **Mexico: Selected household expenditure in urban (high density) areas, 1977, 1984, 1992 (per cent)**

Concept	1977		1984		1992	
	Housh.	Exp.	Housh.	Exp.	Housh.	Exp.
Clothing and shoes	88.77	10.54	83.24	7.40	88.05	7.79
Furniture and appliances[a]	62.66	3.83	23.62	1.60	32.75	2.04
Recreation[b]	49.31	3.32	32.98	1.32	27.60	1.57
Parties	n.a.d.	n.a.d.	3.28	0.66	3.42	0.49
Touristic expenditures	n.a.d.	n.a.d.	0.99	0.15	2.20	0.46
Temporary lodging	6.41	0.86	4.26	0.43	4.90	0.54
Housing repairs	n.a.d.	n.a.d.	n.a.d.	n.a.d.	n.a.d.	n.a.d
Housing repair materials	n.a.d.	n.a.d.	11.89	0.90	11.33	1.10
Housing repair & enlargement	n.a.d.	n.a.d.	4.19	0.50	7.14	0.99

Source: For the 1977 data: SPP, 1977; for the 1984 and 1992 data: INEGI, 1989a and 1993a.
Key: Housh. = Percentage of households reporting the expenditure.
Exp. = Percentage of expenditure in total expenditure.
[a] In 1984 and 1992 it includes only recreational services.
[b] The concept in 1977 is broader and thus not comparable with the other two years.
n.a.d.: No available data.

In the same way, expenditure on temporary lodging (hotels and similar) goes down from 6.4 per cent to 4.3 per cent percent and recovers only partially, rising to 4.9 per cent in 1992. Housing repairs[45] in 1977 cannot be compared with the other two years. Nevertheless, there is a clear trend between 1984 and 1992 whereupon one can see, bringing together the two concepts included in the table, that 1984 represents a low point in these expenditures (1.4 per cent of all expenditures *vis à vis* 2.1 per cent in 1992). Something similar happens with respect to the percentage of households reporting expenditure in the items.

8.4. Household Borrowing Capacity

Three years after the 1982 economic crisis, in 1985, more than 25 per cent of households in my sample resorted to borrowing some money in order to meet ends. Almost 74 per cent of households that resorted to borrowing money stated that the prime reason for borrowing was to buy food. By 1994 the percentage of households that resorted to borrowing money slightly declined to 23 per cent. The relevance of borrowing money in order to buy some food also declined to 66 per cent, thereby increasing the percentage of other reasons for asking for money (e.g. transportation, rent, etc.).[46] This reinforces the evidence in the direction of the reduction of real income during the eighties.

8.5. Education

It has been claimed that one of the population groups most affected by economic crisis and adjustment were young people, particularly those finishing secondary school, who were obliged to discontinue their education in order to earn money to contribute to the reduced household income. Benería (1992:92) affirms that, as a result of the severity of the 1982 economic crisis, schooling interruption was probably permanent for many teenagers. However, the findings of this study show little evidence of children leaving school in order to work.

In Xalpa the educational levels for those who were 6 years of age and over were as follows: 5.4 per cent were illiterate,[47] 45.1 per cent had primary school education, 33.4 per cent had secondary school education, and 16.1 per cent had higher school education. In keeping with the improvement trends in education at the national and city level in spite of the 1982 economic crisis, the data suggests that in Xalpa the educational levels of the sample population were rising. For instance, the percentage of the population that had completed primary school education rose. Dividing the population by age groups I found that 35 per cent of the group who were between 31 and 35 years of age had studied no farther than primary school education. This percentage declined to less than 20 per cent for the group who were between 26 and 30 years of age, and to less than 10 per cent for the group who were between 16 and 20 years of age. The remaining percentages had studied at least a year of secondary school education or more.

Educational improvements are clearly observed when intergenerational changes are analysed. While around 10 per cent of parents were illiterate, this percentage was only 1.4 per cent for sons and 2.3 per cent for daughters (see table 3.14). Moreover, the majority of parents had only primary school education (62 per cent of fathers and 55.3 per cent of mothers), while the majority of children had secondary school and above (68 per cent of sons and 60.3 per cent of daughters).

Table 3.14. Educational level of household members

	Total	Fathers	Mothers	Sons	Daughters
Illiterates	5.4	10.0	9.0	1.4	2.3
Primary	45.1	62.3	55.3	39.8	37.4
Secondary.	33.4	21.1	25.2	41.4	38.9
Preparatory	8.7	2.2	3.0	12.3	12.2
University	6.3	2.2	7.5	4.3	9.2
Not specified	1.1	2.2	----	0.8	----
Total	100.0	100.0	100.0	100.0	100.0

Source: Own household survey

In general, my findings show that the majority of sons and daughters remained in school at least until the end of secondary school, and a larger proportion of them went on to the preparatory college (high school), compared to their parents. At the time of the interviews, which coincided with the summer vacations, some children were involved in family petty retail trade activities, or selling newspapers, but for most of these children such employment was restricted to holidays.

In addition, the percentage of children dropping-out from school was 6 per cent, a percentage similar to that observed at the national level (5 per cent for primary school and 7 per cent for secondary school, Friedmann, *et al.* 1995; table 9-14). However, I did not find children dropping out from school as a result of a general deterioration in living conditions during adjustment. This process was more associated with "household crisis", e.g. desertion by the father, or sickness or death of the main breadwinner.

Gender studies show that in general women have poorer education levels as compared to those of men (see Roldán, 1985). My data show that women had higher educational levels than men did, as a whole, particularly in the older generation, where mothers had a much better level of education than men did. This is particularly noteworthy in the percentages of persons with university education, where mother's level is almost 3.5 times that of fathers, and daughters' level is more than twice the level of sons. Additionally, the younger generation of women was much better educated as compared to their mothers. (See table 3.14).

It can be argued that in spite of economic crisis and of stabilisation and structural adjustment policies, sons and daughters were not prematurely sent into the labour market and households were able to afford children spending longer periods of time in the educational system. Therefore, for children, educational levels have improved compared with that of their parents, even during stabilisation and adjustment. The links between educational improvement and employment status will be explored in chapter 5 (section 2) for the population of Xalpa.

Although I do not have income data for my sample, the findings presented in this chapter reinforce the evidence found previously at the national level and at the Mexico City Metropolitan Area. On one hand, the evidence shows that living dimensions like education continued to improve during the eighties. On the other hand, I found evidence of income deterioration in that expenditures on discretional areas like housing or recreation were at their lowest in the eighties.

9. SUMMARY

Taking into account the contradictory trends of income and other welfare indices in Mexico during the period 1982-1994, is it possible to hold that poverty increased after the 1982 economic crisis as well as during the years of stabilisation and adjustment? To answer this question I have looked at: first, the consistency and reliability of the data sources from which conclusions on poverty have been arrived at and presented in published studies; second, the methodologies applied to measure poverty; third, the poverty incidence trends that derive from available poverty measurements at the national level; fourth, I calculated poverty trends in Mexico City based on a methodology that allows the examination of the different forces that determine the level of poverty; and, finally, I contrasted the general trends I found for Mexico and Mexico City with the data derived from fieldwork.

I have already pointed out the main weaknesses of the ENIGHs with respect to their comparability and reliability. For example, in the ENIGHs, household income tends to be underreported compared with that estimated by means of national accounts (e.g. 46.7 per cent in 1984 and 38.7 per cent in 1989). Therefore, measuring poverty by means of the original survey data may lead to an underestimation of the living standards of households.

Inasmuch as household income is underreported in the ENIGH, when poverty is estimated using the original raw data of the surveys one finds that income poverty declined in the period 1984-1989. This contradicts most of the evidence, which shows a deterioration in income during that period. For instance, national accounts report that average earnings, consumption per capita, as well as GDP per capita were at their lowest level in those years, compared with their 1982 level (see chapter 2). Because of this inconsistency, most scholars and official agencies calculate income poverty adjusting the ENIGH's household income to National Accounts.

An additional problem in the measurement of poverty by means of the ENIGHs is that the nearest survey carried out before the 1982 crisis was the 1977 ENIGH, and the nearest one after the crisis, the 1984 ENIGH. That means that there are no empirical data on household income on which we can rely in order to assess the impact of the economic crisis. To do this, data on 1981 or 1982 would be required.

If raw income data are used to measure changes in household income, one finds that income increases in the poorest 60 per cent of the population between 1977 and 1984, despite the economic crisis. The conclusion would be that the economic crisis hardly affected the income level of the poorest strata of the population, and, therefore, poverty was reduced. Nonetheless, if income figures are adjusted to NA the level of poverty remains almost constant (58 per cent and 58.5 per cent, respectively). This means that, if poverty was reduced during the oil boom period, the 1982 economic crisis eliminated such progress.

With regard to poverty trends after the 1982 crisis, studies on poverty at the national level have different findings. This diversity is explained by the use of different methods to measure poverty, different definitions of poverty lines, and the varied methodologies used to adjusting household income of the ENIGHs to national accounts (including non adjustment). While almost all studies affirm that poverty increased between 1984 and 1994, some of them contend that poverty reached its highest level in 1989 and then began to decline. To the contrary, Boltvinik (1998b) argues that poverty continued to increase up to 1992 and then remained constant up to 1994.

This disagreement has important implications with regard to policy reform in Mexico. The implicit corollary in the contention that poverty began to decrease from 1989 onwards is that the policies followed by the Mexican government after the 1982 economic crisis helped the economy to eventually recover. Therefore, it is possible to reduce poverty by means of these policies. On the other hand, for analysts who affirm that poverty did not decline in the entire period, the implicit corollary is that the policy reforms were unable to benefit the poor.

As mentioned before, there is a consensus that income poverty increased between 1984 and 1994. In contrast, all social indices show that poverty, as measured by the Unsatisfied Basic Needs method, declined during adjustment in Mexico. Moreover, infant mortality and life expectancy improved. Similarly, it has been observed that there was an improvement in the quality of shelter, and in health and educational levels. These findings seem to contradict the idea of a decline in income. This paradox has to be explained.

After analysing different methods used to measure poverty (PL and UBN) I arrived at the conclusion that none of them alone can be taken as a reliable indicator of poverty trends. While poverty lines are normally defined in terms of income, which is an indirect measure of consumption, poverty tends to be overestimated since not all consumption is monetised. Moreover, there is a growing stream of criticism of those measurements of poverty that rely entirely on income. Reliance on income has been criticised 'on the grounds that low income is not a reliable measure of exclusion arising from lack of resources' (Nolan and Whelan, 1996:2). Nolan and Whelan also point out that there are long-term factors that influence households' current situation, which cannot be assessed with the analysis of income dynamics from one year to the next (*Ibid.*:220). Therefore, it is difficult to gauge what was the impact of adjustment on poverty relying on income exclusively.

On the other hand, to focus entirely on deprivation measures of poverty (e.g. UBN) equally poses some problems. As noted, in its usual applications in Latin America, the poor identified by means of UBN, among other problems, tend to increase as the number of basic need categories rises.

Taking into consideration the contradictory trends of poverty in Mexico (measured by income and other welfare indices) and the criticism of the PL and UBN methods, I decided to make use of an approach to identify the poor which incorporates both income and deprivation in the measurement of poverty (the IPMM). The particularly of the IPMM is that it takes into consideration not only income and basic needs deprivation as the forces that lead to specific levels of poverty, but also how the time devoted to extra-domestic work affects household living standards.

My point of departure was to compare the IPMM poverty level in Mexico and Mexico City. The trends between 1984 and 1992 point to an increase in poverty both in the city as well as nationwide. However, between 1984 and 1989 the increase in poverty was more pronounced in the former than in the latter. The increase in poverty concentrated in social groups with the lowest levels of income; in this sense, extreme poverty in Mexico City almost doubled between 1984 and 1989. In the 1989-1992 period, while IPMM poverty continued to grow at the national level, there was a slight reduction of poverty in Mexico City.

Looking at the evolution of the two main dimensions of IPMM I found, once again, the paradox of declining UBN poverty and rising income-time (YT) poverty. These paradoxical trends of the two main dimensions of poverty have already been found in multidimensional studies of poverty for other countries of Latin America and for some Anglo Saxon countries, including the United Kingdom and Ireland As noted in section 7.3, poverty studies including both income and direct measures of deprivation have shown a rather looser income-deprivation association than commonly supposed.

I found that while income poverty increased in the City from 32.5 per cent of the population to 52 per cent between 1984 and 1992, the percentage of the population whose basic needs were unsatisfied fell from 60.8 per cent to 56.2 per cent in the same period. Part of this paradox may be explained by two main factors. On one hand, social spending in Mexico was not reduced in real terms, and therefore more people had access to health and education services. On the other, some improvements in certain income needs measured by the UBN method may also have improved by the fact that, with the opening of the Mexican economy to external competition, the price of some basic household durable goods (e.g. electrical appliances) was reduced. Although more empirical research needs to be done on this important issue, my data show that the improvement in those income needs measured by the UBN method mainly took place between 1984 and 1989, that is, a period during which the Mexican economy was opened to external competition (in 1986). In Mexico City, the Basic Durable Goods Gap fell from 0.12 in 1984 and to 0.02 in 1989, and slightly increased in 1992, when the Mexican economy was recovering. Therefore, it seems that household improvements in certain areas of welfare are associated not only with income but also with other economic and non-economic factors.

There are other factors that may explain improvements in the material conditions of dwellings in Mexico City (the Housing Poverty Gap went down from 0.47 in 1984 to 0.36 in 1989, and after this important decline, it remained at the same level from 1989 to 1992). For instance, there was increased coverage in the provision of public services in the city, and, as my fieldwork in Xalpa showed, improvements in the material conditions of dwellings were associated with the provision of these services. Moreover, the use of concrete brick became widespread, which is much cheaper than traditional brick. This allowed poor families to improve their dwelling's precarious conditions with the use of a low-cost durable material. However, these hypotheses have to be tested.

With regard to my findings based on fieldwork, I found that there seems to be an improvement in certain aspects of household living conditions during the period of stabilisation and adjustment in Xalpa. Households saw improvements in particular areas associated with shelter and household equipment. It was also observed, for example, that a larger proportion of households continued to spend money on social activities, such as family visits and holidays. Education for the younger generation in my sample also improved, with more children remaining in education beyond primary and secondary school. It was also found that the reasons for children dropping out of school were not associated with a general trend of a decline in living conditions, but, rather, with a particular household's circumstances.

These findings confirm the general trend observed for the city and for the nation as a whole with regard to the material conditions of dwellings and other welfare indicators. However, it should be noted that my data also suggest a reduction in household capacity to carry out dwelling improvements and to acquire household appliances and furniture during the 1980s, that is, the decade when the Mexican economic was most affected by the economic crisis. In contrast, household capacity to improve its living conditions resumed in the period 1990-1994, when GDP per capita began to recover.

In summation, my findings suggest that during the stabilisation and adjustment periods there were opposite forces affecting the welfare of the population during the process of policy reform. It seems that while the improvement of social indicators was relatively protected, household income was not. Some policies (e.g. trade liberalisation) may have had a positive impact on household consumption by lowering the prices of some basic goods (e.g. household durables). There may also be other forces (e.g. technological changes), that have led to improvements in household living conditions, which are not related to policy reform.

Turning to another of the central issues of this book, I introduced in this chapter the analysis of the time deprivation index, which will help us to measure to what extent there was an increase in the labour force participation of household members in response to the decline in income. For Mexico City I found that income deteriorated to a much larger degree than time deprivation. I also found that the increase in the time deprivation index took place between 1989 and 1992, a period during which income poverty remained almost constant. This means that, as income declined, households incorporated a much less significant additional work effort than that suggested scholarly studies published by other authors. Moreover, the trend of this index suggests that extra work is not factually associated with income decline. However, as we will see in the next chapter, employment figures point to an increase in the level of employment, despite the decline in income.

Notes

[1] As noted above, for poverty measurement purposes income figures are normally adjusted; however, this is a controversial issue, which is on debate.
[2] It is necessary, nevertheless, to point out that since the food baskets in both the INEGI-CEPAL study and the UNDP-CEPAL study are based on observed diets of non-undernourished population, the food baskets thus defined are time and place specific, i.e., culturally determined. In this sense, these studies cannot be labelled as belonging to the biological approach. On the other hand, the World Bank studies, where the

3   definition of the extreme poverty line is based on the cost of a food basket that reflects the diets of the poor, are much closer to the biological approach.
4   Nevertheless, this is not necessarily so. In the Beccaria, *et al.* (1992) study, Brazil was subdivided into several regions for which specific food baskets and poverty lines were calculated. For a presentation of these results consult CEPAL, 1986.
5   This is the approach adopted by CEPAL. It has been called by Bo.tvinik (1998b) the reference stratum sub-variant of the Standard Food Basket (SFB) PL method. Nevertheless, there are other possible choices for the Engel's Coefficient. Molly Orshansky (1965), who may be regarded as the "inventor" of the methodology used in the official U.S. poverty measurement method, adopted the Engel's Coefficient of the average population. The Engel's Coefficient of the poor population might also be selected. However, in the case of the INEGI-CEPAL study, the poverty line was calculated by multiplying by two the extreme poverty line.
6   Coordinación General del Plan Nacional de Zonas Deprimidas y Grupos Marginados (COPLAMAR - General Coordination of the National Plan for Depressed Zones and Marginalized Groups).
7   However, the last-mentioned authors took as their poverty line what COPLAMAR regarded as the extreme poverty line, i.e. the cost of food, food implements and fuel, education, health and housing.
8   For instance, to calculate the amount of money required to acquire toothpaste, the quantity of toothpaste required by a person in order to wash his teeth three times a day was determined by conducting experiments with the toothpaste.
9   As a matter of fact none of these items is included in the COPLAMAR basket. Instead, it includes launderette service.
10 As noted, the poverty line in the COPLAMAR study considers, for example, the quantity of toothpaste needed by any person to wash his teeth three times a day and not the amount of money spent on toothpaste by the seventh decile.
11 Levy obtains around 80 per cent poverty incidence in 1984 because he does not adjust income figures from the ENIGH to National Accounts, whereas COPLAMAR does adjust.
12 This description is further complemented in the second section of the Methodological Appendix 1.
13 An ENIGH was not conducted for 1981. However, Hernández-Leos estimated poverty assuming that the composition of household income distribution was not modified between 1977 and 1981. He then applied the increase in the level of consumption as reported in National Accounts to estimate the shift in the income distribution curve.
14 It should be noted that the 1977 and 1984 ENIGHs are not comparable because the survey questionnaires are different. Moreover, while the 1977 ENIGH reports data only on monetary income, the 1984 survey also includes non-monetary income.
15 According to Cortés's figures (1996, table 8:22), the ENIGHs report a very substantial increase in real income per capita for the whole population between 1984 and 1989, from 808.3 thousand pesos to 934.6 thousand pesos. After adjusting to National Accounts, this evolution is reversed as will be emphasised in the text.
16 Nonetheless, the poverty gap increased and inequality within the poor also increased (*Ibid.*).
17 In this poverty index, the poverty gaps of each household are squared before adding them up, thus exaggerating the importance of the very poor.
18 In this study the poverty gap for moderate poverty went down from 10.6 per cent in 1989 to 10.2 per cent in 1992 and the Foster-Greer-Thorbecke index from 5.53 to 5.16 (Pánuco-Laguette and Székely (1996, table 8:198).

18 These figures were calculated based on the IMSS-COPLAMAR reports regarding a programme that provides basic health-care to uninsured families in poor rural areas (Friedmann, et al., 1995). This source, which reports a universe of 1 million children under the age of five, is not based on a representative sample and therefore its results should be taken with care.
19 These data are based on surveys carried out in rural areas in 1978 and 1989 by the Mexican National Nutritional Institute (see Friedmann, et al., 1995).
20 These studies were carried out by the Secretaría de Salud (National Nutrition survey-Health Ministry), and by the INNSZ (Boltvinik, 1998a:320).
21 Note that average consumption per capita in all groups is below normative requirements, which CEPAL-UNDP (1992: 340) defined for Mexico in 1980 as 2139 kilocalories per day. Moreover, note that caloric intake does not seem to be associated with a social strata's socio-economic level. These two features and the fact that the sample is not statistically representative cast serious doubt on the reliability of these figures.
22 The procedure to estimate health service capacity consists in defining a number of people for whom each unit of health resource is able to service adequately. For instance, one doctor was defined, on the base of a comparative analysis of international health indicators, as capable of providing adequate services to 1100 persons. The other resources included were nurses, beds, laboratories, operating theatres, and X ray cabinets.
23 Boltvinik (1994c) defined crowded dwellings as those having more than 2 persons per room in urban areas and more than 2.5 persons rural areas.
24 The National Consumers Institute carried out a follow-up family survey between June 1985 and February 1988 in Mexico City. The survey began with a non-representative sample of 258 families and ended with 172 families. In the survey, families were interviewed six times. The information collected was on: household members' demographic characteristics (main activity, age, etc.); household income and expenditure; and household consumption. This survey has several problems: 1) As the number of families varied in each stage, the original panel idea is lost (in November 1985, 280 families were interviewed, and in August 1986 this number increased to 518 families, INCO, 1987:2); and 2) only 172 families were interviewed in February 1988, therefore the well-known selection problem might be present and the results might be biased.
25 In the INCO study families were classified according to their income level and according to whether the household head was working in the formal or informal sector. Formal sector workers were regular salaried employees, who had social security. Informal sector workers were self-employed workers, or workers who had no legal contract and no social security.

There were five income groups: two low-income groups (one formal and one informal), composed of households whose income ranged between 0.8 to 1.5 minimum salaries; one formal low-middle-income group, made up of households whose income ranged between 1.5 and 2.5 minimum salaries; one formal middle-income group (households whose income ranged between 2.5 and 3.5); and one informal middle-income group, comprised of households whose income ranged between 1.5 and 3.5 minimum salaries (INCO, 1987).
26 It is important to note that Benería's study is based on a non-random sample of women working in subcontracting in the manufacturing sector and therefore this author's conclusions cannot be taken as representative of poverty trends in Mexico City. This study compares household data of a survey conducted between 1981 and 1982 with another survey conducted in 1988. A total of 140 households were interviewed in 1982

and 55 households in 1988. In this last year, half of the interviewed households (27) belonged to the original sample, and the other half were included through a snowball technique.

[27] Boltvinik followed Cortés's (1997) methodology for adjusting income to National Accounts. As Cortés has stated, the changes in the methodology used for constructing the National Accounts, which were introduced in Mexico in 1994, make it almost impossible to obtain a comparable series with the previous years. For instance, as a result of the new methodology, there is a significant increase in the percentage share of salaried income in total value added. That is why no attempt was made to include 1994 in the following calculations, despite the fact that an ENIGH was carried out on that year. This might not be important either, given the great deal of consensus among scholars that from 1992 to 1994 there was almost complete stability in the level of poverty at the national level. It is very likely that the same findings would result in Mexico City. Thus, 1992 can be regarded, with all due precaution, as showing the end of my period of analysis.

[28] There are various caveats in the data which have been analysed in section 2. At this point suffice it to note that the sample size in 1984 is much smaller than in 1989 and in 1992, which of course makes the errors larger in 1984. In 1984 the number of households in the sample was 542, whereas in 1989 it was 1793 and in 1992 it was 1770. These household sample sizes, given the average household number of members of 4.99, 4.59 and 4.50, results in 2705, 8230 and 7965 persons surveyed in each year.

[29] Indigents were defined as individuals who meet less than 50 per cent of the overall normative score; very poor, individuals who meet from 50 per cent to 66 per cent of this score; finally, moderately poor, individuals who meet more than 66 per cent of the normative score, but less than 100 per cent.

[30] The extremely poor are defined as the sum of the indigent and the very poor.

[31] Income is combined with time by dividing household income by an index of Excess Working Time (EWT) prior to comparing it with the poverty line. EWT is an index which at the normative level is equal to 1. In the case that EWT is equal to 1 the income of households that do not overwork or underwork remains unchanged. Households that overwork will have an EWT greater than 1, they will be time poor and their income will be lowered when divided by EWT. Households that underwork will have an EWT less than 1, they will be time non-poor and their income will be increased. It should be noted that the income of households, whose income is below the poverty line and who are time non-poor, is not adjusted since it is assumed that they underwork for involuntary reasons (e.g. unemployment).

EWT is obtained with the following formula for each household j:

$EWT_j = (1+W_j) / (k^*_j W^*) = (1+W_j)/(k^*_j 48)$, where W_j are the hours of extra domestic work by the household members; W^* is equal to 48 hours of work, which is the Mexican weekly standard of hours of work and k^*_j are the normative extra domestic workweeks in the household j. k^*_j is calculated as follows:

$k^*_j = N^{15-69}{}_j - h_j |$ when $h_j < N^{15-69}{}_j$;

$N^{15-69}{}_j$ is the number of household members aged 15-69; h_j represents household members who are excluded in the calculation of a household's normative extradomestic workweeks. The excluded household members are the following: 1) members who did not work during the reference week, despite having a job (and therefore the number of hours worked recorded by the survey is equal to cero); 2) members who are permanently disabled; 3) part of the time of members who are students (0.5833); and 4) a calculated number of workweeks required for domestic work. To calculate the workweeks required for domestic work, Boltvinik (1998b, Methodological Appendix) developed an index of

Intensity of Domestic Work, which is calculated by combining three indicators: Water Carrying, Deprivation of Labour-saving Domestic Equipment and Deprivation of Day Care Services for Children. The combination of these indicators with the number of members in the home and the presence of children less than 10 years of age defines the number of workweeks excluded from extradomestic work, inasmuch as these workweeks are required for domestic work.

[32] As NA does not provide data at the city level, income data for Mexico City were adjusted to NA with the same coefficients used to adjust income figures at the national level. Using the same coefficient for all areas in the country is the usual practice among those who adjust income figures.

[33] As noted, this gap is the weighted average of the income-time gap (YT) and the global UBN gap, where the weights, based on participation in costs, are 0.626 for the former and 0.374 for the latter.

[34] It should be kept in mind that my household sample is representative for the neighbourhood and not for the city as a whole. Moreover, as the household data was collected by means of a retrospective survey, there are some limitations when comparing data over time. Therefore, conclusions should be taken with extreme caution (see Damián, 1999, Methodological Appendix 1).

[35] The ejidal lands were established in Mexico after the revolution. The lands were handed over to landless communities, who could use the land but not sell it.

[36] Illegal in this case refers to the process of invading the land, or selling the land with no legal documentation, or without meeting planning regulations.

[37] Household expenditure includes food, transportation, electricity, gas, rent (where applicable) and other expenditures, such as medicines, clothes, shoes, and so on, that depend on a household's budget.

[38] The exchange rate at the time of the interview was approximately 6 Mexican pesos per US dollar.

[39] The number of equivalent adults was calculated taking children of up to 12 years of age and adults of 65 years and over, who were taken to represent 75 per cent of the expenditure required for household members aged between 13 and 64 years. Therefore each child and each old person counts as 0.75 equivalent adults.

[40] The dependency rate is the number of equivalent adults who depend on a household member who works and contributes to the household budget. It is calculated by dividing the number of equivalent adults in the household by the number of working members.

[41] The household's participation rate is the proportion of household members between 16 and 65 years old who are working (employed).

[42] For a description of the main characteristics of this study please refer to endnote 25.

[43] Most of the families in my sample (75 per cent) had been living in Xalpa for more than 10 years.

[44] The number of rooms considers the kitchen, since in many dwellings the cooking and eating area are together.

[45] This item is classified as a capital transaction in the surveys and not, as the rest, as a current transaction, so that the division by total current expenditure is somewhat unorthodox.

[46] At the time I carried out my fieldwork (July 1995), seven months after the 1994 financial crisis in Mexico, the percentage of households that resorted to borrowing money in order to make ends meet had increased to almost 40 per cent of my sample.

[47] Illiteracy in Xalpa was slightly higher than that for Mexico City in 1990 (4.0 per cent).

4 Labour Force Participation Trends (1979-1994)

1. INTRODUCTION

Despite that some authors, during the 1970s, recognised the relevance of demand side-factors in explaining changes in the level of labour force participation rates in Mexico (e.g. Muñoz: 1975), there was widespread concern about employment conditions in Mexico. It was said that the Mexican economy was unable to create enough jobs for the growing Economically Active Population (EAP).[1] This perception was reinforced by the fact that, during the 1970s, the industrial growth rate began to decline. This was seen as a sign of economic stagnation. Scholars then suggested that the economy's ability to generate employment had declined. Since then, there has emerged widespread concern over employment conditions in Mexico.

The eruption of the 1982 economic crisis reinforced the pessimistic appraisal of labour market conditions in Mexico. However, contrary to all expectations, employment statistics showed that employment grew after 1982. This was interpreted by many scholars as a sign that more household members entered the labour market to counteract the losses in income suffered as a result of the 1982 debt crisis and of the economic policies implemented by the government. This interpretation is based implicitly on the idea that the supply of labour is counter-cyclical. As Escobar (1996:549) — an outstanding proponent of what I have called the Labour Survival Strategy Current of Thought (LSSCT) — has stated, "a group of anthropologists, socio-demographers, and human geographers have focused on the household as the significant social unit defining the amount of extra work performed by individuals ... To some (González de la Rocha, Escobar, Tuirán, Cortés) additional work is countercyclical: the economically active population (EAP) tends to grow under crisis and restructuring."[2]

In this chapter, I start by reviewing the available sources on employment data and the restrictions and problems such sources impose to the study of the labour market in Mexico in the 1982-1994 period (section 2). I then discuss the prevailing interpretations of the increase in the labour force participation rate during our period of study and confront these interpretations with a new look at the empirical evidence provided by the employment surveys (ECSO/ENE/ENEU) both at the national level and the Mexico City level (section 3) and the empirical evidence provided by the national household income and expenditure surveys (ENIGHs), again for both levels, nationwide and Mexico City (section 4). In section 5 I discuss trends in labour force participation rates in women's work and in section 6 I discuss the trends in work by adolescents. Section 7 concludes my discussion on this topic by incorporating some important evidence derived from the poverty measurement exercise of the Integrated Poverty Measurement Method (IPMM) presented in chapter 3 (section 8) which highlights the interaction of income and time deprivation.

2. EMPLOYMENT DATA SOURCES AND EMPLOYMENT DEFINITIONS

Although several attempts have been made to define the concepts of employment and unemployment; the complexity of the labour market makes it very difficult to construct an objective concept of employment/unemployment. Employment has generally been defined as the number of persons who are engaged in any economic activity for pay, profit, or family gain. Unemployment has been defined as the number of persons who are not working, but who are willing and able to work and who are seeking a job. However, because willingness and ability to work depend on economic, social and cultural factors, they are not absolute concepts. Moreover, there is an ongoing debate over other definitions of particular concepts of employment, such as self-employment and unpaid work.[3]

There are several basic statistical sources on employment in Mexico. However, few of them are consistent over time regarding the definition of variables, coverage, quality or reliability of the data. The challenge in using this statistical material to analyse changes in labour force participation during the period of stabilisation and adjustment is particularly great.

2.1 Population Censuses

Population censuses, which are normally considered to be the sources that provide consistent information about employment, have been challenged on several grounds. First, there are serious doubts concerning the reliability of the 1980 National Housing & Population Census, for even total population was apparently greatly overestimated, especially in some cities such as Mexico City (Camposortega, 1992:3).

García (1994:12) has stated that the 1980 Population Census "overestimates" the Economically Active Population (EAP). In Mexico, the EAP is defined as the number of persons aged twelve years of age or older who are employed or unemployed. Employment is defined as the number of persons who were engaged in any economic activity in the reference week (in this case, the previous week). Unemployment was defined as the number of persons who did not work and did not have a job in the reference week, but who were looking for a job. However, as I will explain below, the censuses have introduced changes in the definition of the weekly number of hours of work to be considered as the minimum criterion for being employed.

In the 1970 Population Census, in order to identify the EAP, a person's economic activity was linked explicitly to the number of hours worked during the preceding week.[4] In the 1980 Population Census, however, that link was lost.[5] In 1970 the EAP comprised persons who earned income and worked at least *one* hour during the previous week and persons who did not earn income and worked at least *fifteen* hours during the previous week. In 1980, persons who worked without earning income were included in the EAP regardless of the number of hours that they had worked. The changes in the definition of the EAP resulted in an increase in the labour force participation rate beyond the expectations of the experts. Thus, between 1970 and 1980, the labour force participation rate rose from 71.6 per cent to 75.1 per cent for males, and from 16.4 per cent to 27.8 per cent for females (García, 1994, table 1.2:15).

Another difficulty in examining changes in employment figures based on the 1980 Population Census is the large percentage of the EAP which was classified as "insufficiently specified". For instance, the percentage of workers whose economic activity was classified as "insufficiently specified" accounted for 29.8 per cent of the total employed population (*Ibid*. table 1.6:18). Therefore, there are several difficulties encountered in comparing the 1980 Population Census with other Population Censuses.

In an effort to overcome some of the problems of the 1980 Population Census, the 1990 Population Census modified the employment questions included in its questionnaire. Nonetheless, it seems that such changes led to an underestimation of the EAP. It seems that what most affected the measurement of the EAP in 1990 was the removal of some questions concerning the identification of "unpaid workers".[6] As a result, only workers who perceived their activity as a job were included in the total of the EAP (García, 1994:19-20). According to García (1994:24), this may have affected the level of participation, since the definition of "work" depends on economic, social and cultural factors. García notes that several studies have shown that some workers, particularly women and children, perform certain types of economic activities that they do not recognise as "work" per se. This may lead to an underestimation of the labour force, as seems to have occurred in the 1990 Population Census, particularly concerning women's participation, which was highly underestimated. According to the Population Censuses' figures, between 1980 and 1990 the labour force participation rate declined from 75.1 per cent to 68 per cent for men, and from 27.8 per cent to 19.6 per cent for women. Thus, neither the 1980 nor the 1990 Population Censuses are thought to be reliable sources of employment data. Accordingly, these statistical sources are regarded as useless for examining the changes in the composition of the labour force during the adjustment period.

2.2. Employment Surveys (ECSO, ENE, and ENEU)[7]

According to expert opinion, the most reliable statistics on employment at the national level are the Continuous Survey on Occupation (ECSO for its acronym in Spanish) and the National Employment Survey (ENE for its acronym in Spanish), and, more specifically, on urban employment, the National Urban Employment Survey (ENEU for its acronym in Spanish).[8] Through these surveys, statistical data on the employment characteristics of household members are collected. The ENE applies two questionnaires, one for urban areas, and another one for rural areas. The ENEU applies the same questionnaire used for urban areas by the ENE.

An analysis of the impact of the 1982 economic crisis and structural adjustment policies on the labour market in Mexico based on such surveys poses serious difficulties. The nearest employment survey at the national level conducted before the 1982 economic crisis was the 1979 ECSO survey, and the first available survey after the crisis was conducted in 1991 (ENE).[9] These surveys have been used to measure employment trends during the 1980s in Mexico.

Concerning the labour market in Mexico City, the 1979 ECSO and the 1986-1994 ENEU surveys provide data on employment. However, there are some published employment data on the 1980-1987 period which I will use as well.[10] In order to measure and analyse the impact of the 1982 economic crisis and the effects of stabilisation and adjustment, I analysed the database of the 1986-1987 ENEU and compared it with the 1979 ECSO published data.

Despite the fact that the majority of the variables are comparable between the ECSO and the ENE/ENEU surveys, several problems arise for the analysis of the changes in the composition of the labour force during the period of adjustment. First, the representative quality of the employment surveys has been challenged, since this depends on the reliability of the population census from which the sampling frame for all surveys is built (e.g., from the 1980 Population Census). Second, the sampling frames tend to become obsolete as years go by and new localities or new neighbourhoods are left out. This fact introduces biases into the samples. Third, for the expansion of the sample to the universe, surveys have to rely on population projections whose errors grow as more years go by. That is, if the survey is conducted within only a few years following the population census, the results are more reliable than the results of another survey conducted several years later after the population census. For instance, the sample frame of the 1979 ECSO was drawn based on the 1970 Population Census, which was nine years old, and population totals were based on projections for a nine-year period as well. Therefore, the biases and errors are expected to be larger than the ones in the 1993 employment survey, which is based on the 1990 Housing & Population Census, which was three years old.

Comparability problems between the ECSO and the ENE/ENEU arise because the definitions of some of the employment categories were modified. While in the ECSO survey the definition of unemployment also includes persons who did not work in the reference week but who stated that they would begin to work within a thirty-day period, the ENE defined this type of person as "employed". Moreover, the definition of employment in rural areas according to the ENE definition also includes persons who did not work, but who stated that they would begin to work within a seven-week period. Therefore, as the period of reference to define the EAP in the ENE survey was expanded, an "artificial" increase of the employed labour force may have been the result. These differences affect the rate of employment at the national level and in rural areas.

Another conceptual problem with regard to the definition of employment is the concept of unpaid work. There has long been a debate among scholars concerning the definition of unpaid work. The conventional classification of unpaid work is difficult to apply when children's and women's "unpaid" work is highly integrated into domestic activities (see, Turnham, 1993). Another problem with this category is the heterogeneity of people classified as "unpaid". This category may include owners, business partners, and "family" workers with no regular earnings.

There have also been some changes in the definition of unpaid work in Mexico. While the ECSO survey defined unpaid workers as persons who worked at least 15 hours or more without being paid in the reference week, the ENE/ENEU survey includes in this employment category persons who worked without being paid for at least one hour in the reference week. These changes resulted in another "artificial" increase in the proportion of workers considered to be working in "marginal" activities, as well as in the overall labour force participation rate. The number of non-salaried workers is higher than would have been expected without changing the employment definitions and survey questionnaires. This not only increases the labour force participation rate, but also changes the composition of the EAP by economic sector, as the "marginal" workers tend to be concentrated in certain activities (e.g., petite retail trade and agricultural activities). As a result, from 1979 to 1991 the annual rate of growth in the number of unpaid workers at the national level appears to be 6.3 per cent, compared to 3.7 per cent for the entire labour force. (table 4.A.2 statistical appendix to this chapter).

Changes in the definition of unpaid work mostly affected the number of female workers and their distribution by economic activity. The number of unpaid female workers appears to have increased overall by 13.6 per cent annually and in agriculture by 18 per cent. In other words, whereas in 1979 there were nearly 350,000 unpaid women workers, by 1991 the statistics give the impression that there were more than 1.6 million. (table 4.A.1, statistical appendix to this chapter). The percentage of unpaid female workers within total female employment appears in 1991 (14.3 per cent) as almost twice the level recorded in 1979 (7.6 per cent) (see table 4.1). Consequently, the distribution of female workers by occupational category was entirely modified and, in some cases, the degree of change is difficult to believe. For example, in agricultural activities in 1979 unpaid female workers accounted for 27.3 per cent of the labour force in that sector and by 1991 this percentage had risen to nearly 52 per cent.

Experts on employment also claim that, as a result of the decline in the demand for labour in the formal sector, workers have had to rely on the informal sector (see García and Oliveira: 1994; Jusidman: 1988).[11] According to these authors, the increase in self-employment during the 1980s demonstrates the inability of the formal sector to generate employment. However, national figures on employment do not support this idea. Self-employment decreased from 25.4 per cent in 1979 to 24.3 per cent in 1991. Conversely, the number of employers who are sometimes considered to be part of the "formal" sector more than doubled (from 3.4 per cent to 8.1 per cent, respectively; see table 4.1).

Table 4.1. Mexico: Percentage of workers by position at work, 1979, 1991-1996

Position at work	1979	1991	1993	1995	1996
Total	100.0	100.0	100.0	100.0	100.0
Employer	3.4	8.1	4.2	4.5	4.9
Self-employed worker	25.4	24.3	27.5	26.1	24.5
Salaried worker	62.9	56.3	56.4	58.8	60.1
Unpaid worker*	8.2	11.1	11.7	10.6	10.5
Other and not specified	n.a.d.	0.3	0.1	0.1	0.1
Male workers	100.0	100.0	100.0	100.0	100.0
Employer	4.1	10.5	5.4	5.8	6.2
Self-employed worker	27.0	26.2	29.2	27.3	25.8
Salaried worker	60.5	53.2	54.4	57.7	59.0
Unpaid worker*	8.5	9.7	10.8	9.1	8.9
Other and not specified	0.0	0.3	0.2	0.1	0.1
Female workers	100.0	100.0	100.0	100.0	100.0
Employer	1.3	2.3	1.6	1.5	2.1
Self-employed worker	20.5	19.6	23.3	23.6	21.7
Salaried worker	70.7	63.7	61.1	61.1	62.4
Unpaid worker*	7.6	14.3	13.9	13.8	13.8
Other and not specified	0.0	0.1	0.1	0.1	0.0

Source: Own calculations based on table 4A.1, statistical appendix to this chapter.
* Figures refer to unpaid workers who worked 15 hours or more in the reference week.
n.a.d.: No available data.

According to García (1994:30), rather than a decline in the percentage of self-employment, this category was underestimated in the 1991 ENE. The author argues that a large proportion of agriculture workers classified as employers should have been classified as self-employees. Additionally, according to the author, self-employed workers in agricultural activities hire a casual labour force during harvest time when the workload increases, and, therefore, she argues, this does not make them employers. This example shows how the vagueness of employment concepts may affect the distribution of workers by position at work.

2.3. Other Sources to Measure Employment

2.3.1. National Survey of Household Income and Expenditure –ENIGHs

Although the main purpose of this survey is to measure household income and expenditure (see chapter 3), the ENIGH (Encuesta Nacional de Ingresos y Gastos de los Hogares –National Survey of Household Income and Expenditure) has been another data source used by some scholars to analyse labour force participation in Mexico. As the survey sample is drawn based on the Population Censuses, criticism that was already expressed with regard to the ENE/ENEU sample also applies to the ENIGH sample (see previous section). On the other hand, comparability problems among the ENIGHs arise since the definition of urban/rural areas is different in each survey. (For a more ample discussion on this topic see section 2 in chapter 3).

The nearest ENIGH conducted before the economic crisis of 1982 is the 1977 ENIGH, and the nearest one following the crisis is the 1984 ENIGH. These two surveys have been used to measure the impact of economic crisis on household income. During the period of structural adjustment, three additional surveys were conducted: in 1989, in 1992, and in 1994.

The data provided by these surveys on employment cannot be compared with those of the ENE/ENEU employment surveys, as the definition of Economically Active Population is different. In the ENIGH survey, the period of reference for identifying the EAP is longer than that of the ENE/ENEU survey. In the former, people are asked whether they worked during the *last month*[12] for at least one hour, while in the latter people are asked whether they did so during the *last week*. Therefore, as the period of reference is longer in the ENIGH survey, the labour force participation rate would tend to be higher than that of the ENE/ENEU. This may be compensated by the fact that another relevant difference between these surveys is that while in the ENIGH there is only one question to identify the EAP,[13] the ENE/ENEU surveys have more than one question to identify the EAP. In the ENE/ENEU, although the interviewee answers that he/she did not work,[14] another three questions are asked to find out whether or not that person should be considered as economically active.[15]

Although the ENIGH surveys cannot be compared with other employment surveys, they provide information related to the number of occupied members in the household. Moreover, since the ENIGH surveys capture income more systematically than the employment surveys, they allow for an analysis of the interaction of income poverty and working time deployed in the household. I will use this advantage extensively in section 7 of this chapter.

2.3.2. Economic Censuses

It has been suggested that the National Economic Censuses in Mexico provide valuable information on recorded or "formal" activities. However, these censuses are not recommended for analysing the overall changes in the composition of the labour force because, despite efforts to expand coverage over time, the coverage of small establishments has been limited.

The 1981 Economic Census is the nearest census conducted before the 1982 economic crisis. In order to measure the likely effects of the economic crisis on the recorded sector of the economy, this census can be compared with the 1985 Economic Census. During the adjustment period, two other Economic Censuses were conducted (in 1988 and in 1993). However, comparability problems arise, since the coverage of small establishments has been expanded. The impact of the increase in economic census coverage has not been evaluated (Rendón and Salas, 1992a: 22). Nevertheless, it can be said that the expansion in the coverage of this type of establishment may have raised its proportion with respect to the total, rather than reflecting a real increase of small establishments. Moreover, the economic censuses do not provide data on self-employment, on petite retail trade, and on home-based production.

Economic censuses provide information at the national and state levels. However, given that the Metropolitan Area of Mexico City is composed of the Federal District (D.F.) and some municipalities of the State of Mexico, there are several difficulties to aggregate the data for the city as a whole. Therefore, in this chapter, I will analyse only economic census information at the national level.

The following sections will discuss the trends in labour force participation in Mexico and in Mexico City during the stabilisation and adjustment periods. The discussion will be based on the available surveys on employment and on household income and expenditure. In order to assess the findings presented in what follows, the difficulties posed by different employment sources should be borne in mind.

3. LABOUR FORCE PARTICIPATION RATES I (EMPLOYMENT SURVEYS)

Employment surveys and economic censuses report a number of transforming trends in the labour market during the 1980s and the first half of the 1990s. These trends indicate increases in the following areas: labour force participation rates; women labour participation rates; children's work; the importance of the self-employed and of small businesses; and the weight of services and the commercial sector. These trends have been interpreted as an indication of a lack of demand for labour. In this and the next section, the first trend will be discussed. Women and adolescent's work are discussed in sections 5 and 6. The last two trends are discussed in chapter 5.

3.1. Mexico

It is widely held that, as a result of household income decline, more children, women and elderly persons were forced to engage in paid activities (Jusidman, 1988; Cortés and Rubalcava, 1990, and 1991; García and Oliveira, 1994; Benería, 1992; INCO, 1989, and Tuirán, 1992). This interpretation has been based on an increase in the labour force participation rate (LFPR) reported by employment surveys (ECSO/ENE/ENEU) during the 1980s, as well as data derived from micro-social studies.

Employment figures show that the LFPR, without making any correction to the data taken from the surveys (which is the prevailing practice among labour market specialists), increased from 45.5 per cent in 1979 to 53.6 per cent in 1991 (see table 4.2). This represents a 17.8 per cent increase in the rate, which means a 3.9 per cent annual rate of growth in the EAP. If the figures on the nineties are corrected to make them comparable with the 1979 ECSO (which means excluding unpaid workers who worked less than 15 hours a week), the result is that the LFPR rose from 45.5 per cent in 1979 to 52.5 per cent in 1991, a 15.4 per cent increase, implying an annual rate of growth of 3.7 per cent in the EAP, that is, a lower rate of growth than the previous calculation (table 4.2). It should be noted that the 1979-1991 period is difficult to analyse because during this period the economy experienced an oil boom, an economic crisis and an economic recovery, making it therefore difficult to separate the impact of the economic crisis on the level of employment during the 1980s. Unfortunately, there are no usable national employment surveys in the eighties. Therefore, it is not possible to differentiate the changes in the labour market associated with the outbreak of the 1982 economic crisis from those that took place during the stabilisation and adjustment periods. The alternative source could have been the ENEU surveys which are available year by year since 1987; however, this is not possible as the 1979 ECSO, which is not available as a database, does not distinguish urban from rural areas.

Table 4.2. Mexico: Economically active population (EAP) and labour force participation rates (LFPR), 1979, 1991, 1993, 1995 and 1996

Year	EAP (000's)[a]			Labour force participation rate		
	Original	Corrected	Equivalent workers[b]	Original	Corrected	Equivalent LFPR[b]
1979	19, 839	19,839	16,793	n.a.d.	45.5	38.5
1991	31,229	30,593	24,045	53.6	52.5	41.2
1993	33,652	32,869	25,449	55.2	53.9	41.7
1995	35,558	34,645	26,970	55.6	54.1	42.1
1996	36,581	35,863	28,680	55.4	54.3	43.4

Source: 1979, SPP (1980), table:2A:37; 1991, INEGI and STPS (1993), table:2:36; 1993, INEGI and STPS (1994), table 2:44; 1995, INEGI and STPS (1996), table 2:40; 1996, INEGI and STPS (1997) table 3.4:53.

[a] EAP: Economically active population. EAP in the "original" column as published; in the "corrected" column it excludes unpaid workers who worked less than 15 hours in the reference week.

[b] See text for an explanation of these concepts.

n.a.d.: No available data.

Between 1991 and 1993, when the Mexican economy was growing around 3 per cent annually, the employment rate of growth of the EAP (again with uncorrected figures) was 3.7 per cent per year. However, between 1993 and 1995, when the financial crisis erupted in Mexico, the employment rate of growth decreased to 2.7 per cent. When the analysis is done with uncorrected figures, the 1994 crisis and the policies adopted seem to have adversely affected the employment pace of growth, suggesting, for the time being, that during an economic recession the EAP tends to grow slower, not vice versa as claimed by some scholars.

Some scholars also suggest that as income declined during stabilisation and adjustment, there was an intensification of work by working a longer number of hours (see González de la Rocha, 1993:9-11). However, employment figures show an opposite trend. Between 1979 and 1991, there was a sharp increase in the percentage of workers who worked less than 40 hours a week (from 20.4 per cent to 31.5 per cent) (table 4.3). Furthermore, the percentage of workers who worked more than 40 hours a week decreased from 79.6 per cent in 1979 to 67.9 per cent in 1991. This means that, although the labour force participation rate increased during the 1980s, persons were working a relatively lesser number of hours. This is expressed in the average number of hours worked in the reference week, which decreased from 43.2 in 1979 to 40.4 hours in 1991 (see table 4.3).

The change in the number of hours worked shows that the sheer number of employed population is not homogeneous enough to grant comparability over time. In order to attain a higher degree of homogeneity I have standardised the working population on the basis of weekly hours of work, which results in what I have called equivalent full time workers (or for brevity "equivalent workers") and equivalent participation rates.[16] Table 4.2 presents the calculations of these two concepts.

The evolution of equivalent workers in the 1979-1991 period is slower than the corresponding evolution of the two versions of the EAP presented above. In 1979 equivalent workers were 16.8 million and in 1991 they had increased to 24.0 million. This implies an annual rate of growth of 3.0 per cent, substantially lower than the 3.9 per cent and 3.7 per cent of, respectively, the original and the corrected EAP, but still large enough to reflect a slow increase in the equivalent participation rate. This rate changed from 38.5 per cent in 1979 to 41.2 per cent in 1991, that is, a 7 per cent increase in the 12-year period, less than the 15.4 per cent calculated above for the comparable EAP figures, and also less than the 17.8 per cent with the uncorrected EAP figures. In conclusion, participation rates, once standardised and the sources made comparable, did grow during the 1979-1991 period, but at a much slower pace than previously assumed by scholars. The corrected figures look more compatible with basic economic principles. That is, as GDP during the 1979-1991 period increased by an annual rate of growth of 2.4 per cent, still below the rate obtained in equivalent workers (3 per cent), but very far from the 3.9 per cent or 3.7 per cent of the original and the corrected EAP.

Thus we may conclude that productivity per equivalent worker in the economy decreased at a 0.6 per cent rate annually during this period.[17]

Table 4.3. Mexico: Percentage of workers according to number of hours worked in the reference week, 1979-1996

Num. of hours worked	1979	1991	1993	1995	1996
1 to 24 hours	8.5	12.5	14.2	13.2	12.1
25 to 39 hours	11.9	18.9	18.2	18.3	17.3
Less than 40 hours (subtotal)	20.4	31.5	32.4	31.5	29.4
40 to 48 hours	54.1	45.6	40.9	39.7	40.7
More than 49 hours	25.5	22.3	26.0	28.6	29.8
More than 40 hours (subtotal)	79.6	67.9	66.9	68.5	70.6
Not Specified	0.0	0.6	0.8	0.2	0.1
Total	100.0	100.0	100.0	100.0	100.0
Average number of hours of work	43.2	40.4	40.3	41.2	41.9

Source: Own calculations based on table 4.A.7, statistical appendix to this chapter

From 1991 to 1993, while GDP grew by 2.8 per cent annually, barely above the rate of growth of population, equivalent workers increased by 2.9 per cent annually. From 1993 to 1995 GDP decreased, on average, 1 per cent annually and equivalent workers increased from 25.4 million to 27 million, which also implies a 2.9 per cent rate of growth. Accordingly, in this last period there is no clear relationship between economic growth and employment growth.

I will return to the question on whether there was an increase in working effort (as expressed both in number of persons and hours per person) as a result of income losses by the main breadwinners (section 7). In the next section, however, I will look at the evolution of workers and participation rates in Mexico City with and without standardisation (section 3.2).

3.2 Mexico City

There are some studies on Mexico City that also hold that after the 1982 economic crisis there was an increase in the labour force participation rate.[18] Jusidman (1988:249) claims that the labour force participation rate is a "stable"[19] employment index that tends to decline as income per worker increases. Based on this proposition, Jusidman argues that the increase in the labour force participation rate in Mexico City between 1983 and 1985 (from 46.7 per cent to 52.8 per cent, see table 4.4) resulted from a greater incorporation of "secondary" workers[20] into the labour market in order to make up for income losses (*Ibid.* 246). However, if we look carefully at the employment figures and associate them with the behaviour of the economy and with average earnings per occupied person, this conclusion may become opaque.

Table 4.4. Mexico City: Labour force participation rates, 1979-1994*

Year	Total	Male	Female
1979	50.5	70.5	32.5
1980	49.9	n.a.d.	n.a.d.
1981	49.5	n.a.d.	n.a.d.
1982	49.9	n.a.d.	n.a.d.
1983	46.7	n.a.d.	n.a.d.
1984	48.1	n.a.d.	n.a.d.
1985	52.8	n.a.d.	n.a.d.
1986	52.3	n.a.d.	n.a.d.
1987	51.6	70.8	34.0
1988	51.9	71.0	34.5
1989	52.9	71.6	35.8
1990	53.0	71.5	34.7
1991	54.0	74.1	35.8
1992	55.1	73.9	37.9
1993	55.5	74.8	37.5
1994	54.4	75.0	35.6
1995	54.4	73.5	37.1

Source: 1979, SPP (1980), table 2A: 205; 1982-1985 Jusidman (1988), table 4:247; 1986-1995, own calculations based on ENEU databases, INEGI.
* Employment figures refer to April-June of each year, except for 1979.
n.a.d. No available data.

During the oil boom (1978-1982), when the Mexican economy was growing by 6 per cent to 8 per cent annually, the labour force participation rate in Mexico City fluctuated at around 49 per cent. After the 1982 economic crisis, the labour force participation rate went down to 46.7 per cent in 1983 (see table 4.4). This exemplifies that under the impact of economic crisis, labour force participation shrank, rather than increase, as claimed by some scholars. Based on the employment figures displayed in table 4.4, I can state that the changes in labour force participation rate in Mexico City have been positively (i.e. directly) associated with the economic performance of the country from 1983 onwards.[21]

As noted in chapter 2, the Mexican economy had a brief recovery during 1984 and 1985 (after a strong decline between 1982 and 1983, GDP grew annually by 3.6 per cent and 2.7 per cent). In 1984, the labour force participation rate began to recover, and in 1985 this rate increased to 52.8 per cent. This change in labour force participation may be explained by improvements in macroeconomic indicators. At the same time, average earnings by the occupied population, as reported by national accounts, were stable during this period. At the end of 1986, international oil prices declined, adversely affecting the rate of growth of the Mexican economy which became negative. At the same time, average earnings declined quite sharply. From that year on, the labour force participation rate in Mexico City began to decline again. Between 1987 and 1988, this rate fluctuated at around 51 per cent. Between 1988 and 1994, when the Mexican economy grew again and average earnings increased as well, the labour force participation rate also recovered, reaching 55.5 per cent in 1993, its highest level since 1979 (see table 4.4 for LFPR; and see chapter 2 of this book and Boltvinik 1998a, table 3: 342-343, for figures on average earnings).

In Mexico City there was a similar behaviour to the one noted for the national level –in the previous sub-section– regarding the inverse relation between the labour force participation rate (LFPR) and the weekly hours of work. Between 1979 and 1986 the LFPR increased from 50.5 per cent to 52.3 per cent (table 4.4) and the average number of hours worked in the reference week decreased from 42.5 to 40.8 hours. During the adjustment period, weekly working hours stagnated during many years (1987 to 1992), recovering in 1993 and 1994, years in which they almost reached the 1979 level (table 4.5).

As these figures (as well as those for the country) are calculated on the basis of pre-stratified groups of hours of work (as explained in the note to table 4.5), a test was performed processing ENEU databases to make sure there were no strong biases. I was able to do this for 1986, 1989, and 1994. The comparative results of both procedures of calculation are presented in table 4.A.10 in the statistical appendix to this chapter. The pre-stratified source yields results which are slightly higher, around 2 per cent, than the ones obtained with the micro-data, but this difference is maintained throughout the observed years with very little variation as shown in the referred table. Given the stability of the differences, the evolution of the results is similar. This validates the procedure used for Mexico City as well as for the national level.

Table 4.5. Mexico City: Average number of hours worked in the reference week, 1979, 1986-1994*

	1979	1986	1987	1988	1989	1990	1991	1992	1993	1994
Total	42.5	40.8	40.8	40.9	41.3	41.4	41.4	41.0	41.7	42.0
Male workers	44.1	43.1	42.7	42.6	43.2	42.9	43.4	43.2	43.7	44.2
Female workers	39.4	36.6	36.9	37.5	37.8	37.9	37.7	36.9	37.9	37.9

Source: Own calculations based on table 4.A.9, statistical appendix to this chapter.

* The average hours worked in the reference week was calculated as follows: the middle point of each range of number of hours worked was multiplied by the percentage of workers of each range of hours worked. The average number of hours represents the sum of the values obtained in each range of hours worked. In order to test the consistency of these figures, the average number of hours worked was calculated based on ENEU database, INEGI, 1986, 1989 and 1994 (see table 4A.7.1, statistical appendix to this chapter).

Based on the information of number of hours worked in the reference week, I calculated the equivalent labour force participation rates, which were explained above when such rates were presented for the country level[22] (table 4.2). Table 4.6 shows that between 1979 and 1987 (for years 1980-1986 this equivalent rate could not be calculated) the equivalent rate decreased (from 40.7 per cent to 39.0 per cent), while the non-adjusted participation rate rose (from 50.5 per cent to 51.6 per cent). I contended, when analysing table 4.4, that, after 1982, participation rates have been positively associated with economic growth. Equivalent participation rates are also associated positively with economic growth. From 1979 to 1987, a period during which per capita GDP decreased, equivalent participation rates decreased as well (table 4.6). During the 1987-1988 sub-period, per capita income stagnated and the equivalent rates stagnate as well. From 1988 to 1993 equivalent rates grew very quickly (an increase from 39.5 per cent in 1988, to 43.1 per cent in 1993) during a period in which per capita income grew steadily (except in 1993). Therefore, there seems to be an almost perfect and positive association between these variables, which confirms the non-validity of interpretations which assume households were able to increase their working effort during periods of economic recession, thus postulating the counter-cyclical nature of participation rates.

Table 4.6. Mexico City. Labour force participation rates (LFPR) and equivalent LFPR, 1979, 1987-1993

Year	Labour force participation rates	Equivalent participation rates*
1979	50.5	40.7
1987	51.6	39.0
1988	51.9	39.5
1989	52.9	41.6
1990	53.0	40.6
1991	54.0	42.7
1992	55.1	42.2
1993	55.5	43.2

Source: 1979, SPP (1980), table 2A:205; and 1987-1993, own calculations based on ENEU databases, INEGI.
* Number of equivalent workers divided by the population of 12 years of age and above.

From 1989 onwards there was a real increase in the amount of work performed by the entire population. Not only the (non-corrected) labour force participation rate increased, but also the average weekly hours increased, both factors being expressed in the equivalent participation rates, which went up in the first part of the nineties. In conclusion, it can be said that as economic conditions improve, persons have a greater possibility to increase their work effort.

4. WOMEN'S WORK

During the 1980s in Mexico, both the male and female labour force were growing quickly. However, this increase was particularly important for women, whose labour force participation rate rose from 21.5 per cent in

1979 to 30.4 per cent in 1991,[23] that is, almost 10 percentage points in 12 years (table 4.2). Since there is a consensus among scholars that labour demand shrank during the 1980s, the increase in female labour supply has been seen as a result of women's survival strategies. For instance, Selby *et al.* (1990:175) have suggested that, during the period of economic crisis, women were brought into the work force in unprecedented numbers, and their work was overwhelmingly in unregistered jobs in the informal sector. The authors point out a very important paradox they observed in the city of Oaxaca in 1987: "Employment is down .... observation and interviews show that informal sector activity is much reduced from 1982 levels, even though more people, especially more women, are employing themselves in these activities." (*Ibid.*:169.)[24] This paradox had been analysed thoroughly by the regional agency of the International Labour Organisation (ILO) in Latin America for the study of employment, called PREALC. These analyses have been synthesised by the UNDP (1991: 37):

> Crises compress the monetary mass of wages (employment and/or wage levels) and therefore family income. Demand directed to small units (which has a high-income elasticity of demand) falls abruptly. In parallel new entrances to independent jobs increase and the most precarious small units multiply themselves. Aggregated supply by small units of all types increases. This produces, therefore, a collapse of average income of self-employed and of small bosses. This effect is transmitted to its employees...

García and Oliveira (1994:227-28) have stated that the sharp increase in the number of women with children and with little or no education participating in the labour market observed in the 1980s indicates a deterioration in family living conditions. According to the authors, before the economic crisis, young and childless women comprised a major proportion of the female labour force; however, after the 1982 economic crisis this trend changed.[25] These scholars affirm that poor women were forced to engage in paid activities in order to fulfil their families' and children's basic needs.

García and Oliveira (1994:226-227) have recognised that part of the increase in female labour force responds to a secular trend observed since the 1970s. A study of the labour market in Latin America found that more women were participating in the labour market. The contribution of women to the increase in the EAP during the 1980s in eight Latin American countries — Brazil, Colombia, Costa Rica, Chile, Mexico, Uruguay and Venezuela — was 42 per cent (see Infante and Klein, 1991).

Buvinic (1983) has pointed out that evidence in the mid-1970s shows that the supply variables (i.e. fertility, education) were powerless to explain the participation of women in the labour market. More women with children were participating in the labour force regardless of the number of children or of their marital history. Since then, research began to focus on the demand for, rather than on the supply of, women workers and the variables that may restrict this demand.

Table 4.7. Mexico: Employment growth rate by sex, 1980-1985, 1985-1988 and 1988-1993 (per cent)

Period	Total	Salaried employment
1980-1985		
Total	4.2	4.4
Male workers	4.4	4.2
Female workers	4.0	5.0
1985-1988		
Total	3.6	3.8
Male workers	2.5	2.4
Female workers	5.8	7.0
1980-1988		
Total	4.0	4.2
Male workers	3.6	3.5
Female workers	4.7	5.8
1988-1993		
Total	6.8	5.9
Male workers	5.7	5.0
Female workers	8.7	7.8

Source: Own calculation based on national economic censuses, INEGI, 1981, 1986, 1989, and 1994.

In Mexico, there is some evidence to suggest that the increase in the number of women participating in the labour market may be explained by changes in the demand for labour. According to the National Economic Censuses, between 1980 and 1988 women's participation in the universe of activities captured by these censuses grew faster than that of men (annually by 4.7 per cent and 3.6 per cent, respectively, see table 4.7). This increase was particularly high between 1985 and 1988, when women's employment grew annually by 5.8 per cent, as compared to 2.5 per cent for men. During the period of structural adjustment (1988-1993), women's participation in recorded activities grew even faster, at a rate of 8.7 per cent annually (see table 4.7).[26]

Table 4.7 shows that between 1980 and 1993, there was an increasing demand for women in the salaried employment category. This may reflect a change in the demand for labour. These changes may have implied an increase in the demand for women with little education; they do, however, also indicate that there were more working opportunities for women in the salaried sector during the period of stabilisation and adjustment in Mexico. Nevertheless, this evidence is not very consistent with the widely-held idea that the increase in female participation in the labour market can be explained by a deterioration in household income, i.e., that women were forced to work predominantly in "marginal" or "informal" activities.

Table 4.8. Mexico City: Income per hour and employment growth rates by sex, 1986-1994

	Income per hour growth rate (per cent)			Employment growth rate (per cent)		
	1986-1989	1989-1994	1986-1994	1986-1989	1989-1994	1986-1994
All workers	-1.4	3.8	1.8	3.9	2.3	2.9
Male workers	-1.4	3.7	1.8	4.0	2.0	2.7
Female workers	-3.0	4.6	1.7	3.6	3.0	3.2

Source: Own calculations based on ENEU databases, INEGI, 1986-1994.

Official figures do not support the opinion of some experts that women's labour force participation has a counter-cyclical tendency (e.g. Jusidman, 1988: 246); that is, that it grows during recession and shrinks during economic growth. In other words, more specifically, women's participation rates grow when household income decreases and shrink when income increases. What the figures show is that there is no fixed relation between both set of variables in Mexico City. According to the ENEU surveys, during the 1986-1989 period, average female income per hour declined at a rate of −3 per cent annually, much more than the equivalent male income, the rate of which declined −1.4 per cent annually).[27] In this case, female labour supply did behave counter-cyclically and women entering the labour market grew by 3.6 per cent annually (table 4.8). However, from 1989 to 1994, when hourly income recovered, the number of women participating in the labour market behaved pro-cyclically, not counter-cyclically, and continued to increase. Between 1989 and 1994, when income per hour for female workers increased by 4.6 per cent annually (a higher increase than the equivalent for men, at 3.7 per cent), the female labour force grew at a rate of 3 per cent annually (table 4.8). As a consequence, the rate of participation of women in the labour force did not decline; on the contrary, it rose (table 4.8).

The increase in the number of women participating in the labour market in Mexico City seems to have responded to female labour demand, especially in the formal sector. Studies on other cities in Mexico (e.g., Queretaro, Puerto Vallarta and León) and on cities in other countries have also shown that the demand for female labour has affected the level of women's participation in the labour market (e.g. see Chant, 1991:Ch. 3). In these studies, it has been suggested that the increase in the number of women participating in the labour market was correlated with a rise in real wages for women (e.g. see Pahl and Wallace, 1985).

Nevertheless, as was shown in section 3, the labour force participation rate is an indicator which gives the same weight to a person who works few hours a week and to a person who works 48 or more hours weekly. Thus, I introduced the concepts of equivalent workers and equivalent participation rates. These are particularly important in the case of women as their average hours of work are substantially below that of men. In effect, while 27.8 per cent of men worked less than 39 hours a week in 1991, the corresponding percent for women was 45.3 per cent (table 4.A.9 statistical appendix to this chapter).

The evolution of uncorrected and equivalent participation rates for both sexes can be seen in table 4.9. Non-standardised female participation rates increased spectacularly, from 21.5 per cent in 1979 to 30.4 per cent in 1991 — a 41.4 per cent increase in 12 years (at an annual rate of growth of 2.9 per cent). When the rate is standardised, it changes at a more moderate but still quick pace, from 16.1 per cent to 20.7 per cent — a 28.7 per cent increase (an annual rate of 2.1 per cent). Thus, female participation rates increase substantially even when they are standardised, meaning that hours of extra-domestic work performed by women grew faster than the increase in the number of women in working ages throughout the entire 12-year period of 1979-1991. Unfortunately, as has been mentioned before, this period is too long: it includes two boom sub-periods (1979-1981 and 1989-1991); one sub-period of recovery (1984-1985); and two crisis (1982-1983 and 1986-1988). In 1991 GDP was 33.5 per cent higher than in 1979, representing an average annual growth rate of 2.4 per cent, slightly higher than the population growth rate. In consequence, GDP per capita in 1991 was only 1.9 per cent higher than in 1979, which means practically stagnation.

Table 4.9. Mexico: Evolution of female and male participation rates and equivalent participation rates, 1979, 1991, 1993, 1995, 1996 (per cent)

Concept	1979	1991	1993	1995
Female participation rates (original)[a]	n.a.d.	31.5	33.0	34.5
Female participation rates[b]	21.5	30.4	31.7	32.9
Female equivalent participation rates	16.1	20.7	21.1	22.1
Male participation rates (original)[a]	n.a.d.	77.7	78.9	78.2
Male participation rates[b]	71.3	76.6	77.7	77.0
Male equivalent participation rates	61.8	61.0	60.8	61.1

Source: 1979, SPP (1980, table:2A:37); 1991, INEGI and STPS (1993, table:2:36); 1993, INEGI and STPS (1994, table 2:44); 1995, INEGI and STPS (1996, table 2:40).
[a] Figures include unpaid workers who worked an hour or more in the reference week.
[b] Figures include unpaid workers who worked 15 hours or more in the reference week.
n.a.d.: No available data.

The 1991-1995 period featured a sharp decline in GDP per capita, particularly in 1995. Therefore, I may characterise this period as recessionary (even the 1991-1993 sub-period was one of very slow growth in GDP, registering a decline in GDP per capita), a period during which GDP decreased slightly and GDP per capita fell by 8 per cent. Nevertheless, uncorrected female participation rates grew from 30.4 per cent to 32.9 per cent, representing an average annual growth rate of 4 per cent, quite higher than the observed rate of growth in the 1979-1991 period. Female equivalent participation rates grew at an annual rate of 3.3 per cent between 1991-1995, a higher rate than the one observed in the

1979-1991 period. If the 1991-1995 period is divided into two sub-periods, then the pace of growth of the uncorrected participation rates decelerates slightly from the first to the second sub-period, though the equivalent participation rates accelerate substantially, indicating that the average hours worked by women during 1995 was higher than prior to the crisis.

Thus, with this division of periods it turns out that equivalent female participation rates increased faster in a period of recession (1991-1995) than in a period of stagnation (1979-1991), supporting the interpretation that female labour growth is explained as a survival strategy, i.e., as a supply-driven phenomenon. But part of the growth in female participation during the 1979-1991 period was negatively offset by a slight decrease in male equivalent participation rates. When one looks at the uncorrected participation rates this trade-off remains hidden, inasmuch as male participation rates also increased between 1979 and 1991. Nevertheless, male equivalent participation rates, which were 61.8 per cent in 1979, slightly decreased to 61.0 per cent in 1991. Moreover, during the 1991-1995 period, male participation rates remained stagnant while female rates grew.

Table 4.10. Mexico City: Equivalent labour force participation rates by sex, 1979 and 1987-1993

Year	Male workers		Female workers	
	Labour force participation rate	Equivalent participation rates*	Labour force participation rate	Equivalent participation rates*
1979	70.5	59.3	32.5	29.3
1987	70.8	57.1	34.0	29.2
1988	71.0	57.3	34.5	29.7
1989	71.6	59.4	35.8	31.9
1990	71.5	58.3	34.7	30.5
1991	74.1	61.7	35.8	32.5
1992	73.9	60.4	37.9	33.2
1993	74.8	61.6	37.5	33.0

Source: 1979, SPP (1980, table 2A:305); 1987-1993, ENEU databases, INEGI.
* Number of equivalent workers divided by the population of 12 years of age and above.

But the available national information, as already noted at the beginning of this chapter, does not provide any employment data for the decade of the eighties. Moreover, the resulting initial period (1979-1991) is too long, encompassing too many different stages in the Mexican economy, to be able to determine any fruitful association between economic performance and labour force participation rates. Information for Mexico City includes the publication of three survey results for the eighties, of which two were obtained before the economy started to grow again. In what follows, I will refer to this evidence from Mexico City regarding participation rates by gender. This is presented in table 4.10.

If one were to look at the participation rates in the 1979-1991 period, one would find a similar pattern for Mexico City to the one I have just described for the country. In effect, both the female participation rate and the equivalent participation rates grew. But if this period is divided into two sub-periods, one notes that during the 1979-1988 sub-period, which can be called a mild recessionary sub-period, there was a slight decrease in GDP per capita (-2.5 per cent in the whole period); by contrast, during the 1988-1991 sub-period there was a 4.5 per cent increase in GDP per capita.[28] Looking again at the female rates for these two sub-periods, the resulting uncorrected participation rate increases in both of them, while the equivalent participation rate remains stagnant in the first sub-period, growing substantially in the second sub-period. With the equivalent participation rates and the best period cuts available, the conclusion is that female labour participation is pro-cyclical and thus demand driven. On the contrary, if one compares the uncorrected participation rates at the start and at the end of the 1979-1991 period, one would be tempted to interpret the rapid rise in the rates to reflect survival strategies in response to the crisis of the eighties. Moreover, it should be noted that during the 1991-1993 period, when GDP for the country recovered, the female equivalent labour force participation rate increased steadily. Therefore, based on these findings we cannot conclude that women's labour supply is counter-cyclical, for the evidence presented here favours a pro-cyclical trend.[29]

5. WORK BY ADOLESCENTS

Informed opinion claimed that after the 1982 economic crisis more children entered the labour market. There are several difficulties in measuring child labour. One of these problems is that child labour is not legally allowed. In the case of Mexico, there is not enough evidence to support the idea that, as households became poorer, more children entered the labour force. Employment surveys do not ask questions related to child labour, since it is legally forbidden to hire children under twelve years of age. Therefore, it is impossible to measure changes in the participation of children in the labour force. Moreover, if surveys were to inquire into this topic, there would be serious difficulties in collecting reliable data on child labour, since an adult's perception of child work may vary with cultural traditions and the willingness to report the truth might be deterred by shame in some cases.

In view of the almost complete absence of information on children, I will restrict the analysis of this section to work by adolescents on which there is available information. The 1979 ECSO and ENE surveys provide employment data on adolescents (i.e. persons between twelve and nineteen years of age). Nevertheless, at the national level I had no access to the ENE database, so I could not correct the classification of active and inactive population to make it comparable with the one applied in the 1979 ECSO. The ECSO survey considers as active unpaid workers who worked at least 15 hours in the reference week; the ENE survey, however, does not consider this working time restriction. Unpaid work is particularly important at these ages, whereupon, without the correction, the data cannot be compared. If one takes the published data at face value one ends up with dramatic but absolutely biased results (García, 1994, tables 2.19 and 2.23: 65 and 67). A very impressive increase in adolescent participation in the labour force would be observed. Male adolescents would increase their rate from 35.4 per cent in 1979 to 47.8 per cent in 1991, while female adolescent participation rates would increase from 15.4 per cent to 22.6 per cent. The absurdity of these results can be tested indirectly by the fact that I did have access to the ENEU database for Mexico City and could correct the classification to make it comparable with the 1979 one.

The evidence on Mexico City, based on the same definition of active population for all years, shows a decline in teenage non-standardised labour force participation. Between 1979 and 1987, a period which can be considered to be one of stagnation given the fact that GDP per capita remained virtually constant, declining very slightly (less than 2 per cent for the period as a whole), the labour force participation rate of adolescents between 12 and 19 years of age decreased from 24.9 per cent to 22.4 per cent. This decrease was almost completely explained by the change observed for female teenagers, whose labour force participation rate decreased from 20.4 per cent to 15.7 per cent. In the case of male teenagers the rate remained almost constant at 29.6 per cent and 29.2 per cent respectively (see statistical appendix, table 4.A.11).

Contrary to the idea that as income recovers "secondary" workers leave the labour force (as suggested by Jusidman, 1988: 246), during the period of adjustment (1988-1994), when the ENEU figures indicate a recovery in income per hour, and GDP per capita grows, the labour force participation rate of all adolescents, male and female, increased from 22.4 per cent in 1987 to 26.9 per cent in 1993. This increase is observed both for males and for females, but while teenage males end up with a 34.7 per cent rate, well above the 1979 rate, the teenage female rate in 1993 is still below the 1979 level. However, this increase resulted from a greater participation of adolescents between 15 and 19 years of age, while the number of adolescents between 12 and 14 years of age declined from 7.1 per cent in 1987 to 5.1 per cent in 1994 (see statistical appendix, table 4.A.11).

It is difficult to assume that the increase observed in the 1987-1993 period resulted from a deterioration in household living conditions. It is important to take into consideration other factors (e.g., labour demand) that determine, to a great extent, the level of employment. For instance, it has been found in Puerto Vallarta (a beach resort city on Mexico's Pacific coast), that, although household income declined at the end of the 1980s to the beginning of the 1990s, households were unable to increase the number of members participating in the labour market because of the lack of overall demand: "No matter how much people may wish to protect incomes, the growing scarcity of viable employment options makes it difficult for [household members] to do so" (Chant, 1994:220). Nevertheless, the general increase in adolescent participation in the labour force might imply diminished opportunities to continue studying.

In any event, what becomes clear is that non-standardised adolescent participation rates behave more pro-cyclically than anti-cyclically and therefore there does not seem to be any solid basis for the contention that there was an increase in the work performed by teenagers. But we have to keep in mind that the analysis carried out for adolescents has not incorporated the equivalent rates of participation, because available information does not allow it. As we have seen in many of the analysis carried out up to now, such a standardisation leads to quite different results.

6. LABOUR FORCE PARTICIPATION RATES II (INCOME AND EXPENDITURE SURVEYS)

6.1. Mexico

The studies that focus on the actions and coping mechanisms of households after the 1982 economic crisis assume that the added work or effort on the part of the working class and the poor in general is counter-cyclical. According to Escobar (1996: 549), added work or effort grows under economic stagnation and contracts during economic growth. If this holds true, then it is expected to find a higher labour force participation rate during an economic crisis than during economic growth.

Cortés (1997:58-59) measures this phenomenon through the changes in the number of household earners.[30] In another study, Cortés and Rubalcava (1990:115-116) found that, according to the ENIGHs, the poorest strata of the population (70 per cent) were less affected by the economic crisis because, as income deteriorated, more children and women participated in the labour market between 1977 and 1984. Based on the above-mentioned findings, these scholars argue that more household members were forced to participate in paid activities in order to counteract income losses (Cortés, 1997:68, and Cortés and Rubalcava, 1990: 116).

However, these findings can be challenged on several accounts. First, let us consider the nature of the 1977-1984 period. From the point of view of economic growth, this period cannot be regarded as a period of recession or crisis as it includes four years of oil boom (1978-1981) and then two years of the debt crisis (1982-1984). According to national accounts, private consumption per capita increased from 37.6 thousand pesos (pesos of 1980) in 1977 to 45.8 thousand pesos in 1981 and then decreased to 41.1 thousand pesos in 1984. Thus, when comparing 1977 and 1984 one has to view it as a period of growth inasmuch as in 1984 consumption per capita and GDP per capita were higher than the 1977 level, by 9.3 per cent and by 16.4 per cent, respectively. According to Hernández-Laos (1992), from 1977 to 1984 income poverty incidence remained practically at the same level (58 per cent in 1977 and 58.5 per cent in 1984), notwithstanding that minimum wages declined by −33.8 per cent and average earnings per occupation (national accounts concept) decreased over that same period by -22 per cent. Moreover, according to the same author, the poverty gap increased very little, from 0.374 to 0.382. Income distribution (adjusted to national accounts) was also very similar in both years (the Gini coefficient was 0.462 in 1977 and 0.461 in 1984). Hernández-Laos calculations include a table (*Ibid.*:89) which shows that in

1984 average income per household was lower in all deciles compared to the 1977 level. But the average drop was not very large: 12 per cent. Amongst the deciles it ranged from 18 per cent in the fifth decile to 3.1 per cent in the second decile.

Hernández-Laos's results do not look totally consistent with aggregated GDP behaviour. It does not seem consistent, among other things, for private consumption from national accounts in 1984 to be larger than in 1977 (by 9 per cent) and at the same time for household income (adjusted ENIGH results) to be smaller by 12 per cent. On the other hand, the consistency of falling wages with consumption growth is explained in national accounts by the lower participation of wages in GDP, so that it is implicitly assumed that consumption was financed increasingly from other income sources (e.g. entrepreneurial rent or government income). So we can end up saying that the period includes a lot of seemingly paradoxical changes which have not been made thoroughly consistent, at least not in the literature on Mexican development. At any rate, there does not seem to be enough evidence to regard this period as one of a dramatic decrease in household income, and, therefore, there is no reason to expect a huge response of households to these changes.[31] Certainly the dramatic change was experienced from 1981 to 1984, but unfortunately this cannot be measured directly by means of the ENIGHs.

Second, there is a critical discrepancy between the figure on average earners per household provided by Cortés and the one provided by the 1977 survey publication. In effect, as can be seen in tables 4.11 and 4.12, the figure taken from Cortés (1997) is 1.60 and the one derived from the 1977 survey publications is 1.53.[32] As will be seen below, this fact changes the trajectory of this indicator in the 1977-1984 period.

Third, the indicator used to measure the labour effort made by households (number of household earners) does not reflect the number of household members participating in the labour market. This indicator includes not only household members who work, but also household members who receive retirement pensions or remittances from household members working somewhere else. For this reason this indicator is influenced by other factors, for instance, the relative increase in the elderly population or the emigration of Mexicans to the U.S.A.[33]

Fourth, it should be noted that income figures by Cortés refer only to monetary income, partly as a consequence of the non-availability of figures on non-monetary income and partly to the fact that figures on non-monetary income are even less reliable than monetary income figures.

Table 4.11. Mexico: Monetary income per capita and earners per household by decile, 1977, 1984, 1989 and 1992

Decile	Household income[a] (000's pesos august 1989)					Household earners per household[b]				
	1977	1984	1989	1992	1994	1977	1984	1989	1992	1994
I	96	143	137	112	129	1.17	1.17	1.26	1.25	1.28
II	205	248	268	245	253	1.30	1.30	1.33	1.31	1.45
III	290	340	356	360	355	1.34	1.38	1.31	1.33	1.42
IV	395	416	439	431	447	1.49	1.35	1.45	1.42	1.45
V	476	509	529	523	542	1.42	1.39	1.49	1.54	1.53
VI	606	614	641	613	627	1.52	1.50	1.70	1.73	1.76
VII	759	733	737	735	753	1.58	1.59	1.83	1.87	1.94
VII	936	906	918	894	946	1.81	1.91	2.08	2.09	2.10
IX	1,261	1,110	1,178	1,238	1,287	1.97	2.05	2.27	2.23	2.26
X	2,468	2,013	2,797	2,979	3,143	2.35	2.16	2.26	2.12	2.16
Total	865	808	935	946	993	1.60	1.58	1.70	1.69	1.73

Source: [a]For 1977-1992 income data: Cortés (1996), table 8:22; and for the 1994 data, Cortés (1997), annex 2.2: 216; and [b]Cortés (1997), table 2.4: 33.

With these objections in mind, in what follows I will look at the results obtained by Cortés.

Period 1977-1984. The average number of earners per household reported by Cortés's table declined from 1.60 in 1977 to 1.58 in 1984 (table 4.11),[34] according to published ENIGH data, it increased from 1.53 to 1.58 (table 4.12). According to the data processed by Cortés, the decline (or stagnation) in the number of household earners was observed in five of the six lower household deciles (the poorest). For the majority of households in a better economic position, this number increased between 1977 and 1984 (except for the 10 per cent of the richest households). As table 4.11 shows, income in the poorest 60 per cent of the population increased between 1977 and 1984 (while the corresponding income in the highest deciles decreased), which would show an improvement in income distribution. This trend, as has been seen above with Hernández-Laos's data, is modified when the figures are adjusted to national accounts. That is, all deciles see their income reduced and inequality remains almost constant. At the end of the day one is left with at least three areas of uncertainty. The first is the characterisation of the period for which contradictory evidence was analysed above. The second is whether earners per household increased or decreased. The third is whether income of the lower deciles increased or decreased. In conclusion, with so many uncertainties, very little can be ascertained for this period.

Table 4.12. Mexico: Selected household demographic features, 1977, 1984, 1989, 1992, 1994 and 1996

	1977	1984	1989	1992	1994	1996
A Household size	5.54	5.07	4.93	4.72	4.60	4.52
B Adults per household	3.51	3.32	3.42	3.29	3.25	3.20
C Workers per household	1.60	1.51	1.63	1.63	1.69	1.72
D Participation rate = (C) / (B)*100	45.58	45.48	47.66	49.54	52.00	53.75
E Earners per household	1.53	1.58	1.67	1.69	1.73	1.77
F Children per household	2.03	1.75	1.51	1.44	1.35	1.31
G % of children = (F) / (A) *100	36.64	34.52	30.63	30.51	29.35	28.98

Source: 1977, SPP (n/d), table P1.11: 47; 1984, INEGI (1989a), table 8:6; 1989, INEGI (1992d), table 2:3; 1992, INEGI (1993b), table 1.2:8; 1994, INEGI (1995), table 12:13; 1996, INEGI (1998), table 1.15.

Period 1984-1989. A recessionary period according to national accounts, in which income per capita, consumption per capita, average labour earnings (national accounts concept) and minimum wages, all drop, while earners per household go up in all but the third decile. Average earners per household increased from 1.58 to 1.70, according to Cortés's figures (table 4.11), and to 1.67, according to published ENIGH data (table 4.12). The income figures in table 4.11 show that income per capita increased in all but the first decile. This trend, opposite to the one portrayed by national accounts, is explained because the underestimation of income was sharply reduced between the 1984 and 1989 surveys (Cortés, 1998:133-142). Thus a decrease in household income, disregarding the ENIGH results, is associated with an increase in average earners as expected by Cortés. However, it turns out to be impossible to analyse this association by decile without resorting to ENIGH.

Period 1989-1992. GDP per capita increased and private consumption per capita increased even faster. This is congruent with the increase in average household income captured by the ENIGHs (table 4.11). Nevertheless, ENIGH figures show a sharp increase in income inequality. In this case, we have, once more, a trend discrepancy. If the figures by Cortés are used, earners per household show, on average, a very slight decrease (from 1.70 to 1.69). But if published figures are used, average earners increased (from 1.67 to 1.69). The behaviour among those deciles which saw their income per capita reduced, without adjustment to national accounts (as presented in table 4.11), is a very mixed one. While household income declined for the first eight deciles (with the exception of the third) the average number of household earners rose in the third decile and in the fifth to eighth deciles, but declined in the first, second and fourth deciles (see table 4.11). Again, however, there are various uncertainties regarding the change in earners per household and the real movement in income distribution, whereupon nothing can be concluded on this period. The first area of uncertainty can be eliminated by broadening the period to 1994.

Period 1989-1994. When the period is thus broadened, it becomes clear that earners per household increased (from 1.67 or 1.70 — depending on the source used — in 1989, to 1.73 in 1994) in a period of somewhat slow economic growth (3.9 per cent annual rate), in which average earnings (national accounts concept) grew. In this same period, average income for all households in the ENIGH grew by 2.26 per cent annually. Thus, in this case there was an increase in both average earners per household and income, an event that is contrary to what Cortés would expect.

Let us now look at the relationship between changes in income per capita and in the number of household earners by income decile. Household income per capita of deciles I, II, III and VI decreased during the period, while earners per household increased in all of them. But, in the rest of the deciles, in which income increased, earners per household increased as well, with the exception of decile IV, where it remained constant. In this way, the increase in earners per household was not associated with income decreases. When analysed by deciles, it rather seems to be independent of income during this period.

The above evidence supports Cortés's argument of the labour force participation in the 1984-1989 period, but only if one disregards income evolution and income by decile in the ENIGH. In the other two main periods either nothing can be concluded (1977-1984) or the evidence is not conclusive (1989-1994). Nevertheless, let's see if the evidence resists the necessary corrections in the indicators used.[35]

First, using household workers instead of household earners, we can see in table 4.12 that similar trends prevailed. The average number of workers per household declined between 1977 and 1984 from 1.60 to 1.51, increased in the 1984-1989 recessionary period, stagnated in the 1989-1992 growth period, increased in the 1992-1994 slow growth period, and continued to grow in the crisis years of 1994-1996 in which the Mexican economy's GDP suffered a severe reduction and real earnings by the population also suffered drastic reductions. As can be seen, the only reduction in workers per household took place during the 1977-1984 period; from then on, one finds a steady tendency to increase (with one sub-period of stagnation) regardless of recession, like the 1984-1989 and the 1994-1996 periods, or growth, like the 1989-1994 period.

In table 4.12 I have added additional demographic data in order to highlight two important demographic tendencies. In the first place, the tendency of household size to reduce. This tendency is systematically observed throughout the period and has meant the reduction of average household size from 5.54 in 1977 to 4.52 in 1996. In the second place, the reduction in 1.02 members per household is explained by 0.72 children's reduction and 0.31 adults' reduction. This implies a very important structural change in the adult-children relation. The number of adults per child (quotient adults/children) was 1.73 in 1977 and rises to 2.44 in 1996. This demographic change amplifies the opportunities for extra-domestic work for the adult population and has to be considered as a force behind the tendency of number of workers per household to grow despite the reduction in the number of adults (table 4.12).

The workers per household index is still an unsatisfactory indicator of effort performed as household size is changing over time. A better indicator is "household labour force participation rate" (HLFPR) calculated by dividing the number of workers per household by the number of adults (household members of 12 years of age and above).[36] The HLFPR remained almost constant in the 1977-1984 period (45.58 per cent in 1977 compared with 45.48 per cent in 1984, table 4.12). Between 1984 and 1989, the HLFPR increased despite the fact that this was a period of recession. However, when the economy began to recover (1989-1994), this proportion continued to increase (table 4.12), in spite of the idea that as income recovers, some household members leave the labour market. After the 1994 "tequila" crisis, the same trend prevails.

From 1984 to 1996 the HLFPR increased very impressively from 45.5 per cent to 53.8 per cent. Again, this alternative indicator on the extra-domestic working effort shows that the HLFPR seems to increase both in growth and in recessionary periods, i.e., both when earnings per occupied person are increasing and when they are decreasing.

Thus we arrive at the same conclusion from which I had departed in section 3.1, in the sense that the evidence from the ENE/ENEU surveys shows a clear trend for uncorrected participation rates to increase. In that section I found that the increase in participation rates was associated with a decrease in the weekly hours of work from 43.2 to 40.4 hours in the 1979-1991 period and ends in 1996 in 41.9, below the 1979 level. This trend in weekly hours made necessary the standardisation of the number of workers by the number of working hours. Thus I arrived at the concepts of equivalent workers and equivalent participation rates. In that moment I stated, based on the figures in table 4.2, that equivalent workers still grew above the rate of growth in GDP, and above the rate of growth in working age population (2.4 per cent annually), so that equivalent participation rates increased during the 1979-1996 period, but the rate of growth of equivalent workers is substantially below that of the EAP.

One would expect the same trend to be found in the ENIGHs. Cortés (1997, table 3.2: 61) gives some relevant figures he obtained processing the data bases of the surveys of 1984, 1989, 1992 and 1994. Besides data on weekly hours of work, Cortés gives the average number of jobs held by occupied people, which is a seldom quoted figure, and which shows a rapid downward trend: 1.33, 1.15, 1,16 and 1.13 in the four years mentioned, respectively. Average weekly hours of work, according to Cortés's data, remained almost constant from 1984 through 1992 (47.8, 47.9 and 47.8 respectively), while there was a substantial decrease in the 1994 survey (45.8 hours). Weekly hours of work in ENIGH are higher than in ENE/ENEU. In table 4.3 I presented average hours in this last source and they ranged, in the nineties, from around 40 to 42 hours. One reason for this difference is that ENIGH includes both main and secondary occupations, while in ENE/ENEU only hours worked in the main occupation are captured. Cortés shows that weekly hours in the main occupation were 43.4, 44.6, 44.5 and 43.1 in 1984, 1989, 1992 and 1994 respectively. These figures are closer to the ones in ENE but are still higher. Weekly hours of work in secondary occupations, for the same years, are 4.4, 3.4, 3.2 and 2.7, showing a definitive downward trend as a consequence of the above-noted downward trend in jobs per person.[37] These findings make Cortés (*Ibid.:* 62) conclude that "household members did not look for additional jobs nor did they intensify their labour workdays." In terms of the above-stated question on whether my findings of section 3.1 are confirmed by the ENIGH results, I did not find a downward trend in weekly working hours, although this can perhaps be explained by the fact that we lacked an ENIGH survey in the late seventies (when the economy was booming).

On the other hand, the trend derived from Cortés's data (1997, table 3.2: 61) on the reduction of jobs per occupied person raises a very important question. If this trend is really prevailing (i.e. that it is not only an ENIGH result, and, consequently, a product of internal problems of the survey), and given the fact that ECSO/ENE surveys capture only hours worked in the main occupation, then total hours worked would have descended in a faster way than described in section 3.1. In that case, even the slow increase I have obtained in the equivalent participation rate might be cancelled.

Unfortunately, the ECSO does not provide information on secondary occupation, so we are left only with the 1991-1996 period for analysis of this variable, and only for urban areas of 100,000 inhabitants or more.[38] In 1991, 3.3 per cent of the occupied population in these cities had two jobs. In 1993 the figure was 3.4 per cent; in 1995 it was 3.1 per cent; and 2.9 per cent in 1996. Despite the very few observations available, it can be pointed out that, in the 1994-1996 crisis, the proportion of persons holding two occupations in large cities goes down very clearly. On the contrary, for the 1991-1993 period, when the economy was growing, this percentage goes up. I will analyse this variable later on for Mexico City, for which I was able to build a larger series (1987-1995). We can anticipate that in the common years the same trends hold.

Thus, although with restricted evidence, I can postulate tentatively that the proportion of people having two jobs behaves pro-cyclically. Given the fact described above, that weekly hours of work in the main job also behave pro-cyclically, the interaction of both variables must have translated into an even slower evolution of the real number of equivalent workers, which might be expressed in the stagnation of the equivalent participation rate. If this were true (unfortunately the data do not allow for an explicit calculation) it would constitute an additional challenge to the interpretation that households mobilised additional working effort in response to the reduction in real earnings.

6.2. Mexico City

In order to analyse the changes in household labour force participation rate, given the fact that not all the ENIGH survey publications allow city level analysis, I was unable to construct a similar time series of workers per household for Mexico City as the one presented at the national level (table 4.6). However, with the available data, it can be seen that there has been a tendency for the rate of workers per households to increase in Mexico City. In 1977, 44.3 per cent of working age household members were participating in the labour market, compared to 47.5 per cent in 1989 (see table 4.13). However, this period covers the oil boom and the 1982-1989 sub-period of crisis, stabilisation and the early years of adjustment. Therefore, it is difficult to discern how the economic crisis affected labour force participation in Mexico City households. Nonetheless, table 4.13

shows that during the period of economic recovery that took place at the end of the 1980s and the beginning of the 1990s, the proportion of workers by household increased from 47.48 per cent in 1989 to 48.17 per cent in 1992. This is the same pattern encountered at the national level.

Table 4.13. Mexico City: Number of occupied members per household, 1977, 1989 and 1992

	1977	1989	1992
Household size	5.50	4.59	4.45
(a) Adults per household	3.66	3.37	3.28
(b) Workers per household	1.62	1.60	1.58
(c) Participation rate (b) / (a)	44.26	47.48	48.17

Source: 1977, SPP (n/d), table P1.11:47; 1984, INEGI (1989a), table 8:6; 1989, INEGI (1992d), table 2:3; 1992, INEGI (1993b), table 1.2:8.

There are two micro-studies that have been conducted on Mexico City which analyse the impact of the 1982 economic crisis on the poor (Tuirán, 1992, and Benería, 1992).[39] Based on a survey of low-income families in Mexico City, Tuirán (1992:183) claims that, between 1985 and 1988, in the capital, the number of household earners increased.[40] According to the author, during adjustment, loss of income by the main breadwinner imposed severe budgetary constraints. As a result, a large proportion of households experienced an increase in the number of household members participating in the labour market. Tuirán then suggests that this was a strategy followed in households in which the family head suffered a decline in income (*Ibid.* 183).

Tuirán calculates the percentage of households that made total or partial use of their male and female labour force.[41] However, there seems to be some analytical shortcomings in regard to the measurement of the working effort of households. While the percentage of households with women who were not engaged in paid activities declined in most of the strata groups between 1985 and 1988, that of households not utilising their male labour force increased in the same period. It would seem that the final result was not an increase in the number of household members engaged in paid activities, but a change in the gender composition of those who work.

150 *Adjustment, Poverty and Employment in Mexico*

Based on Tuirán's figures, I calculated the household labour force participation rate (HLFPR) in order to confirm whether or not there was an increase in this rate.[42] Despite the fact that the average number of household earners increased from 1.6 to 1.9 persons (Tuirán, 1992, table 2: 184), I found that the labour force participation rate did not increase in all of the strata groups. This was as a consequence of a concomitant increase in the number of household members who were old enough to be economically active, that is, members between 15 and 64 years of age (*Ibid.*: table 6:193).

Table 4.14. Changes in income of the household head, income per capita and household LFPR in a group of households of Mexico City, June 1985-February 1988

Households by social strata	Income of the household head[a]		Per capita income [a]		Household's LFPR (per cent)[b]	
	June 1985	February 1988	June 1985	February 1988	June 1985	February 1988
Formal						
Low income	100	95	100	94	47	54
Low-middle income	100	84	100	99	43	55
Middle income [c] *	100	67	100	72	50	45
Informal						
Low income*	100	104	100	109	47	54
Middle income*	100	84	100	93	51	49

Source: [a]Tuirán (1992), table 5:190; [b]own calculations based on *Ibid*, tables 2:184 and 6:193.
[c] The formal-middle-income group had the highest level of household income in Tuirán's sample (between 2.5 and 3.5 minimum wages, see endnote 25, chapter 3). It should be noted, however, that the average income range of this population group (3 minimum wages) is almost equal to the poverty line derived from the NBES which situated the poverty line at 2.96 minimum wages in June 1985 and 2.95 in February 1988 (own calculations based on Boltvinik, 1998a, table 5: 350).
* Family groups in which labour force responses did not follow a counter-cyclical pattern.

Table 4.14 shows that in three out of five family groups (marked by an *), the labour force participation rate did not respond inversely to the changes in income, as suggested by Tuirán. For instance, in the "middle income" families of the "formal" sector, although the household head suffered a decline in his/her salary, the labour force participation rate (LFPR) also decreased from 50 per cent in 1985 to 45 per cent in 1988. In contrast, in "low-income" families of the "informal" sector, there was an increase in their labour force participation rate together with an increase in the real income of household heads. It should have become clear that, based on this evidence, no general conclusion can be drawn on the relationship between household labour responses and changes in household income during the period of economic crisis and adjustment.

7. INTERACTION BETWEEN INCOME POVERTY AND WORKING EFFORT

In this section I will examine the relationship between working effort and income in an internalised manner, so to speak. This is done by analysing the interaction between time poverty and income poverty. In chapter 3 I presented a poverty measurement exercise in which I compared the results obtained from applying the Integrated Poverty Measurement Method to Mexico City data for the 1984, 1989 and 1992 ENIGHs with the national results obtained by Boltvinik at the national level (table 3.7, chapter 3). In that same chapter I also arrived at the conclusion (table 3.8, chapter 3) that both time poverty (or Time Deprivation Index)[43] and income poverty increased in Mexico City during the period of analysis, although the increase observed in income was much larger than the one observed in time. I noted that the time poverty gap (EWT: excess working time) for the population classified as poor in terms of the IPMM declined during the 1984-1989 period at the same time that the income poverty gap increased very quickly (from 0.17 to 0.31). On the contrary, the time poverty gap increased very quickly (from 0.15 to 21) during the 1989-1992 period with the income poverty gap remaining stagnant (see table 3.8, chapter 3). I concluded that this evidence does not seem to confirm those authors who have interpreted the evidence on rates of participation to indicate that persons responded to income deterioration by making an additional working effort. In this section I will examine this evidence more in depth as I regard it to be essential for understanding the interaction between income and working time at the household level.

If one classifies the population by the level of its time deprivation indicator,[44] as shown in table 4.15, one finds that the time-deprived population grew from 37.8 per cent in 1984 to 40.3 per cent in 1989 and then remained unchanged at that very same level in 1992. The average gap, or time poverty intensity for the deprived, remained quite constant, around 0.68. The time deprivation magnitude, which is the product of both numbers, increased from 0.23 in 1984 to 0.27 in 1989, remaining unchanged in 1992.

Table 4.15. Mexico City: Time deprivation evolution, 1984, 1989 and 1992

Poverty indices	1984	1989	1992
1 Time deprivation incidence (per cent) (H)	37.8	40.3	40.3
2 Time deprivation intensity (I)*	0.68	0.66	0.69
3 Time deprivation magnitude (HI) = 1 x 2	0.25	0.27	0.27

Source: Own calculations based on ENIGH database, 1984, 1989, and 1992.
* For persons time-poor deprived.

Two comments are necessary. In the first place, this evidence, which will be reinforced later on, if seen superficially seems to support such authors who have held that persons responded to the decrease in wages by working harder (see preceding sections of this chapter). Note, however, that the time-deprivation index is not simply an index of working hours; it also takes into account the overall domestic setting in terms of a number of determining factors of the domestic work requirements. Note, also, that my finding is that the increase in time deprivation is additional to the growth in income poverty, not a substitute.

In the second place, it is important to consider one characteristic of Boltvinik's procedure: the fact that of the four possible groups formed by the combinations of income and time deprivation depicted in table 4.16 for Mexico and in table 4.17 for Mexico City, in one group income is not adjusted as in the case of the other three groups. For the latter three groups, household income was divided by EWT (the index of excess working time), before comparing it with the poverty line. This adjustment is not done in the group depicted in the shaded cells (table 4.16 and table 4.17). Boltvinik argues that the "free time" of this group is non-voluntary, so that an adjustment could make it non-poor simply because the persons classified in this group may be unemployed or underemployed.

As can be seen in table 4.18 below, the four categories into which the population is classified, according to their condition as poor or non-poor by income and time, are the following: A) income and time poor; B) income poor and time non-poor; C) income non-poor and time poor; and D) income and time non-poor.

Table 4.16. Mexico: Time and income poverty matrix, 1984, 1989 and 1992. Percentage of population (H) and income-time poverty gap

	1984		1989		1992	
	Time poor	Time non-poor	Time poor	Time non-poor	Time poor	Time non-poor
Per cent of the population						
Income poor	20.5	20.8	26.6	28.9	29.6	28.2
Income non-poor	28.2	30.5	19.9	24.3	19.0	23.2
Income-time poverty gap						
Income poor	0.6242	0.4197	0.6715	0.4605	0.6745	0.4663
Income non-poor	-0.0138	-0.3933	0.0081	-0.3901	0.0281	-0.4008

Source: Own calculations based on ENIGH database, INEGI, 1984, 1989 and 1992.

Starting from D, clockwise and analysing the changes in the extreme years in tables 4.16 and 4.17, we obtain the following results.

The consistently non-poor (D) diminish their share in the population (from 30.5 per cent to 23.2 per cent in Mexico and from 42.9 per cent to 33.5 per cent in Mexico City); over the same period. Moreover, during that same period, the group's highly negative[45] time-income gap fluctuates in Mexico City and is very stable in Mexico.

The time poor but income non-poor (C) is a group whose share in the total population shows a reduction during the period: from 28.2 per cent to 19.0 per cent in Mexico; and from 25.2 per cent to 18.5 per cent in Mexico City. The average gap of this group remains very close to zero in both geographical areas.

Table 4.17. Mexico City: Time and income poverty matrix, 1984, 1989 and 1992. Percentage of population (H) and income-time poverty gap

	1984		1989		1992	
	Time poor	Time non-poor	Time poor	Time non-poor	Time poor	Time non-poor
Per cent of the population						
Income poor	12.6	19.3	20.0	28.9	21.8	26.2
Income non-poor	25.2	42.9	20.3	30.8	18.5	33.5
Income-time poverty gap						
Income poor	0.5822	0.3080	0.5892	0.4237	0.5974	0.4132
Income non-poor	-0.0392	-0.3968	-0.0210	-0.4319	-0.0079	-0.3884

Source: Own calculations based on ENIGH, INEGI database, 1984, 1989 and 1992.

Table 4.18. Identification of cells for tables 4.16 and 4.17

	Time poor	Time non-poor
Income poor	A	B
Income non-poor	C	D

As for the income and time poor group (A), which can be called the consistent poor, its share of population grows throughout the period: in Mexico from 20.5 per cent to 29.6 per cent; and in Mexico City from 12.6 per cent to 21.8 per cent. Its average income-time gap increases: from 0.62 to 0.68 in Mexico; and from 0.58 to 0.60 in Mexico City.

Concerning the time non-poor and income poor (B: shaded cells in the tables), which is the group for which the time adjustment is not performed (an adjustment would make its situation better off), its share of the population grows very quickly during the 1984-1989 period: from 20.8 per cent to 28.9 per cent in Mexico; and from 19.3 per cent to 28.9 per cent in Mexico City. Thereafter, its share decreases in both levels of analysis: down to 28.2 per cent in Mexico in 1992; and down to 26.2 per cent in Mexico City also in 1992. But its income-time poverty gap, which in this case is equal to the income gap (as the negative time gap is not used to adjust income), increases throughout the entire period: in Mexico, from 0.42 in 1984 to 0.47 in 1992; and in Mexico City it rises steeply in the 1984-1989 period, from 0.31 to 0.42, thereafter falling slightly to 0.41 in 1992 (see tables 4.16 and 4.17).

Note that for Mexico City groups A and B are the only two groups which, judging them by their average income-time gap, turn out to be income-time poor. The C and D groups have a negative mean income-time poverty gap, thereby denoting, on average, a non-poor (in income-time terms) status.[46]

The substantial growth in the presence of the B group and its overwhelming importance[47] in the total of income poor population challenges the idea that as income declines more household members enter the labour market in order to counteract income losses. The mere existence and size of this group constitutes very strong evidence against the contention that the generality of households followed a strategy of compensating income losses with a greater working effort. If all households acted in this way there would be no households which, in addition to being income poor, also have some time available that is not utilised in extra-domestic work (this is the meaning of being non poor in the time dimension).

Figure 4.1 Mexico: Plausible net flows, given empirical results, 1984-1992

	Time poor	Time non-poor
Income poor	A +9.1 points	B +7.4 points
Income non-poor	C −9.2 points	D −7.3 points

(9.1) (0) (0.1) (7.3)

In order to understand the dynamics implied by the "labour survival strategy current of thought" as well as to contrast it with the dynamics implied in my empirical results, I have drawn two simplified contingency tables, which highlight the percentage points lost or gained by each group, for results in Mexico. In the first contingency table (Figure 4.1), arrows have been drawn to show the plausible *net flows* between cells, given the empirical results. In the second contingency table (Figure 4.2), the arrows show the logical flows derived from the "labour survival strategy current of thought" in the face of a generalised fall in income.

Figure 4.2   "Labour Survival Strategy Current of Thought" logical flows

		Time poor	Time non-poor
Income poor	A		B
Income non-poor	C		D

Flow coherent with successful "Labour Survival Strategies": ⟶

Flow which implies a failure of the strategy: ⤏

In the first diagram there are four possible net flows going out of the cells loosing points (two from each of the bottom cells) and entering the cells gaining points (two into each of the top cells). The empirical results draw the limits of value within which these arrows can move.

The flow from C to B is one which can be generated when (among other factors) someone in the household looses his job (or ceases working) and remains unemployed (or not active), so that the household becomes income poor and, having available time, also becomes time non-poor. But unemployment in Mexico in the dates of the ENIGHs, according to this source, decreased between 1984 and 1992, from 4.4 per cent to 3.8 per cent. Thus we can assume, with some confidence, regarding the possible flow generated by unemployment, that this net flow was zero (empirically it was almost zero, 0.1) in this period. This assumption allows us to calculate the remaining three net flows, which then are as follows: CA=9.1, DB=7.3 and DA= 0. (This does not mean that there were no other flows among cells; such flows, however, cancel out and are not reflected in the *net flows*). The most likely event is that the highest flow went from C to A, which represents households which were already time poor and became income poor. Another portion, 7.3 per cent, of the population (the

DB flow) meant that most of the previously consistently non-poor, in the face of an income loss, simply became income poor. Consequently, this flow (DB) implies simply becoming income poor with no apparent change in working habits.

In figure 4.2 I have drawn the logical flows which one would expect under the "Labour Survival Strategy Current of Thought" in the face of a generalised decrease in income. Only flows implying a change of cell have been drawn. Let us start from cell D and look at the consequences of the income loss. Naturally, for the very rich (for whom income is unconnected to work performed) the income loss would not imply a response if they continue to be consistently non-poor. They would remain in the same cell. Movements from D to A or to C have been classified as the logical flows one would expect from the standpoint of this current of thought. In effect, consistent non-poor households (apart from the very rich) would respond to a decrease in income, which threatens their non-poor status, by working harder, and this would continue up to the point where either they exhaust their free time (and they become time poor, moving to the left-hand column) or they avoid becoming income non-poor and thus stay in the lower row. These two options imply staying in the same cell (in which case there is no flow), that is, moving to C and thus avoiding income poverty by becoming time poor, which can be considered a successful labour survival strategy. Naturally, the households could get to the limit of available time and still be income poor, in which case they would fall into income poverty (the DA flow), which would be classified as a strategic failure. Thus the DB flow would be inconsistent, for it implies that households do not respond to a drop in income even when this implies becoming income poor. According to this current of thought, because this flow should be zero, it has not been drawn in Figure 4.2. My empirical findings, on the contrary, identify this flow as the most important one.

The households which confront the income shock from cell C could be pushed to A or to B. If the income shock takes the form of a drop in earnings without loss of employment, the household would be pushed to A. If the income shock takes the form of someone loosing his (her) job, they would be pushed to B. In response to these threats, the current of thought we are examining would forecast, in the first case, the work by additional members of the family, and, in the second case, a new job by the unemployed. In the latter case, if this implies lower earnings which threatens the status of the household, the current of thought would forecast additional work by other members. The CA flow could be a result of a strategic failure (as income poverty was not avoided). The CB flow would be inconsistent with this theory as it implies idle time. Thus it has not been drawn.

From A nobody would exit as a result of a survival strategy because this population group is already time-poor and households do not have available members to send to the labour market. Therefore, no arrow has been drawn going out of A (if they could exit to C now that income has fallen, then, *a fortiori*, they would have also have been able to do it previously).

The mere presence of households in B would be abnormal for this current of thought.[48] Outgoing flows from B to C or to A (expressing an intensification of work) as a consequence of an income shock would be inconsistent because, as happened with the flow from A to C, if they can do it now they could as well have done it before (they were already income poor and had the motive and the available human resources). Thus no outgoing arrows have been drawn from this cell. As has been said, flows from D to B or C to B as a consequence of an income shock would be inconsistent with the theory. Empirically, however, I have found DB to be a very strong flow, while I have assumed CB to be zero given the rates of unemployment in 1984 and 1992 (and empirically the flow was almost equal to zero, 0.1).

Summing up, the only logical and successful flow consistent with the "labour survival strategy" is the DC flow. The additional flow drawn in Figure 4.2, the DA flow, implies strategic failure: the intensification of work is unable to prevent income poverty. All other movements are either inconsistent with the theory or are illogical (if it is possible now, it was possible before). The DC and DA flows have not been found to exist empirically. So the rest of the empirical flows have been found to be inconsistent with the forecasts of the labour survival strategies. In effect, moving from D to B or from C to A appears as a mere consequence of the fall in income. Particularly the DB flow is completely inconsistent with this current of thought: having available time and not using it to avoid income poverty is inconsistent with the main premise of the theory, i.e. that households respond to income losses by intensifying the extra-domestic work carried out by the household.

8. SUMMARY

The literature on the impact of adjustment on the labour market assumes that the expansion of the labour force between 1982 and 1994 was not a result of an increase in the demand for labour, but rather of survival strategies adopted by those who lost their jobs or suffered income losses. This interpretation implies that work is always available, and that the supply of labour is able to create its own demand.

There are two sources of these interpretations. One is the few micro-studies conducted in Mexico that hold that as income declined households set in motion labour survival strategies; the other is the statistical employment material, which show a rising trend in the labour force participation rate. However, this statistical material poses serious problems of comparability and reliability.

The lessons learnt, in this chapter, in addition to the empirical ones on the relationship between economic performance and labour force participation rates, are methodological. At least five aspects have to be considered in order to arrive at a correct conclusion:

1) In order to achieve a transparent association with the dependent variable (in this case, participation rates), the periods of analysis have to be homogeneous in terms of the independent variable (which in this case is GDP per capita, or even better, earnings per occupied person). This means that one simple period should not include recessionary and growth years.
2) No conclusions can be derived from one period of observation, as the assumed dependent variable might be determined by secular forces and might be moving in a certain direction which is not determined by the independent variable.
3) No conclusions can be derived for a part of the whole labour force (e.g. female labour force) without looking at the total and/or at its complement (e.g. male labour force).
4) The observed dependent variable has to be comparable among periods, which requires the same definitions and homogeneity (e.g. the same definition of active population and standardised or equivalent workers).
5) It is necessary to divide the population into segments that in principle one would expect to respond differently to an income loss. The standard of living of these groups (e.g. poor and non-poor, and each one divided by strata) is a good way to go for such a classification. One would expect wealthy households to respond differently to a crisis than poor households.

Many authors do not observe these rules and thus their results are not reliable. I have tried to come close to them but I have had many restrictions from the availability of data. Sometimes I have complied with some of these rules and sometimes with some others, but I have never been able to comply with all of them completely.

In order to clarify whether there was an increase in a household's work effort as a response to income decline, I standardised employment data and analysed other employment indices. I found that there is not an association between a decline in income and an increase in the labour force participation rate (LFPR). I will now explain how I arrived at this conclusion.

One of the main problems I found when analysing employment trends by means of the available employment surveys is that there is no employment statistical material available to build a consistent time series, which captures the transformation suffered by the Mexican economy throughout my period of analysis (1982-1994). At the national level, there is no statistical material to analyse employment in the 1980s; therefore, I had to rely on the 1979 ECSO and the 1991 ENE to assess employment trends in the decade. However, as I noted above, during the 1979-1991 period Mexico went through an oil boom, two economic crises (in 1982 and 1986), and two periods of economic recovery (1984-1985, 1989-1991). This means that the Mexican population may have suffered various drastic changes in household income, which may have produced different labour responses during the decade, and which cannot be captured by one survey at the end year of the period.

Although for the country as a whole the non-corrected Labour Force Participation Rate (LFPR) seems to grow regardless of changes in the GDP trend (that is, the LFPR grew during periods of economic crisis, of stagnation or of recovery), I found some evidence to believe that the demand for labour did not increase at the same pace. First, when we look at the Equivalent LFPR (standardised LFPR by 48 working hours per week), the increase is half of that observed by using the uncorrected LFPR. Second, although there was a higher corrected LFPR (ELFPR) in 1991 than in 1979, the proportion of workers who worked less than 40 hours in the reference week also increased. This means that although more persons were working, they were working a lesser number of hours. This is clearly reflected by the decline in the average number of weekly working hours, which went down from 43 to 40.4 hours between 1979 and 1991.

I was able to analyse the employment trends observed in Mexico City during the 1980s. This exercise highlighted the relevance for the analysis of employment trends to be able to identify particular homogeneous periods in which only one drastic economic change occurs (rule 1, above). With regard to the changes of the LFPR and the ELFPR in Mexico City I found that when rule 1 is complied with, these rates are more closely associated with changes in GDP growth. Comparing the city's labour force participation rate between 1979 and 1991 (as I did for the country as a whole) the conclusion would have been that the labour force participation rate increased, despite the economic crisis. However, if we compare the LFPR of 1979 and 1983, the conclusion is that the 1982 economic crisis adversely affected the level of employment in Mexico City, since the LFPR rate went down from 50.5 per cent to 46.7 per cent. This evidence does not support the idea of a massive entry of women, children and elderly people to the labour market as a response to income decline. Performing the same standardisation as I did for the national LFPR, I found that it was not until 1989 that the equivalent LFPR recovered, as compared with that in 1979. In this case, the ELFPR went down from 40.7 per cent of the population of 12 years of age and above, to around 39 per cent in 1987 and 1988. This means that employment in the city did not increase faster than the working age population, a finding that contradicts the propositions of the labour-survival-strategy current of thought. A decline in the ELFPR means that although more people may be participating in the labour market, they worked, on average, a lesser number of hours per week. I also found that changes in the level of employment in the city were not counter-cyclical. The Equivalent LFPR rose considerably between 1989 and 1993 (from 41.6 per cent to 43.2 per cent) as economic conditions improved. In this case, there were not only more people participating in the labour market, but also the average weekly number of hours of work increased.

Up to here it should have become clear that while at the national level we can not draw any strong conclusion with regard to the trends of labour force participation during the 1982-1994 period, for Mexico City the evidence indicates that households were not able to increase their work effort in order to counteract income losses.

Another source of evidence that has been used by those who hold that there was an increase in the number of household members in the labour market, despite a decline in income and wages, is the number of earners reported by the ENIGHs. In the analysis of employment trends by means of the ENIGH I also encountered several problems with the analysis of employment by periods, since the number of surveys is limited. As the nearest surveys conducted before and after the 1982 economic crisis were the 1977 and 1984 ENIGH surveys, these two surveys are compared in order to analyse the impact of the crisis on the population. As was seen above, the evidence on the overall balance in this period is not conclusive. On the one hand, it is not clear whether poverty increased in this period. For instance, despite the fact that GDP per capita and consumption per capita were higher in 1984 than in 1977, Hernández-Laos estimated that poverty increased slightly. Nonetheless, ENIGH raw data report an average decline in income but an increase in the income of the poorest 60 per cent of the population. Therefore, according to the original ENIGH figures, poverty was reduced. On the other hand, although the number of earners per household increased, the number of workers per household declined and the household labour force participation rate (HLFPR) remained constant. Therefore, ENIGH surveys do not provide enough evidence of an increase in the work effort of households during the period. Moreover, no conclusive evidence exists on changes in household income between 1977 and 1984.

When analysing the relationship between income and household labour force participation for the 1984-1989 period, the proposition of labour survival strategies seems to be supported if the ENIGH income figures are adjusted to national accounts. That is, as income declined, both the number of workers per household and the HLFPR increased. However, in the survey there is an employment figure that seems to contradict this trend: the number of jobs held per worker declined in the same period.

If the data for the 1984-1989 period seem to support the labour-survival-strategy current of thought, the evidence for the 1989-1992 or 1989-1994 period contradicts this current of thought. As we have seen, during the 1989-1994 period there were clear signs of economic recovery. GDP per capita, income per capita, and average wages began to increase. However, contrary to the idea that labour force participation is counter-cyclical, the ENIGH surveys report an increase in the number of workers per household (or at least a stagnation between 1989-1992) as well as an increase in the household labour force participation rate. Therefore, in this case, household labour effort was pro-cyclical. When analysing the changes in the number of earners per household by deciles of income, I did not find any clear relationship between income changes and the number of earners per household. This number changes when either income per capita in the relevant decile increases or decreases.

In summation, the ENIGH surveys do not provide consistent evidence to support the interpretation that, as income declines, more household members enter the labour market in order to counteract income losses. This is because there is no association between changes in income and in number of workers (or household earners) per household or in HLFPR.

With regard to women's labour force participation, I found that national data confirm the proposition that female labour supply is counter-cyclical. This seems to be so because women's LFPR grew faster during economic recession (1991-1995) than during stagnation (1979-1991). However, when analysing female employment figures for Mexico City, for which data on employment during the 1980s is available, I found that between 1979 and 1988, when GDP per capita showed a slight decline, women's labour force participation rate remained relatively at the same level. In contrast, between 1989 and 1991, when GDP per capita increased, women's participation in the labour market also increased In this case we cannot assume that women's labour supply is counter-cyclical as suggested by some scholars. There are other indicators that may explain an increase in women's participation in the labour market. For example, the economic censuses report a significant increase in female salaried employment. This increase was not only explained by the growth of the "maquiladora" sector, but, as we will see in the next chapter, in service activities.

Another idea held by the labour-survival-strategy current of thought is that, as a result of the economic crisis, more children entered the labour market. However, as we saw, there are no employment data on children in Mexico. Nonetheless, I analysed data for adolescents in Mexico City and my conclusions are that their labour force participation rate is pro-cyclical (particularly for adolescents between 15 and 19 years of age), that is, that it increases as GDP grows. For adolescents between 12 and 14 years of age, their labour force participation rate does not have a clear pattern, since it grows and shrinks regardless of the direction of economic change. Nonetheless, it should be pointed out that in 1994 this population age group had its lowest level of participation since 1987.

I ended this chapter by analysing the relationship between household income and work effort, based on poverty estimates using the IPMM method, which were presented in chapter 3. In the present chapter I analysed more closely the relationship between household income and extra-domestic work. In order to do so, I designed three contingency tables (for Mexico, Mexico City, and an hypothetical one) composed of the income poor/non-poor and time poor/non-poor categories. In the case of the observed data for Mexico and Mexico City, I found that a major proportion of the population classified as income poor was classified as time non-poor. That means that, although they were poor from the point of view of income, they were not mobilising all human resources which could be engaged in the labour market in order to escape poverty. The existence of this group and its steep increase between 1984 and 1989 (when the Mexican economy went through an economic recession) contradict in principle the proposition that when income declines, households engage in labour survival strategies.

The observed changes in the percentage of the income-time poverty categories were contrasted with the likely responses of households to income decline, under the principles of the labour-survival-strategy current of thought. I found that the net flows among income-time categories did not follow the likely labour responses of households proposed by this current of thought. For instance, this current of thought believes that, as income declines, households set in motion labour strategies in order to avoid poverty. However, data on Mexico and Mexico City show that between 1984 and 1989 a major proportion of consistent non-poor households (measured by income and time availability) became income-poor, but remained time-non-poor. That means that they did not attempt (or were not able to) make additional use of their available human resources to perform extra-domestic work. Therefore, the proportion of the income-poor and the time non-poor increased sharply. This population group was the largest one, and the one which had the highest increase in the 1984-1989 period, and, as noted, its mere existence contradicts the survival-strategy current of thought.

My main conclusion is that there is not enough evidence to support the idea that households responded to income losses by intensifying the extra-domestic workload. This does not mean that they did not attempt to perform additional work, but that, as data suggest, if they did, they were not necessarily successful. These findings have very important implications against the idea that work in Latin American countries is always available, and that, irrespective of the prevailing economic conditions, persons will be able to find or create their own jobs. I have found that standardised employment data, for the appropriate period of analysis, do not support this idea in the case of Mexico and Mexico City.

Notes

[1] According to Gregory (1985), this view was influenced by international concern over a problem of employment in developing countries. This author points out that contrary to the idea of the existence of a large volume of under-utilised labour, the evidence at the end of the 1970s suggests that there were unmistakable signs of labour shortages in many sectors and regions of Mexico (Gregory, 1985:3).

[2] I included within the Labour-Survival-Strategy Current of Thought scholars who explained the growth in the number of household members participating in the labour market during the 1980s, partially or totally, as a response to household income loses (e.g. González de la Rocha, 1993, 1994; Benería, 1992; Tuirán, 1992; García, 1994; García and Oliveira 1994; Cortés and Rubalcava, 1991, Cortés, 1997). For a detailed discussion on the propositions of this current of thought please refer to Appendix 1 to this chapter.

3   For instance, some scholars argue that household work should be taken as productive work, since it makes possible the performing of other economic activities. Others claim that, for labour force measurement, household work should be counted as work only if the household work contributes directly to household income (for this discussion see Turnham, 1993).
4   In the 1970 Population Census, the questions to identify labour force participation were as follows: Last week, did you work for an hour or more for a wage or salary, or as a self-employee?; In the preceding week, did you work in a family business for fifteen hours or more, without receiving any payment for it?; and, Did you not work, although you had a job?
5   The employment questions in the 1980 Population Census were as follows: Last week, did you work as a salaried worker, as an employer, as a self-employee, or in a production co-operative?; How many hours did you work?; Did you work helping on a property, in a manufacturing concern, a shop, or in the workshop of someone in your family without receiving any payment for the work?; How many hours did you work?; Did you not work, although you had a job, because you were on vacation, sick leave, maternity leave, on a permit, because there was bad weather, because workers were on strike, or because you were waiting for sowing/harvest time to begin?, and Although you did not work, were you looking for a job, and have you had a job before?
6   The employment questions in the 1990 Population Census were as follows: Did you work last week?; Did you have a job, but did not work?; Are you a student?; Are you a housewife or is your activity related to housekeeping?; Are you handicapped and, therefore, unable to work?, and Did you not work for other reasons?. As can be seen, the 1980 Population Census eliminated the question on unpaid work (see endnote 3 of this chapter).
7   ECSO: Encuesta Continua Sobre Ocupación (Continuous Survey on Occupation); ENE: Encuesta Nacional de Empleo (National Employment Survey); ENEU: Encuesta Nacional de Empleo Urbano (National Urban Employment Survey).
8   The ENEU provides information on the main urban areas in Mexico. Its coverage has been extended over time and it has been conducted since 1986. The questionnaire of this survey is the same that has been used in the ENE; therefore, all comments made with regard to the ENE apply also to the ENEU.
9   Although there was another ENE conducted in 1988, the data provided by this survey cannot be compared with the 1979 ECSO, since national tables for many employment categories are not available (see García, 1994, Ch. 1).
10 Relying on Jusidman (1988) and the household surveys she quotes (Encuesta Nacional de Hogares) I will be able to provide a year by year evolution of labour force participation rates throughout our period of analysis.
11 The informal/formal definition generally associates large firms with the formal sector and small firms with the informal sector. Other definitions of the informal sector rely on occupational categories (e.g., self-employment), conditions of employment (e.g., casual work), and form of remuneration (e.g., non-wage-earning work). The definition of informal/formal sector has been challenged on the grounds of its arbitrariness and internal contradictions (see Kannapan, 1988 and 1989). Moreover, most of the studies on the informal/formal sector have been based on inadequate, highly aggregate, and often unreliable data.
12 In the 1977 ENIGH, the reference period to define the EAP is even longer: people are asked if they worked for money or without being paid (at least for a third of the working day) during the past six months (from January 1 to June 30).

[13] Did you work, or did you carry out any activity from which you received any income, or from which you were expecting to receive any money or pay in kind during the past month?
[14] Last week, did you work at least one hour in order to support your family or to pay for any of your own expenditures?
[15] The other three questions are: Although you have told me that you did not work last week, do you have any job or business of your own from which to earn a living?; Are you going to start a new business?; and, Last week, did you work without being paid in a family member's or other person's business (or on their property)?
[16] Equivalent workers are the result of standardising all workweeks in terms of weekly hours of work, expressed as a proportion of the standard workweek in Mexico, which is 48 hours. This means that, for example, 24 hours of work during the week is converted into 0.5 equivalent workers. The equivalent participation rate is the result of dividing equivalent workers into the working age population. Unemployed population and persons who were employed but did not work last week, as they worked zero hours, are not considered as equivalent workers.
[17] It should be noted that the level of productivity would have declined much more markedly if productivity had been calculated per occupied person.
[18] The three major studies on household members' labour responses are Jusidman (1988), Tuirán (1992), and Benería (1992).
[19] In Spanish, "tradicionalmente estable" (or, literally, traditionally stable).
[20] Children, women and elderly persons.
[21] Although there is no information on the performance of the Mexico City economy, we can assume with confidence that it behaved very similarly to the Mexican economy as a whole.
[22] The equivalent labour force participation rates are the result of dividing equivalent workers (instead of EAP) by adult population. Equivalent workers is a standardised unit where workers are converted into equivalent workers by multiplying them by the quotient of their working hours and 48, which are the normative weekly working hours in Mexico.
[23] This is the result obtained when the figure in 1991 is corrected for comparability with the 1979 ECSO by excluding unpaid workers who worked less than 15 hours a week. In the uncorrected comparison, the resulting growth is still larger, from 21.5 per cent to 31.5 per cent, exactly 10-percentage points and a 46.5 per cent increase in only 12 years.
[24] Selby et al. (1990:11-13) carried out a household survey between 1977-1978 in ten cities of Mexico (9,458 households). The aim of their study was to study physical living conditions of the family. Additionally, a second interview of 213 households was carried out in order to analyse the social and economic situation of the household, along with a detailed inventory of its membership and some questions concerning attitude. Ten years later (1987), the authors carried out a follow-up study in Oaxaca, interviewing 604 households and conducting 50 in-depth surveys that covered topics on household organisation during the crisis (*Ibid.*: 169). However, the study did not specify whether or not the same households were interviewed in both surveys.
[25] The García and Oliveira study is based on fertility surveys carried out in 1979, 1982, and 1987. Employment data refers to women between 20 and 49 years of age; therefore, findings cannot be taken as representative of the female labour force as a whole (women of 12 years of age and above). There also are some comparability problems because of changes in the question related to women's employment in the surveys (see Appendix 1 to this chapter and García and Oliveira, 1994, Appendix I).

Labour Force Participation Trends 167

[26] There are some clarifications that have to be made on these data reported by the economic censuses. First of all, they exclude agricultural activities, so that they reflect "urban activities". Second, the censuses capture activities which are carried out in specialised establishments, thereby omitting activities carried out on the street without a fixed installation and activities carried out at dwellings. Third, there has been a great effort by INEGI to broaden the coverage of censuses, so it is likely that part of the growth reflected in the text is a result not of real employment growth but of expanded coverage by the economic censuses.

[27] The reliability of the income figures of the ENEU has not been tested. Nevertheless, I have argued in section 4 of this chapter that the evolution of income levels derived from the ENIGHs is not reliable. Given the fact that ENIGHs are the specialised surveys on income, it looks very likely that the ENEU would also turn out to be non-reliable as a source to measure the evolution of real income for earners and households.

[28] There are no available GDP data for Mexico City. Changes in GDP refer to data at the national level; therefore, conclusions should be take with caution.

[29] It should be noted that, although for the country as a whole the equivalent female labour force participation rate seems to have behaved counter-cyclically during the 1993-1995 period, such behaviour cannot be analysed in isolation, as male participation rates went down.

[30] "Household earners" refers to all household members who receive an income either by working or by receiving a retirement pension or remittances from other household members working away from the household's locality.

[31] For a wider discussion on which household are expected to respond according to the labour-survival-strategy current of thought, please refer to Appendix 1 to this chapter.

[32] Cortés's figure is derived from the database of that survey; the database and the published figures apparently are not entirely consistent.

[33] It should be noted that Cortés's study used the number of household earners as one of the variables to be taken into consideration in the analysis of income distribution.

[34] For additional empirical analysis by this author, please refer to Cortés (1995a, 1995b and 1995c).

[35] Conclusions obtained in a previous study (Cortés and Rubalcava, 1991) are not comparable with the conclusions of the 1977 study analysed in the text, because in the former they used published deciles which are based on total household income, whereas the present analysis relies on deciles based on per capita income.

[36] The optimum procedure would be to calculate this rate by social strata (e.g. the poor, the non-poor, and so on).

[37] In order for the two averages (in main and in secondary occupations) to be amenable for aggregation, average hours in secondary occupations have to be calculated by dividing the sum of hours worked by total occupied persons

[38] Although I was unable to build the series 1991-1996 for the country as a whole, owing to the lack of this variable in 1991 for localities of less than 100,000 inhabitants, it should be pointed out that the proportion of people having two occupations in these localities is much larger than in large cities: 9.9 per cent in 1995 and 9 per cent in 1996. In 1993 people occupied in agriculture were excluded in the calculations in these localities and, as a consequence, the proportion falls to 5 per cent. Among what the ENE 1993 (Table 117) calls agricultural producers, the percentage of people having two occupations goes up to 29.5 per cent. Consequently, the conclusion derived from this evidence is that the proportion of people holding two jobs in small cities and in rural areas is biased by the inclusion of agricultural producers, for which the questionnaire is different, with different reference periods. Thus, the best thing is to analyse this variable only for cities.

[39] In this section I will analyse Tuirán's study, while Benería's research will be discussed below.

[40] As noted in chapter 3, Tuirán's study is based on a follow-up survey conducted by the National Consumers Institute (INCO), the first interview was conducted in June 1985 and the last one conducted in February 1988 in Mexico City. The survey began with a non-representative sample of 258 families and ended with 172 families. In the survey, the households were interviewed six times. Households were classified according to their income level (low, medium-low and medium), and according to whether the head of the household was working in the formal/informal sector. The head of the household was classified within the formal sector if he or she was an employee, received a regular salary, and had social security. In addition to the problems regarding the definition of the formal/informal sector, it seems that in this study job mobility of the household head was not taken into consideration. It is unclear whether workers remained in the same type of job (formal/informal) during the period of analysis. Therefore, we do not know whether changes in the level of income of the household head resulted from job-to-job mobility.

[41] Tuirán calculates an index of a household's utilisation of labour force to measure the proportion of male and female household members who are engaged in economic activities. Tuirán classified households according to the following criteria: a) whether they made use of their total available labour force (that is, if all working age members were engaged in paid activities); b) whether they made partial use of their household labour force (not all working-age members age are working); and b) whether they do not use their available labour force at all.

[42] The HLFPR was estimated dividing the average number of household earners by the average number of household members who were between 15 and 64 years of age (Tuirán, 1992, Table 2 and Table 6).

[43] Boltvinik has named his excess working time (EWT) index a Time Deprivation Index, for, by including not only extra-domestic working time, but also domestic working time and time for education within non-free time, it comes close to that. For a detailed explanation of this index see endnote 31 in chapter 3, and the Methodological Appendix to this book.

[44] In this case households are ordered by their time deprivation indicator, whereas in the material presented in Table 3.8, chapter 3, they were ordered by their IPMM poverty gap.

[45] A negative gap indicates welfare above the standards. The more negative the gap is, the greater the implied welfare.

[46] Naturally this s not the procedure that was used in my calculations to estimate income-time poverty incidence. I did it household by household. Consequently, the results are different.

[47] Considering the total population of income poor to be 100 per cent (A and B groups), with regard to Mexico City persons who are also time poor account for 60.5 per cent of that total in 1984 and for 54.6 per cent of that total in 1992; with regard to Mexico, the percentage shares of that total range from 50.4 per cent to 48.7 per cent.

[48] Except for a small fraction of households, which I have not calculated, that have no able adults for extra-domestic work and that the EWT procedure classifies as non-time poor. Naturally, in the case of Mexico these type of households represent a small minority.

Appendix 1. The Labour Survival Strategies

In the current of thought of the Labour Survival Strategies (LSS), as I have thus referred to it in my book, I have included researchers who have explained, partially or totally, the increase in the number of household members participating in the labour market (or the increase in the labour force participation rates) as a response to the decline of income suffered during the 1980s (e.g., González de la Rocha, 1993, 1994; Benería, 1992; Tuirán, 1992; García, 1994; García and Oliveira, 1994; Cortés and Rubalcava, 1991; Cortés, 1997).[1] Without detriment to the effort that this could have signified for some households, the assumption that the latter have the capacity to respond with a greater utilisation of their labour force has led to thinking that this strategy prevents, or at least reduces, the deterioration in family living conditions in periods of crisis and adjustment.

Cornia (1987: 90) has pointed out that "for the majority of low-income households (whether part of the informal sector or not), adjustment entails a variety of adaptations — known as survival strategies — in the creation and use of resources (labour force participation, migration, consumption, etc.). These survival strategies are often attributed with the potential of reducing welfare losses during periods of decline." Within what this author calls "Strategies aiming at the generation of resources" we find the strategy of "increasing the supply of labour to the economy" (*Ibid*.: 94). Based on a series of research reports on developing countries regarding the crisis of the 1980s, Cornia concluded that "it appears, therefore, that the economic crisis has increasingly drawn members of the 'non-primary' labour force into market production" (*Ibid*.: 95). Given the fall of GDP in developing countries during the 1980s and the ensuing reduction in the overall demand for labour, the phenomenon described by Cornia would be giving us indications that employment in developing countries is (or was) determined by the supply of labour, regardless of the conditions of the demand for it. This raises a number of questions about such strategies.

1) Is it possible for employment to increase in periods of crisis?

2) Which social groups responded to the drop in income?
3) Which household members were the ones who entered the labour market?

Bearing in mind the above-stated questions, in what follows let us review some of the research studies that observed this phenomenon in Mexico during the 1980s.

1. THE COUNTER-CYCLICAL NATURE OF THE LABOUR SURVIVAL STRATEGIES

Researchers attribute a counter-cyclical nature to the LSS. As Escobar (1996:549), a prominent exponent of this current, has asserted, "To some (González de la Rocha, Escobar, Tuirán, Cortés), additional work is counter-cyclical: the economically active population (EAP) tends to grow under crisis and restructuring."

González de la Rocha (1990, 1991) carried out one of the first micro social research studies on survival strategies in Mexico with a non-representative sample of households in the city of Guadalajara.[2] According to this author, the results of her study show "a rational-collective response to the economic crisis ... [through] ... the intensification of salaried work ... by a greater number of members in the labour market" (González de la Rocha, et al., 1990:358). However, despite that her study finds an increase in the number of workers per household between 1982 and 1985 (from 2.13 to 2.69) there are indications that part of this increase was due to changes in household size and age structure. In that same study, the author argues that the household units grew "above all, thanks to the incorporation of working age members and to the withholding of their able members. The households have also grown by 'natural' ways (thanks to the development of the domestic cycle), but, from 1982 onwards, the incorporation of members capable of generating income has been the key to protecting consumption" (González de la Rocha, et al. 1990:358). This assertion requires two comments. Firstly, we could say that, in view of the increase in the total number of working age household members, an increase in the number of workers per household is to be expected, without this representing an "intensification of salaried work," if the latter is measured by net household participation rates (that is, the number of workers in the household divided by the number of working age members in the household).[3] Unfortunately, the study does not report age structure data in order to calculate household participation rates. Furthermore, the increase in the number of workers per household owing to the incorporation of "new" working age members does not mean that employment had increased socially, given that in the households which these members come from there was a reduction in the number of workers. This same author presents some data for the period of 1985-1987 which contradict the postulates of the LSS. González de la Rocha (1991: 117) reports a slight decrease in the number of workers per household (from 2.69 to 2.59) between 1985 and 1987, a period during which the Mexican economy was undergoing one of the most severe crises of the 1980s. The author offers as an explanation of this decrease the fact that by 1987 there had been a slowdown in the rate of reduction of wages. Nevertheless, as we saw in chapter 2, between 1985 and 1987 wages and private consumption nearly reached their lowest level compared to that of 1981. In addition, this period featured a sharp drop in GDP, an increase in the annual rate of inflation, which in 1987 soared to nearly 160%, the highest annual rate observed in the 1980s. Therefore, in this period the postulate that asserts that a decline in wages leads to an increase in the number of workers per household was not fulfilled. Hence the supply of labour did not behave in a counter-cyclical manner, as had been postulated.

Chant (1993) carried out another micro social study that suggest the emergence of labour survival strategies during the crisis of the 1980s. A study carried out in the city of Querétaro[4] found that the increase in the number of household members participating in the labour market was very slight, from 2.1 to 2.3, between 1982-3 and 1986 (see Chant, 1993). We can assume that this slight increase could have been due to changes in the demographic structure of the households, which resulted in an increase in the number of working age household members, rather than stemming from labour survival strategies. In this case, we also do not have information enabling us to calculate household participation rates and thereby evaluate whether or not the increase in the number of workers per household was due to the occurrence of a demographic change.

Despite this very small increase, Chant does not reject the idea of labour survival strategies; rather, she proposes the existence of a point in the level of income at which households do not "need" to send more members to the labour market (see Chant, 1993). Paradoxically, contrary to what was to be expected, Chant finds increased earnings of women and young household members. According to the author, "increased earnings of women and young household members probably provides a partial explanation for the relatively small rise in numbers of income earners within households" (Chant, 1993:324-326). However, the increased earnings of these members could give us indications that the demand for labour of these population groups in Querétaro had increased, and that, therefore, their participation in the labour market is pro-cyclical.

Another micro social study for Mexico City along the lines of the LSS is one authored by Tuirán (1992),[5] who contends that "in a context of low and decreasing wages, the greater participation of household members in paid activities constituted one of the strategies most commonly used to protect the family income or to contain its decline ... [thus one notes] ... a growing trend in the average number of income-earners per household in all strata" (*Ibid.*: 183). This study does provide data for calculating household participation rates, and chapter 4 shows that of the five groups analysed, in three of them the changes in labour participation did not have a counter-cyclical nature; rather, labour participation in these groups tends to be pro-cyclical. (For a more detailed analysis of this point, see section 4.2 of chapter 4 of this book.)

As we can so far observe, the micro social studies of labour survival strategies present serious difficulties for evaluating to what extent such strategies occurred, given that the studies talk about an absolute, not a relative, increase in the number of workers per household. In cases in which one has information for evaluating the extent of such a strategy, we have found that it is either very reduced or it is not present in all cases.

At the macro level, the employment surveys show that the labour participation rates rose considerably during the 1980s, especially owing to the increase in female participation (see chapter 4). According to García (1994: 68):

> in a context of a sharp contraction in salaried industrial employment [in Mexico] during the 1980s... the increase in female participation was linked mainly to the expansion of non-salaried activities within the tertiary sector. This increase has been explained, in part, by the greater economic needs of families prompted by the imposition of wage controls resulting from the adoption of economic stabilisation policies. The reduction in wages and in social benefits has led to the incorporation of additional household members to economic activity, especially women and young persons, to contribute to the everyday sustenance of the families. Under these circumstances, many women went out to look for extradomestic work, in addition to continuing to fulfil their family responsibilities (Selva, Cortés, González de la Rocha, García, and Oliveira).

However, as is pointed out in chapter 4 of this book, even though there was a greater number of persons in the labour market, the number of hours worked was reduced drastically during the periods of crises. Therefore, by standardising the participation rates by the number of hours we find that the participation rates tend to behave pro-cyclically.

2. THE SOCIAL SECTORS THAT RESPONDED WITH LSS

In general, it is held that the poor engaged in labour survival strategies. However, in the majority of the studies there is little clarity regarding the social group to be studied. In analysing the studies of the evolution of poverty and the response of the "poor" during the crisis of the 1980s, Escobar (1996: 540-541) has noted that in the case of micro social studies "there are studies of low-income households that may at times lay above a 'poverty line' (González de la Rocha, Tuirán)."

González de la Rocha (1991), for example, in referring to the social group of households included in the sample talks indifferently about working-class domestic groups or about the urban poor (see also Escobar and González de la Rocha, 1995), without these two groups being necessarily synonymous. Furthermore, Benería (1992), in her study of Mexico City,[6] includes middle-class and lower—middle-class groups within the five groups that she identifies according to their level of income (extreme poor, subsistence, poor, lower middle class, and middle class, *Ibid.*, table 4.1: 89).[7] According to Benería (1992: 92), "A common response to the crisis was the increase in the number of household members participation in the labour market in order to contribute to family income."

Tuirán's study (1992) for Mexico City talks about five household strata classified according to their level of income and the characteristics of the employment of the head of the household (if it is formal or informal).[8] Despite that this study includes middle-class strata, the range of average income of the highest-income group (formal-middle) is situated slightly above the poverty line calculated by the Normative Basket of Essential Satisfiers (NBES), which is used for identifying poverty by Boltvinik (1998a). We thus have that the middle point of this stratum's income range was situated at 3 times the minimum wage (tmw), whereas the extreme poverty line was situated at 2.96 tmw in February of 1988.[9] Although almost all households included in this study can be considered as poor, there are differences in their response to the decline of income. According to Tuirán (1992:183), a greater growth in the number of earners per household takes place in the lower income strata (especially, owing to the incorporation of women) than in the middle income strata.

The study by García and Oliveira (1994) of the factors that have had a bearing on the changes in female participation rates[10] defines the social groups according to their *socio-economic status*. According to the authors, the *status* is determined by the characteristics of the employment of the head of the household, assuming that these characteristics determine the economic condition of the women (poor vs. non-poor) (*Ibid.*: 76). In this work the authors define two main social groups: one comprising women of households whose head is an *agricultural* worker and another one comprising women of households whose head is a *non-agricultural* worker. It is implicitly assumed that the agricultural groups are predominantly poor, whereas in the case of the urban groups their condition is defined explicitly. In this way the households of non-agricultural workers are subdivided into two subgroups: non-manual workers (or "middle classes") and manual workers (or "urban working-class groups"), the activity of which may be salaried or unsalaried (*Ibid.*: 77). The idea that the low-income sectors engage in labour survival strategies is expressed by these researchers in pointing out that the sector of unsalaried manual workers is the most heterogeneous of all, inasmuch as it "gathers *highly impoverished groups which create their own employment as a strategy of survival* and other more privileged groups which have a certain room to manoeuvre to deal with the crisis" (*Ibid.*: 78, italics added).

Throughout the text, the authors refer to the economic necessity affecting the most impoverished social groups during the crisis as one of the main reasons that explain the increase in the participation of women in the manual sectors (or urban working-class groups). For example, when analysing the influence of the level of schooling on female participation, they find that in 1987 "the schooling among the most needy non-agricultural sectors loses importance as an explanatory factor of the condition of the activity. The inclination to work of women of the working-class sectors is associated with the necessity for obtaining money income to compensate for the low wages of the other members of the family" (*Ibid.*: 88). It is worth highlighting that with regard to the influence of the number and age of children, the majority of the social groups analysed do not behave as had been expected. García and Oliveira assert that the participation of women with children in the agricultural sector did not change during the period of economic growth (1979-1982) or during the crisis (1982-1987), either (*Ibid.*: 90). That is to say, that in this population group, in which a large percentage of the population is poor, women did not increase their participation in the face of the possible changes suffered in the household's income. Concerning the sphere of the non-agricultural sectors, it is noteworthy that both women with children of the middle sectors and part of those classified as belonging to the working-class sector (unsalaried manual female workers) reduce their participation in the labour market in periods of crisis. In the case of first-mentioned, the authors argue that this could have been due to a reduction in job opportunities for professionals, technicians and office workers, which most affects women of the middle sectors with small children. In the case of women with children in the unsalaried manual sectors (or working-class sectors) the authors express surprise for the reduction in their participation and explain that this behaviour "is not in keeping with the prior hypotheses that had been put forth" (*Ibid.:*91). The only ones who responded "as expected," that is, who increased their participation in the labour force in the face of the drop in income, are the women in the unsalaried manual sectors. The authors tell us that, in this case, the participation of these women was due to "the sharp reduction in wages and the greater need for the female population to supplement the family income" (*Ibid.*:92).

Finally, we have the studies by Cortés (1997) and by Cortés and Rubalcava (1991), whose main objective was to analyse the factors that have a bearing on changes in the distribution of income in Mexico. However, the authors make a clear reference to what I have called in my book the LSS.[11] In these studies the authors use the concept of household earners as a synonym of the concept of labour force.[12] However, the term of earners can not be considered to be an index of the labour effort made by households because it includes not only persons who work but also all persons who receive an income (which may come from pensions, remittances, etc.,), regardless of the person's condition of activity.

According to Cortés and Rubalcava (1991), between 1977 and 1984, the use of labour survival strategies was observed in the deciles of I to VIII; by contrast, Cortés (1997) finds that these strategies occurred in the deciles of IV to VIII. That is to say, the findings of Cortés indicate that it was not the poorest who increased the number of earners per household. According to this author, labour survival strategies (i.e., the use of additional labour force) were observed in the urban working-class sectors (fourth decile to seventh decile) and in middle-class households (eighth and ninth deciles) (*Ibid.*: 71). The difference between the studies may be due to the fact that Cortés (1997) uses the database of the ENIGHS and groups the households in deciles according to income per capita; in Cortés and Rubalcava (1991), however, the information that is used is taken from officially published information, the deciles of which are found distributed based on income per household.[13] Therefore, the idea that the most impoverished sectors of the population responded with such a strategy is called into question. Moreover, as I have pointed out in chapter 4 (sections 4 and 5) of this book, there is little evidence to assume that households had the possibility of increasing considerably their work effort, despite the decline in income.

3. YOUNG AND WOMEN ACTORS OF SURVIVAL STRATEGIES

In general, the studies of the LSS assert that it was predominantly women, young persons, children and elderly persons who engaged in such survival strategies and this response has a counter-cyclical nature. For example, Cortés and Rubalcava (1991: 84) note that "the most modest households partially neutralized the adjustment measure by a greater sale of labour force. Some household members who already earned a salary intensified their workdays and in addition women members were sent out to the labour market (Oliveira and García, García and Oliveira), as well as young persons and even children, depending on the size of the family, on the family's composition by gender, on the stage of the domestic cycle, on the type of family, on the opportunities afforded by the environment (Nolasco)" (*Ibid.*: 84). Cortés (1997: 68), for his part, points out that "the intensification of the productive effort of the households is a direct consequence of the deterioration in the economic conditions of the most disadvantaged sectors of [Mexico], who, to defend their precarious living standards, have no option other than to resort to the work of females, of the elderly, and of school-age members."

Benería (1992:92) also identifies adolescents and women as the population groups which were most affected by this type of response. Selby et al. (1990: 175)[14] finds that in the city of Oaxaca "During the period of the economic crisis, women have been brought into the work force in unprecedented numbers, and their work has been overwhelmingly in unregistered jobs, in the informal sector."

García and Oliveira (1994) also find a greater presence of women aged 25 and above in the labour market in 1987 as compared to 1982; the authors attribute this change, among other factors, to the fact that "with the contraction of the real wage, a larger number of older women began to work in extradomestic activities, in own-account activities, to obtain additional resources" (*Ibid.*: 86).

Jusidman (1988:246), in analysing the participation rates en Mexico City in the 1980s holds that "the increase in a traditionally stable indicator, such as the net rate of participation, reflects the greater entrance of the 'secondary' labour force (children, women, the elderly) into economic activity in order to add to the family group's income." The idea of the counter-cyclical nature of this "secondary work force" becomes apparent when this author asserts that "in the boom years and with the increase in average earnings per employed worker, a decrease in the net participation rate in the Metropolitan Area is observed" (*Ibid.*: 249).[15]

As we saw in chapter 4, there is little evidence to assert that there was an increase in the participation rate of children in the labour market. Nevertheless, in the case of young persons, as in the case of women, the standardised participation rates tend to be pro-cyclical. Moreover, in the case of women, there are strong indications that the increase in their participation was due both to secular factors and to changes in the demand for labour during the 1980s. An indication of the possible changes in demand is found in the study by Chant (1993), which points out that in the case of the city of Querétaro there had occurred an improvement in the income of adult women included in her sample between 1982 and 1986, given that some women "had moved into higher-paid jobs during that period and/or had businesses or activities which were more consolidated and making reasonably healthy profits" (*Ibid.*: 326).

4. THE LIMITS TO THE LABOUR SURVIVAL STRATEGIES

Some of the exponents of labour survival strategies make important observation that would seem to contradict the existence of the same or else show their limitations. For example, Chant (1994)[16] finds that in the beach resort city of Puerto Vallarta, despite that in 1992 the city was experiencing a serious economic crisis, the number of workers per household had not increased with respect to 1986. According to the author, even though some women increased their participation in the labour market (or lengthened their workdays), this was offset by the loss of employment of some household heads and by the impossibility of bringing into the labour market more household members, especially young males, owing to the reduction in the demand for workers in construction, in tourism, and in small business establishments. Thus, Chant asserts that in the case of Puerto Vallarta "no matter how much people may wish to protect incomes, the growing scarcity of viable employment options makes it difficult for them to do so" (Chant, 1994:220).

On the contrary, in the cities of Querétaro and León, Chant finds that, despite that economic conditions in these two cities had improved between 1986 and 1992, "it was in some respects surprising to find that households had actually apparently appeared to retain, and in many respects intensify, most of their crisis-related survival patterns of 1986, such as multiple-earning strategies, household extension and reduced dependency ratios" (Chant, 1994:221). We may assume that the improvement in economic conditions permitted the increase in the number of workers per household in Querétaro and in León, whereby it may be said that this increase had a pro-cyclical nature, not a counter-cyclical nature as the LSS postulate.

Based on the differences observed in Puerto Vallarta, in Querétaro and in León, Chant asserts that the change in the age structure, in conjunction with the economic needs of the households, does not necessarily determine the existence of multiple-employment patterns (or labour survival strategies). This patterns should be seen in conjunction with the broader economic circumstances, which, in the cases of León and of Querétaro, with economic improvement there were greater possibilities for new household members to become incorporated into economic activity (Chant: 1994:221-222).

Benería (1992), for her part, in her study of Mexico City, highlights the little effectiveness of the labour survival strategies when she notes that: "a clear conclusion to be drawn from this information is that, despite the effort at increasing the participation of diverse family members in paid production, there remained a good proportion of untapped labour that was underemployed or working at the margins, including men an women of all ages that could not find a full-time job and other looking for better job opportunities and working conditions" (*Ibid*:93).

Selby *et al.*, (1990: 169) point out an extremely important paradox that appeared in the city of Oaxaca in 1987: "Employment is down ... observation and interviews show that informal sector activity is much reduced from 1982 levels, even though more people, especially more women, are employing themselves in these activities." We coincide with these authors in the sense that, despite that the number of workers increased during the period of crisis, this did not signify an increase in the total work effort made by the households.

5. CONCLUDING REMARKS

With what has been thus far stated, we can say that, despite that diverse studies hold the thesis that *households increment their supply of labour in periods of crisis*, there exist certain contradictions and imprecision within such studies which put in doubt that thesis. First of all, we have situations in which, for example, there was a non-occurrence of labour strategies, despite the decline in income in the households; or else, situations in which the increase in the participation of women and young persons was related to increases in their levels of income; or other situations in which households continued with the so-called labour strategies or intensified them, despite the situation of crisis having been overcome.

We also have some studies that show that the incorporation of new members into the labour market was offset by the loss of employment of other members who had previously been working (in many cases the head of the household, who in general works more hours per week than any of the rest of the members). Furthermore, the increase in the number of workers in some households was due to the incorporation of new members coming from other households, so that the number of workers in the households of origin very probably had been reduced. This situations permit us to assume that employment did not increase socially.

Moreover, there are certain difficulties in the definition of the social strata that responded with LSS. The majority of the studies assert that it was the poor households which responded with such strategies. However, the procedures of identification of the poor are not presented. Furthermore, other studies show that it was not the poorest households which responded with such a strategy.

Finally, certain studies of the LSS show indications of the limits of these. Some of them report a decrease in the labour participation in periods of crisis; others, the impossibility of increasing the work force despite the crisis; or else, a contraction in employment, even though it concerns the so-called informal sector.

Notes

[1] It is important to mention that the objective of these authors was not solely to analyse the changes in the levels of the labour force participation; some of them (like González de la Rocha, Benería or Tuirán) analyse a series of survival strategies (for example, changes in labour force participation, in the size and composition of the households, or in the consumption of food and in spending patterns in general). Moreover, we have

other cases, like the study by Cortés, whose main interest is to study the factors that affected the changes in the distribution of income, and others, like the studies by García, which give us a panorama of the changes observed in the supply of labour.

2   The study was based on a non-representative sample of 100 households of industrial manual workers interviewed in 1981-1982 and, subsequently, in 1985 and in 1987.

3   Sections 3 and 4 of chapter 4 show the importance of calculating the net household participation rates and of standardising the participation rates of the population in general by number of hours in order to be able to have a better perspective of the dynamics of employment in times of crisis and growth.

4   Of a sample of 244 households surveyed in 1982-3, a sub-sample of 22 households was selected (the method is not specified), which were interviewed in depth in 1986.

5   The study by Tuirán (1991) analyses the information of a panel survey carried out by the National Consumer Institute (INCO) in regard to a non-representative sample of low-income households in Mexico City between June of 1985 and February of 1988. The sample began with 258 households and ended with 172, whereby the idea of panel is lost and problems of comparison arise from not knowing the characteristics of the households that were left out in the subsequent interviewing. For more ample information on the INCO sample, refer to endnotes 24 and 25 of chapter 3.

6   Benería (1992: 20) bases her study of survival strategies on a non-representative sample of 55 households of women who worked in industrial subcontracting activities in Mexico City. The households were interviewed in 1981-1982 and subsequently in 1988. Half of the interviewed households in 1988 belonged to the original sample, whereas the other half corresponds to "new" households which were interviewed by applying the snowball technique. To consult the characteristics of the sample and its problems of comparability, refer to endnote 26 of chapter 3.

7   Benería classifies the households by levels of income without specifying clearly the criteria used for the stratification. The author mentions a Minimum Living Basket of Goods (MLBG) and a Basic Basket of Goods (BBG); however, the author does not specify based on what criteria such baskets were determined. The categories in which household were classified are the following: Extreme poor; subsistence; poor but adequate income; lower middle class; and middle class. However, taking into consideration the Normative Basket of Essential Satisfiers (NBES), only the middle class may be considered as non-poor, since it is the only group whose average household income is above the cost of the NBES.

8   The households are divided into the following strata: two low-income strata ("formal and informal" low-income strata); one ("formal") middle-low income stratum; and two middle-income strata ("formal and informal").

9   See chapter 4 of this book, table 4.14.

10 It should be noted that this study is based on fertility surveys, rather than employment surveys. The surveys used by these authors were the Mexican Fertility Survey (EMF), the National Demographic Survey (END) and the National Fertility and Health Survey (ENFES), conducted in 1976-1977, 1982, and 1987, respectively. These surveys present certain problems in terms of comparability. The criterion for the selection of women regarding age, the presence of children and marital status (married or in consensual union) changed between the EMF and the other two surveys. Moreover, the distribution of the population according to size of locality is not modified between 1976-77 and 1982, which contradicts the trend toward the growing urbanisation of Mexico. One of the most serious problems of comparability of these surveys is found in the formulation of the question related to the condition of activity of the interviewed women. Whereas in the question on female work in the 1976 survey the reference period is not made

Appendix 1. The Labour Survival Strategies 181

explicit, in 1982 the survey asks women on their main work in the last year; and in the 1987 survey women are asked if they work currently (see García and Oliveira, 1994, Appendix I). It is to be expected that the changes and the ambiguity of the questions affect the level of female labour participation.

[11] These studies are based on the National Household Income and Expenditure Surveys. For a more detailed discussion, see chap. 4, section 4.1.

[12] For example, in the study by Cortés (1997), in section 3.1.2 , entitled "Growth of the number of earners;" the author says that "the ENIGHs of 1977, 1984, 1989, 1992 and 1994 provide sufficient information so as to be able to form an idea of the effect of the *increase in the use of the work force* on the incomes of the households" (*Ibid.*, 62, italics added).

[13] This form of organising the deciles presents serious deficiencies, given that, in some cases, households with a large number of members occupied in paid activities may be classified in higher-income deciles than what would otherwise be the case if such a classification were done by income per capita.

[14] Selby *et al.* (1990) have published an interesting study of the socio-economic characteristics of households and their dwellings in ten cities of Mexico between 1977-1978. However, given the severity of the crisis of 1982, these researchers carried out a follow-up survey of households in the city of Oaxaca in 1987. They conducted 50 in-depth interviews which covered topics related to the organization of households during times of crisis (Selby, *et al.*: 169). This study does not specify the percentage of households that were included in the original sample or if sample of the later survey was different from the earlier one. Hence we can not evaluate the problems of comparability of the presented data.

[15] Chant (1994:223) also makes a clear reference to the counter-cyclical nature that is attributed to the survival strategies when she asserts that "the evidence from León and Querétaro suggests that adult women's labour is perhaps only mobilised as short-term adjustment mechanism when household needs dictate."

[16] These data are from a study carried out by the author between 1986 and 1992 in three cities: León, Querétaro, and Puerto Vallarta. In this case, the sample comprised 25 households (4 in León, 10 in Querétaro, and 11 in Puerto Vallarta) (Chant, 1994:217).

Appendix 2. Employment Data

Table 4.A.1. Mexico: Number of workers by employment categories and by sex, 1979-1993

Employment categories	1979	1991	1993	1995	1996
Total	19177329	29633459	31801571	32664515	34288245
Employer	656373	2391856	1344958	1456147	1675090
Self-employed	4874368	7187814	8731460	8534197	8404459
Salaried worker	12066488	16695367	17951272	19196716	20588398
Unpaid family worker	1580100	3284262	3733294	3448444	3588124
Other and not specified	-----	74160	40587	29011	32174
Male workers	14558838	20772196	22223010	22446062	23314365
Employer	596994	2185248	1193741	1304015	1449370
Self-employed	3928851	5452577	6496423	6127297	6018119
Salaried worker	8802473	11052713	12097674	12951778	13743933
Unpaid family worker	1230520	2015971	2399718	2039937	2073707
Other and not specified	-----	65687	35454	23035	29236
Female workers	4618491	8861263	9579146	10218453	10973877
Employer	59379	206608	151217	152132	225720
Self-employed	945517	1735237	2235037	2406900	2386337
Salaried worker	3264015	5642654	5854186	6244938	6844465
Unpaid family worker	349580	1268291	1333573	1408507	1514417
Other and not specified	-----	8473	5133	5976	2938

Source: 1979, SPP (1980), table 6:40; 1991, INEGI and STPS (1993), table 19:108; 1993, INEGI and STPS (1994), table 42:126; 1995, INEGI and STPS (1996), table 85:174; 1996, INEGI and STPS (1997) table 3.43:208.

Table 4.A.2. Mexico: Employment rate of growth by employment categories and by sex, 1979-1993 (per cent)

Employment categories	1979-1991	1979-1993	1991-1993	1993-1995	1995-1996	1991-1995	1991-1996
Total	3.7	3.7	3.6	1.3	5.0	2.5	3.0
Employer	11.4	5.3	-25.0	4.1	15.0	-11.7	-6.9
Self-employed	3.3	4.3	10.2	-1.1	-1.5	4.4	3.2
Salaried worker	2.7	2.9	3.7	3.4	7.2	3.6	4.3
Unpaid family worker	6.3	6.3	6.6	-3.9	4.1	1.2	1.8
Other and not specified	n.a.d.	n.a.d.	n.a.d.	-15.5	10.9	-20.9	-15.4
Male workers	3.0	3.1	3.4	0.5	3.9	2.0	1.2
Employer	11.4	5.1	-26.1	4.5	11.1	-12.1	5.0
Self-employed	2.8	3.7	9.2	-2.9	-1.8	3.0	-1.9
Salaried worker	1.9	2.3	4.6	3.5	6.1	4.0	3.2
Unpaid family worker	4.2	4.9	9.1	-7.8	1.7	0.3	-3.6
Other and not specified	n.a.d.	n.a.d.	n.a.d.	-19.4	26.9	-23.0	-4.7
Female workers	5.6	5.3	4.0	3.3	7.4	3.6	3.5
Employer	10.9	6.9	-14.4	0.3	48.4	-7.4	10.5
Self-employed	5.2	6.3	13.5	3.8	-0.9	8.5	1.7
Salaried worker	4.7	4.3	1.9	3.3	9.6	2.6	4.0
Unpaid family worker	11.3	10.0	2.5	2.8	7.5	2.7	3.2
Other and not specified	n.a.d.	n.a.d.	n.a.d.	7.9	-50.8	-8.4	-13.0

Source: Own calculations based on table 4.A.1.

Table 4.A.3. Mexico: Labour force participation rate of the population of between 12 and 19 years of age, 1979-1991 (per cent)

Population of between 12 and 19 years of age	1979	1991
Total workers	25.3	34.8
Male workers	35.4	47.8
Female workers	15.4	22.6

Source: Own calculations based on SPP (1980), table 2A:37, and INEGI and STPS (1993), table 2:36.

Table 4.A.4. Mexico: Percentage of workers by economic activity, 1979, 1991, 1993, 1995 and 1996

Branch of activity	1979	1991	1993	1995	1996
Agriculture	28.9	27.0	27.1	24.8	22.5
Manufacturing, mining and electricity	21.1	17.0	16.4	16.0	17.4
Construction	6.4	6.2	5.8	5.4	5.1
Commerce	13.8	15.9	17.2	18.5	17.4
Service activities	24.8	29.5	29.5	31.4	32.7
Public Administration	4.5	4.3	3.9	3.8	4.5
Other activities and not specified	0.5	0.1	0.1	0.1	0.5
Total	100.0	100.0	100.0	100.0	100.1

Source: Own calculations based on SPP (1980), table 3A:38; INEGI and STPS (1993), table 10 48; INEGI and STPS (1994), table 15:57 40:87; INEGI and STPS (1996), table 40:87; and INEGI and STPS (1997), table 3.27:115.

Appendix 2. Employment Data 185

Table 4.A. 5. Mexico: Number of unpaid workers by economic activity and by sex, 1979, 1991, 1993, 1995 and 1996

Economic activity by sex	1979	1991	1993	1995	1996
Male workers	1580100	2356049	2779006	2428582	2387615
Agriculture	1052773	1726232	2215720	1779440	1679707
Commerce	278643	227036	315900	354438	331083
Other	248684	402781	247386	294704	376825
Female workers	349580	1612596	1781369	1980582	1930101
Agriculture	70994	520333	777963	869128	791179
Commerce	170383	624639	673033	752123	692656
Other	108203	467624	330373	359331	446266

Source: SPP (1980), table 3:38; INEGI and STPS (1993), table 12:59; INEGI and STPS (1994), table 21:75; INEGI and STPS (1996), table 43:90; and INEGI and STPS (1997), table 3.28:118.

Table 4.A.6. Mexico: Unpaid workers rate of growth by economic activity and by sex, 1979-1995 (per cent)

Economic activity by sex	1979-1991	1991-1993	1993-1995	1995-1996	1991-1995	1991-1996
Male workers	3.4	8.6	-6.5	-1.7	0.8	0.3
Agriculture	4.2	13.3	-10.4	-5.6	0.8	-0.5
Commerce	-1.7	18.0	5.9	-6.6	11.8	7.8
Other	4.1	-21.6	9.1	27.9	-7.5	-1.3
Female workers	13.6	5.1	5.4	-2.5	5.3	3.7
Agriculture	18.1	22.3	5.7	-9.0	13.7	8.7
Commerce	11.4	3.8	5.7	-7.9	4.8	2.1
Other	13.0	-15.9	4.3	24.2	-6.4	-0.9

Source: Own calculations based on table 4.A.4.

Table 4.A.7. Mexico: Number of workers by number of hours worked in the reference week, 1979, 1991, 1993, 1995 and 1996

Number of hour worked	1979	1991	1993	1995	1996
(a) Total	18695653	27781258	29350754	30591394	32172898
1 to 24 hours	1580967	3481769	4164889	4023440	3903796
25 to 39 hours	2233044	5259212	5331002	5601165	5570205
40 to 48 hours	10106725	12677627	11992879	12130910	13083154
49 and more hours	4769429	6184106	7627983	8761845	9585254
Not specified	5488	178544	234001	74034	30489
(b) Equivalent workdays*	16792801	24044888	25448599	26969944	28680228
(c) = b/a	89.82	84.61	84.45	85.60	87.20
Male workers	14190797	19927167	21118560	21620117	22433955
1 to 24 hours	848092	2231472	2755038	2508590	2237947
25 to 39 hours	1371191	3298267	3362120	3342741	3195497
40 to 48 hours	8166064	9312087	8705794	8784271	9313881
49 and more hours	3800423	4925918	6083164	6917352	7662320
Not specified	5027	159423	212444	67163	24310
Female workers	4504856	8490494	9015461	9885168	10456594
1 to 24 hours	732875	1886700	2193118	2428749	2383500
25 to 39 hours	861853	1960945	1968882	2258424	2374708
40 to 48 hours	1965129	3365540	3287085	3346639	3769273
49 and more hours	944538	1258188	1544819	1844485	1922934
Not specified	461	19121	21557	6871	6179

Source: Own calculations based on: SPP (1980), table 8 for each geographic region, pp. 53, 69, 85, 101, 117, 133, 149, 165, 181, 213; INEGI and STPS (1993), table 17:96; INEGI and STPS (1994), table 36:114; INEGI and STPS (1996), table 58: 26-9; and INEGI and STPS (1997), table 3.34:163.

* Calculation of the equivalent workdays was carried out as follows: the middle point of each range of number of hours worked was divided by 48, and the resulting value was multiplied by the number of workers in each range. For instance, in the second range, 25 to 39 hours, the middle point, 31.5, was multiplied by 2,233,044 workers. This result is then aggregated with the results in other ranges to obtain (b).

Table 4.A.8. Mexico City: Economic active population and number of occupied workers by sex, 1979 and 1986-1994

Year	Total EAP	Total Occupied	Male workers EAP	Male workers Occupied	Female workers EAP	Female workers Occupied
1979	4243173	3860852	2808236	2569717	1434936	1291135
1986	5376886	4869932	3525348	3188502	1851539	1678245
1987	5465076	4947532	3583169	3301130	1881907	1646499
1988	5740193	5224942	3754302	3462668	1985891	1762396
1989	5972785	5541182	3884972	3633390	2087813	1907917
1990	5984178	5490620	3924588	3614764	2059589	1875972
1991	6261775	5825604	4091884	3815827	2159891	2009775
1992	6500672	5936109	4184909	3851922	2315763	2084457
1993	6626407	6037876	4317893	3953704	2308514	2084311
1994	6710300	6127889	4328372	3925861	2381929	2166443

Source: Own calculations carried out as follows: The absolute figures of employment for Mexico City derived from the ENEU surveys cannot be compared among them because the number of workers reported by the surveys changes drastically from year to year.

In order to be able to compare the employment figures for Mexico City over time, I calculated the EAP and the number of occupied population as follows:

1) First, based on the population rates of growth calculated by Garza (1998, table 1) for Mexico City for 1970, 1980, 1990, and 1995, I calculated the total population of the city for the 1979-1994 period.

2) Once the total population was calculated, I calculated the proportion of the population of 12 years of age and above by sex for Mexico City, based on the distribution of the population by age and by sex derived from the ENEU surveys (except for the 1979 figures that was calculated assuming the same population distribution of the 1977 ENIGH survey, since the ECSO do not provide such information).

3) Based on the calculated population of 12 years of age and above, I calculate the EAP and occupied population by multiplying the labour force participation rate reported by the ECSO/ENEU surveys.

Table 4.A.9. Mexico City: Percentage of workers by number of hours worked in the reference week and by sex, 1979, 1986-1994

Number of hours	1979	1986	1987	1988	1989	1990	1991	1992	1993	1994
Total	100.0	100.0	100.0	100.0	100.0	100.0	100.0	100.0	100.0	100.0
Less than 25 hours	9.1	12.8	12.9	12.0	11.7	11.6	11.9	13.3	12.1	12.5
25 to 39 hours	16.1	18.2	20.0	18.2	16.6	16.9	16.1	18.4	16.4	14.9
40 to 48 hours	48.8	46.1	42.9	48.1	48.9	48.5	48.1	42.6	43.3	42.8
49 and more hours	26.0	22.8	24.1	21.6	22.8	22.9	23.7	25.6	28.0	29.7
Not specified	0.0	0.1	0.0	0.1	0.0	0.1	0.2	0.1	0.2	0.1
Male workers	100.0	100.0	100.0	100.0	100.0	100.0	100.0	100.0	100.0	100.0
Less than 25 hours	6.1	8.2	9.2	9.0	8.5	8.9	8.3	9.1	8.8	8.5
25 to 39 hours	13.7	15.3	17.1	15.0	13.5	15.1	12.9	15.2	13.0	11.7
40 to 48 hours	50.4	49.0	44.6	50.1	51.0	48.4	49.5	43.7	43.8	44.6
49 and more hours	29.8	27.4	29.0	25.8	27.0	27.5	29.0	31.8	34.0	35.1
Not specified	0.0	0.1	0.1	0.1	0.0	0.1	0.2	0.2	0.3	0.1
Female workers	100.0	100.0	100.0	100.0	100.0	100.0	100.0	100.0	100.0	100.0
Less than 25 hours	15.0	21.4	20.4	18.0	17.8	18.2	18.7	21.2	18.4	20.1
25 to 39 hours	20.8	23.7	25.9	24.6	22.5	20.2	22.2	24.2	22.8	21.1
40 to 48 hours	45.8	40.7	39.3	44.1	45.0	47.8	45.6	40.5	42.2	39.5
49 and more hours	18.4	14.1	14.4	13.2	14.7	13.8	13.5	14.1	16.6	19.3
Not specified	0.0	0.1	0.0	0.0	0.1	0.0	0.0	0.0	0.0	0.0

Source: For 1979, SPP (1980), table 7 A:212; for 1986-1994, own calculations based on ENEU databases, INEGI

Table 4.A.10. Mexico City: Average number of hours worked in the reference week. All workers. 1986, 1989, 1992-1994

	1986	1989	1994
a. From database[a]	40.8	41.3	42.0
b. From ranges of hours worked[b]	39.8	40.3	41.2
c. = (b-a/ a)*100	2.4%	2.4%	1.9%

Source: [a]Own calculations based on ENEU databases, INEGI; [b]table 4.A.7

Table 4.A.11. Mexico City: Labour force participation rate by age and by sex, 1979, 1987-1994

	1979	1987	1988	1989	1990	1991	1992	1993	1994
All workers[a]	50.3	51.9	52.9	52.3	54.0	55.1	55.5	53.6	54.5
All workers[b]	50.3	51.0	51.3	52.3	51.7	53.6	54.4	54.9	52.7
12 to 19 years	24.9	22.4	23.3	23.6	23.3	23.7	25.9	26.9	24.3
12 to 14 years	n.a.d.	7.3	6.9	8.8	8.0	6.2	7.6	8.8	5.2
15 to 19 years	n.a.d.	32.4	32.9	32.1	31.2	32.7	35.8	37.2	34.9
20 to 24 years	64.1	63.3	63.1	62.8	62.4	63.2	63.3	63.3	61.0
25 to 34 years	67.4	70.0	71.8	71.4	72.6	70.7	72.5	71.2	68.5
35 to 44 years	67.7	70.1	68.9	71.3	68.8	72.1	71.8	72.4	70.0
45 to 54 years	60.3	61.7	61.7	63.0	62.6	64.8	67.4	68.1	66.6
55 to 64 years	51.4	51.8	46.6	50.8	46.6	49.5	47.4	49.4	46.0
65 years and over	24.3	22.4	27.0	28.2	22.0	26.3	25.2	23.7	20.9
Male workers[a]	70.5	70.8	71.0	71.7	71.5	74.1	73.9	74.8	74.0
Male workers[b]	70.5	70.0	70.5	71.1	70.9	73.8	73.3	74.3	73.3
12 to 19 years	29.6	29.2	30.6	30.1	29.1	31.5	33.7	34.7	31.0
12 to 14 years	n.a.d.	10.0	10.2	11.7	10.5	7.7	10.6	12.8	7.5
15 to 19 years	n.a.d.	42.0	42.3	40.9	39.1	43.9	46.1	46.8	44.4
20 to 24 years	77.5	77.6	77.6	78.0	78.8	79.2	79.1	80.8	78.5
25 to 34 years	97.0	95.4	95.6	95.0	95.8	96.1	95.9	95.2	94.3
35 to 44 years	97.9	98.4	97.4	98.0	97.5	98.1	97.5	98.0	97.1
45 to 54 years	94.3	93.3	92.4	93.3	94.0	94.2	94.0	93.4	93.8
55 to 64 years	82.9	83.6	73.9	80.4	76.2	78.6	75.3	77.6	75.4
65 years and over	44.8	35.6	44.4	48.8	39.2	44.9	40.5	43.1	38.9
Female workers[a]	32.5	34.0	34.5	35.8	34.7	35.8	37.9	37.5	35.0
Female workers[b]	32.5	33.5	33.9	35.1	34.1	35.3	37.1	36.9	33.9
12 to 19 years	20.4	15.7	16.1	17.0	17.5	16.3	18.2	18.9	18.1
12 to 14 years	n.a.d.	4.2	3.9	5.8	5.5	4.8	4.7	4.7	3.1
15 to 19 years	n.a.d.	23.1	23.6	23.3	23.5	22.1	25.4	27.2	26.2
20 to 24 years	51.0	50.0	49.9	48.4	47.0	47.9	48.5	45.9	43.5
25 to 34 years	40.6	47.0	49.2	49.6	50.3	47.4	51.5	49.9	45.7
35 to 44 years	40.3	43.8	43.0	47.4	44.3	49.7	48.7	49.3	46.3
45 to 54 years	32.0	34.0	35.4	38.3	35.9	37.5	43.1	43.8	40.9
55 to 64 years	24.7	26.0	25.8	24.9	21.0	25.0	24.1	24.7	21.0
65 years and over	11.0	13.5	13.7	13.5	10.2	13.2	13.6	10.6	9.0

Source: 1979, SPP (1980), table 2A:205; 1986 to 1993 own calculations based on ENEU figures, INEGI; 1994, Own calculations based on INEGI, 1994.

[a] While in 1979 unpaid workers who worked less than 15 hours in the reference week were not considered part of the EAP, these workers were included as part of the labour force between 1986 and 1994; however I was unable to adjust these figures to make them comparable by age ranges because there is no available data of hours of work by age.

[b] The labour force participation rate was calculated by taking into consideration unpaid workers who worked 15 hours or more in the reference week.

n.a.d. No available data.

5 Labour Markets in Mexico City and Xalpa

This chapter reviews evidence derived from the ENEU surveys in Mexico City and from my own survey carried out in Xalpa. Section 1 looks at evidence on Mexico City regarding some basic trends which some authors have interpreted as symptoms of deterioration in the standard of living (growth in the proportions of self-employed workers, of unpaid workers, of workers in the tertiary sector). In this section some of the evidence is contrasted with that of the country. Section 2 is based on evidence on Xalpa. This section looks at other indicators which have also been regarded as symptoms of the decay in living standards (children's work, abandonment of school as a result of involvement in work, proportions of persons performing unskilled activities, position at work).

1. EMPLOYMENT BY OCCUPATIONAL CATEGORIES IN MEXICO CITY

1.1 Salaried vs. Non-Salaried Employment

One of the main pieces of evidence that support the idea of a deterioration in labour conditions in Mexico City has been the reduction in salaried employment and in manufacturing activities.[1] Employment figures on Mexico City show that during the years that immediately followed the 1982 economic crisis the proportion of salaried work declined. However, when analysing the overall changes in the labour force, there are several theoretical difficulties related to dichotomising self-employment and wage labour. The concept of self-employment has been challenged on the grounds that it involves a certain level of subjectivity regarding how workers perceive their relationship to the labour market. Scott (1979:106-107) has argued that the concept of self-employment includes an idea of "independence" that fails to highlight the situation of a "self-employee" who depends on the demand for the product or services he or she provides. According to Scott, the dichotomy between the self-employed and wage-labour can be broken down "... by a number of varying situations which could be differentiated in terms of their degree of autonomy over the production process, the manner in which they (are) mediated by capital and the concrete form in which they receive their income..." (Scott, 1979:113). Furthermore, Scott suggests that it is possible to place the different employment situations along a continuum that reflects a worker's degree of autonomy as producers and the extent of a worker's subjection to capital. In the case of Mexico City, it was not possible to construct this continuum. Therefore, the analysis will be based on the extreme poles of this continuum, as classified in the ENEU Surveys.

Table 5.1. Mexico City: Percentage of workers by position at work and by sex, 1979, 1986-1994

Position at work and sex	1979	1986	1987	1988	1989	1990	1991	1992	1993	1994
Employer	2.8	3.3	3.5	4.0	3.6	3.2	3.7	3.7	4.3	4.1
Male	3.7	4.7	4.6	5.5	5.0	4.1	4.8	4.9	5.7	5.4
Female	1.1	1.0	1.4	1.2	0.8	1.5	1.5	1.6	1.8	1.7
Self-employed worker	13.6	14.9	15.1	16.4	17.3	17.8	16.9	17.5	16.2	16.0
Male	13.2	13.8	14.5	16.5	17.3	19.1	17.6	18.5	16.3	16.3
Female	14.4	16.9	16.2	16.1	17.7	15.2	15.5	16.2	15.9	15.4
Salaried worker	80.7	78.3	77.8	76.1	74.8	75.8	76.2	75.3	75.4	76.4
Male	81.0	79.4	78.0	75.3	74.9	74.6	75.4	74.7	75.3	76.2
Female	80.1	76.4	77.3	77.5	74.7	77.9	77.6	75.9	75.5	76.6
Unpaid worker	2.9	3.4	3.6	3.5	4.2	3.3	3.2	3.5	4.1	3.5
Male	2.1	2.1	2.9	2.6	2.8	2.3	2.1	1.9	2.7	2.1
Female	4.4	5.7	5.1	5.2	6.8	5.3	5.3	6.3	6.8	6.3
Total	100.0	100.0	100.0	100.0	100.0	100.0	100.0	100.0	100.0	100.0

Source: 1979, SPP (1980), table 6: 210; 1986-1994 own calculations based on ENEU database, INEGI

Salaried work in Mexico City decreased from 80.7 per cent in 1979 to 78.3 per cent in 1986 (table 5.1). The percentage of female salaried workers in Mexico City declined more (from 80.1 per cent to 76.4 per cent) compared to male workers (down from 81 per cent to 79.4 per cent) in the same period. Afterwards, the proportion of all salaried workers, male and female, continued to fall until 1989, when it reached

74.8 per cent. Subsequently, in the years leading up to 1994 that proportion increased to 76.4 per cent, still lower than the level recorded both in 1979 and 1986 (table 5.1).

In contrast, between 1979 and 1986, "self-employed workers", employers and unpaid workers, as a percentage share of total workers, increased: from 13.6 per cent to 14.9 per cent; from 2.8 per cent to 3.3 per cent; and from 2.9 per cent to 3.4 per cent, respectively (see table 5.1). These percentages continued to grow after 1986. Self-employed workers reached their highest percentage share in 1990, thereafter declining, with fluctuations, to end at 16 per cent in 1994, higher than the levels of 1986 and of 1979. The relative percentage share of employers fell in 1989 and in 1990, thereafter again rising, to end in 1994 quite higher than the levels of 1986 and of 1979. As for unpaid workers, their relative percentage share fell from 1989 to 1991, thereafter rising, to end at 3.5 per cent in 1994, similar to the 1986 level but higher than the 1979 level. These trends differ between the sexes. For instance, the percentage of self-employed males virtually did not grow in the 1979-1986 period (from 13.2 per cent to 13.8 per cent), while the percentage of self-employed females increased by 2.5 percentage points (from 14.4 per cent to 16.9 per cent) in that same period.

Up to now I have been looking at the employment structure by position at work, as registered in the ENEU databases. Nonetheless, this type of analysis gives the same relative importance to all occupied persons regardless of weekly working hours. In chapter 4 I standardised workers according to weekly hours of work, arriving at the concepts of equivalent workers and of equivalent participation rates. I will now apply this same standardising technique to the employment structure by position at work in Mexico City, in order to verify if the above-mentioned trends still hold between 1979 and 1986. Unfortunately, this cannot be done to the 1979 ECSO information, so we are limited to the 1986-1994 period, in which I have selected three critical years for my calculations: 1986, 1989 and 1992. The results are presented in table 5.2.

The results shown in table 5.2 confirm the trends described based on unadjusted proportions. Two sub-periods can be distinguished: 1986-1989, and 1989-1994. With regard to the participation in total equivalent workers of each position at work category, the following trends (and the comparison with unadjusted trends presented in table 5.1 for the same sub-periods) are revealed:

1) The percentage share of employers grew in both sub-periods, just as it did with unadjusted figures.

2) The percentage share of self-employed workers grew in the first sub-period and declined in the second, just as it did with unadjusted data. Nevertheless, concerning unadjusted date on self-employed workers, the 1994 level is higher than that of 1986; by contrast, the corresponding figures for equivalent self-employed workers are almost identical.
3) The share of salaried workers decreased in the first sub-period of 1986-1989 and then increased, although in 1994 its share was lower than in 1986. These two trends are the same as the ones observed in table 5.1.
4) Unpaid workers show the same profile as self-employed workers, i.e. their percentage share rises and then falls, with the difference that share of the former is higher in 1984 than in 1986. This is the same trend found with unadjusted data.

Table 5.2. Mexico City: Percentage of equivalent workers by position at work and by sex, 1986, 1989 and 1994

Position at work and sex	1986	1989	1994
Employer	4.0	4.3	4.9
Male	5.3	5.8	6.0
Female	1.1	1.0	2.1
Self-employed worker	13.8	16.0	13.9
Male	13.4	16.7	14.8
Female	14.6	14.2	11.9
Salaried worker	79.2	76.0	78.0
Male	79.6	75.2	77.4
Female	78.4	77.8	79.4
Unpaid worker	3.0	3.7	3.2
Male	1.8	2.3	1.8
Female	5.9	7.0	6.6
Total	100.0	100.0	100.0
Male	100.0	100.0	100.0
Female	100.0	100.0	100.0

Source: Own calculations based on ENEU database, INEGI

Therefore, it turns out that the shares in employment calculated with equivalent workers show the same trends as the shares calculated with workers. It does not follow, however, that the standardisation performed is useless. It is simply a consequence of the non-occurrence of a substantial change in the relative working hours between categories in the period analysed for Mexico City, owing to the fact that hours worked by almost all categories increased similarly throughout the period. A notable exception is the category of self-employed workers, whose working hours increased marginally between 1986 and 1989, thereafter falling in 1994 to a level lower than that of 1986. This explains why the share of self-employed workers in equivalent workers is practically the same in 1994 as in 1986; by contrast, in terms of 'non-standardised' workers that share is larger in 1994 than in 1986. I can now assume that the same stable relation between the number of workers and the number of equivalent workers by position at work observed in the 1986-1994 period is also valid for the 1979-1986 period and, Accordingly, I can interpret the data in table 5.1 with confidence.

The results obtained are highly consistent with the performance of the economy. The economy of Mexico City is a predominantly waged economy, as table 5.1 shows clearly. This means that economic activity is generated mainly by entrepreneurs (of diverse sizes and degrees of formality) who hire labour. Slow or fast growth is determined (mainly) by the behaviour of entrepreneurs. When the total number of employees hired by entrepreneurs (or more precisely, the equivalent total number) grows, production grows. Consequently, it is quite natural that, when this growth is fast, the proportion of salaried workers increases and vice-versa. This assumes, with scant evidence on hand, that the new tendencies of entrepreneurs to subcontract work are not yet quantitatively important and that the subcontracted entrepreneur hires salaried employees as well. Compared with the ECSO survey, the ENEU distinguishes a new position at work called "subcontractor" (which I have aggregated in the category of employers). Quantitatively, the group of subcontractors is very small (0.11 per cent of all workers in 1994), which supports my assumption. This view does not necessarily contradict some studies that point out a positive correlation between the expansion in subcontracting and the economic restructuring that has been taking place in Mexico since the beginning of the 1980s. Sub-contracting represents a method of reducing labour cost, which in turn provides a way of shifting employment toward the "informal" sectors of the economy. For instance, there is some evidence to suggest that, in the manufacturing sector, the phenomenon of subcontracting had begun to spread even before the 1982 economic crisis

(Benería and Roldan, 1987:17). My view is that these trends, however meaningful, are not as yet important in terms of the structure of the labour force.

The 1979-1986 period is a period of recession when judged by GDP per capita, which is lower in 1986 than in 1979. The 1986-1989 period is a period of stagnation of the national economy (because GDP grew at approximately the same rate as population, GDP per capita remained stagnant). Since there is no comparable information on GDP for Mexico City, one has to assume, as indeed I have done so throughout this book, that Mexico City's economy performed over time in the same way as the Mexican economy as a whole did. In the above-mentioned two periods, as expected, salaried workers diminished their share in the total labour force in Mexico City: from 80.7 per cent in 1979 to 78.3 per cent in 1986, and to 74.8 per cent in 1989. The 1989-1994 period, by contrast, was characterized by economic growth, as expressed by GDP per capita. In this latter period, again as expected, the share of salaried workers in total employment recovered part of what it had lost.

But the fact that the decline in the share of salaried jobs is associated with economic performance, does not imply, necessarily, as some scholars have taken for granted, that non-salaried occupations represent a lower level of income for workers than that received by salaried occupations (e.g. García and Oliveira, 1994: 230). I found, based on the ENEU figures, that there seems to be a correlation between the changes in the distribution of workers by employment categories and the income earned per hour. As noted above, after the 1982 economic crisis there was a tendency for self-employment to increase its relative importance. However, table 5.3 shows that in 1986 income per hour of self-employed workers was almost 12 per cent higher than that of salaried workers.[2] On average, self-employed workers were earning (pesos of 1994) 7.5 Mexican pesos per hour (some 2.2 dollars),[3] compared to the 6.7 pesos received, on average, by salaried workers. In 1989, when income per hour for salaried workers reached its lowest level (6.2 pesos, see table 5.3), the income gap with respect to income per hour of self-employed workers increased to 17.7 per cent. This gap in favour of self-employed workers prevailed up to 1993.

Therefore, in terms of income per hour, between 1986 and 1993, being self-employed seemed to be a better option than being a salaried worker. I do not mean to argue here that income per hour is the best basis for a comparison of the standard of living of a salaried worker and that of a self-employed worker. In general, salaried workers, especially those with access to social security, have various security advantages over self-employed workers. They receive payment when sick and unable to work; they have access to free medical assistance; their income flow (although diminished) is not interrupted during retirement age; they are entitled to paid holidays, and so on. Furthermore, the self-employed work, on average, less hours than wage workers (in 1994, 35.8 versus 42.4 weekly hours, respectively, in Mexico City, according to ENEU surveys database). This means that total income per week might be lower for the self-employed than for wage earners. Finally, with some frequency, the self-employed work alongside with unpaid workers. To the degree that the income declared by an individual self-employed worker is the result of her (his) work and the work of unpaid workers, income per worker is overestimated. Despite these disadvantages, in certain circumstances and for certain members of the household it might be more profitable to move from protected waged employment to self-employment, especially when a member in the household is already socially insured.[4]

Table 5.3. Mexico City: Income per hour by position at work and by sex, 1986-1994 (Pesos of 1994)

Employment category	1986	1988	1989	1992	1993	1994
All earning workers	7.1	6.8	6.8	7.5	7.8	8.2
Male workers	7.3	7.1	7.0	7.8	7.9	8.4
Female workers	6.9	6.2	6.3	7.0	7.5	7.9
Employer	15.3	15.2	15.1	17.8	19.3	17.9
Male workers	15.5	15.4	15.1	18.9	20.1	18.2
Female workers	13.5	13.8	14.6	12.5	15.0	16.4
Self-employed worker	7.5	7.0	7.3	7.8	8.2	7.8
Male workers	7.5	7.1	7.5	8.3	8.0	7.9
Female workers	7.6	6.6	7.0	6.8	8.4	7.6
Salaried worker*	6.7	6.3	6.2	7.0	7.1	7.8
Male workers	6.7	6.5	6.4	7.0	7.2	8.0
Female workers	6.6	5.9	5.9	6.9	7.1	7.5

Source: Own calculations based on ENEU database, 1986-1994, INEGI
* Excludes workers by piece rate

Contrary to the idea that women have to rely on self-employment in order to offset income losses, I found that female self-employed workers were earning per hour 15.2 per cent more than female salaried workers in 1986, and that by 1989 this difference was 18.6 per cent (see table 5.3).

Table 5.4. Mexico City: Income per hour growth rate by employment categories and by sex

Employment category	1986-1989	1989-1994	1986-1994
All earning workers	-1.4	3.8	1.8
Male	-1.4	3.7	1.8
Female	-3.0	4.6	1.7
Employer	-0.5	3.5	2.0
Male	-0.8	3.8	2.0
Female	2.6	2.4	2.5
Self-employed worker	-0.9	1.3	0.5
Male	-0.2	1.2	0.7
Female	-2.7	1.7	0.0
Salaried worker*	-2.2	4.6	2.0
Male	-1.6	4.7	2.3
Female	-3.7	4.9	1.6

Source: Own calculations based on ENEU database 1986-1994, INEGI
* Excludes workers by piece rate

During the adjustment period (1989-1994), overall income per hour began to recover (by 3.8 per cent annually), according to the ENEU. At the same time, the income gap between salaried workers and self-employed workers began to shrink. Between 1989 and 1994, hourly income for salaried workers increased by 4.6 per cent annually, compared to 1.3 per cent for self-employed workers (see table 5.4). At the same time, as has been pointed out, the percentage of salaried workers began to increase and the percentage of self-employed workers began to decline. Although, as I have explained, such shifts were due to increased entrepreneurial demand for labour, the incentives for labour to move had to be right, as indeed they were (see table 5.4). A further implication of the ENEU data on income per hour is that, given the fact that income per hour for self-employed workers was higher than waged income, the move to self-employment cannot be taken simply as a result of survival strategies, since for some persons being a self-employed worker may be a better option than being a waged worker. Other studies have also suggested that for some workers the option of being self-employed might be more profitable than that of being a waged worker (e.g. Escobar, 1995; Pacheco, 1994; Kannappan, 1989).

With regard to female labour, it can be seen that the percentage of female salaried workers partially recovered during adjustment and that, during some years, the percentage of female salaried workers was higher than that of men. At the end of the period, in 1994, the percentage of male and female salaried workers was almost the same (around 76 per cent, see table 5.1). Female self-employed workers did not grow as fast as did male self-employed workers. Consequently, the share of female self-employed workers in total employment, which was higher than the respective share of male workers before the crisis (in 1979), ended up being lower in 1994. Therefore, the "informalisation" of work in this respect affected male workers more than it did female workers during the entire 1979-1994 period (table 5.1).

With regard to unpaid workers, this increased more nationally than in the city. Between 1979 and 1991, unpaid workers at the national level rose from 8.2 per cent to 11.1 per cent (see table 4.1, chapter 4), whereas in Mexico City it only increased from 2.9 per cent to 3.2 per cent during the same period. Nevertheless, there is an important difference between the sexes. The share of unpaid female workers in Mexico City increased from 4.4 per cent in 1979 to 5.7 per cent in 1986, while the respective share of male workers (2.1 per cent) remained constant (table 5.1).

The increases in self-employed workers, in unpaid workers and in employers (i.e in non-salaried workers) may have been associated with the growth of other categories of employment, such as the growth of pieceworkers. Benería and Roldan (1989: chapter VI), in their study on subcontracting in Mexico City, highlighted the fact that many "self-employed" women, who were paid by piece-rate, received help from their children, particularly from their female children.[5] In my fieldwork, I also found families who owned a small shop, in which the father identified himself as a self-employed worker, and his children and wife perform unpaid work. I also found in my fieldwork that wives were often in charge of family shops without receiving any "formal" payment. In general, households with small shops were better off than households made up of adults who worked in the "formal" sector. Moreover, there does not seem to be any correlation between the growth of unpaid work and a deterioration in income. At the end of the stabilisation period (1986-1988), the percentage of female unpaid workers remained at the same level, although income per hour declined (see tables 4.7 and 4.8). To the contrary, during the adjustment period (1989-1994), the percentage of female unpaid workers increased, although income per hour grew.

1.2 Employment Structure by Economic Sector

Employment surveys report a decline in the manufacturing sector in favour of higher employment in services and in commerce during the 1980s, both at the country level and in Mexico City (tables 5.5 and 5.6). At the country level, employment in the manufacturing sector (which includes mining and electricity) decreased from 21 per cent in 1979 to 17 per cent in 1991 and to 16.4 per cent in 1993 (table 5.5). In Mexico City, for which there is yearly information available from 1986 onwards, the fall in employment in the manufacturing sector was even sharper: from 30.6 per cent in 1979 to 21.3 per cent in 1993. The share of employment in manufacturing in total employment declined, at least in Mexico City, not only during the 1979-1986 sub-period (characterised by recession), a sub-period during which that share diminished from 30.6 per cent to 25.5 per cent, but also during the 1986-1993 sub-period (characterised by growth in GDP per capita), a sub-period during which that share fell from 25.5 per cent to 21.3 per cent.

Table 5.5. Mexico: Percentage of workers by economic activity, 1979, 1991, 1993, 1995 and 1996

Branch of activity	1979	1991	1993	1995	1996
Agriculture	28.9	27.0	27.1	24.8	22.5
Manufacturing, mining and electricity	21.1	17.0	16.4	16.0	17.4
Construction	6.4	6.2	5.8	5.4	5.1
Commerce	13.8	15.9	17.2	18.5	17.4
Service activities	24.8	29.5	29.5	31.4	32.7
Public Administration	4.5	4.3	3.9	3.8	4.5
Other activities and not specified	0.5	0.1	0.1	0.1	0.5
Total	100.0	100.0	100.0	100.0	100.0

Source: 1979, own calculations based on SPP (1980); and 1991-1996, INEGI and STPS (1993, 1994, 1995, 1996, and 1997)

While the share of manufacturing was declining, the shares of commerce and service activities were increasing. In the period from 1979 to 1993, the share of employment in commerce rose from 13.8 per cent to 17.2 per cent at the national level, and from 16.4 per cent to 21.3 per cent in Mexico City. The share of employment in services increased from 24.8 per cent to 29.5 per cent at the national level and from 37.4 per cent to 43.8 per cent in Mexico City (including transport and communications). If commerce and services are added together, the share of the tertiary sector (excluding public administration) in total employment climbed from 38.6 per cent in 1979 to 46.7 per cent in 1993 at the national level, and from 53.8 per cent (slightly more than half) to 65.1 per cent (almost two thirds) in Mexico City.

Table 5.6. Mexico City: Percentage of workers by economic activity, 1979, 1986, 1989, 1992 and 1993

Branch of activity	1979	1986	1989	1992	1993
Manufacturing, mining and electricity	30.6	25.5	24.6	22.0	21.3
Construction	5.5	4.0	3.8	3.5	4.5
Commerce	16.4	19.2	19.5	21.0	21.3
Service activities	33.4	34.9	36.3	37.0	36.9
Public Administration	7.8	8.9	8.1	7.7	7.8
Transport & communications	4.1	5.8	5.6	7.2	6.9
Other activities and not specified	2.2	1.7	2.1	1.6	1.3
Total	100.0	100.0	100.0	100.0	100.0

Source: 1979 own calculations based on SPP (1980); and 1986-1993, ENEU databases INEGI

The decline of employment in manufacturing activities and the increase in the number of non-waged jobs (often characterised as "marginal" occupations) have been seen as the two main characteristics of the process of "informalisation" of the economy.

In the rest of this section I will look at data taken from the economic censuses (which exclude what would appear to be the most marginal economic activities, those carried out in the streets and in dwellings) in order to verify if the same trends in employment are also present in this more "formal" group of activities. Finally, I will look at more disaggregated data to determine the type of commerce and the type of services in which employment was growing faster as well as the evolution of income per hour in these activities. Unfortunately, such disaggregated data are available only for the 1986-1994 period.

Table 5.7. Mexico: Growth rate (per cent) of total and waged employment in specialised establishments by economic branch, 1980-1994

Period	Manufacturing		Commerce		Services	
	Total	Waged work	Total	Waged work	Total	Waged work
1980-1985						
Total	3.2	3.3	4.5	6.0	5.9	5.9
Male workers	3.0	2.9	5.5	6.4	6.3	6.2
Female workers	4.2	4.7	3.1	5.2	5.2	5.4
1985-1988						
Total	1.1	1.8	4.8	6.3	6.2	7.5
Male workers	-0.2	-0.2	4.1	5.5	6.1	6.8
Female workers	5.2	5.4	5.9	7.9	6.4	8.6
1988-1993						
Total	4.4	3.5	7.3	6.4	9.5	10.1
Male workers	3.1	2.4	6.7	6.3	8.9	9.6
Female workers	7.4	6.4	8.3	6.4	10.6	10.6

Source: Own calculations based on national economic censuses, INEGI (1981, 1986, 1989 and 1994)

The economic censuses in Mexico, which register only economic activities which take place in specialised establishments, show that the trend towards "tertiarisation" is not a phenomenon restricted to marginal activities, in which the impoverished population engaged as a result of survival strategies. The trend towards a faster rate of growth in commerce and in services is also present in the universe registered by the economic censuses. Thus, the largest proportion of new waged jobs, within this universe, was created in commerce and in service activities. Between 1980 and 1985, a period that covers around one year of the oil boom and four years of economic crisis, the rate of growth of waged employment in services and in commerce activities was nearly double the rate recorded in the manufacturing sector (6 per cent compared to 3.3 per cent, see table 5.7).

During the years of stabilisation (1985-1988), waged employment in the manufacturing sector grew by only 1.8 per cent annually, compared with employment in the commercial and service sectors, which grew by 6.3 per cent and 7.5 per cent, respectively. During the adjustment period (1988-1993), economic recovery promoted the growth of employment in all sectors. Waged employment in the manufacturing sector recovered and grew 3.5 per cent a year; nonetheless, its rate of growth was the lowest in the economy. Waged employment in commerce increased annually by 6.4 per cent, and in services by 10.1 per cent (see table 5.7).

Table 5.7 shows that, during the 1980s, the demand for female labour in specialised establishments was growing fast. The increase in the number of women participating in activities which take place in specialised units (or "the recorded or formal sector") was the result of an increase not only in "maquiladora" (in-bond plant) activities, but also in commerce and in services. This evidence indicates that the demand for labour in services and in commerce was expanding, and that this expansion was taking place not just in the most marginal activities, which are those carried out in the street or in the dwellings.[6]

Expert opinion suggests that the 1982 economic crisis negatively affected the economy of major cities, where a large proportion of manufacturing activities is concentrated (Garza and Rivera, 1994:13). The share of Mexico City's industrial GDP with respect to national GDP declined from 37.5 per cent in 1970 to 33.7 per cent in 1990.[7] This process accelerated after the 1982 economic crisis. According to Garza (1990, table 1:18), employment in manufacturing industries in Mexico City, as registered by the economic censuses, declined in absolute terms, falling from 1,059,182 workers in 1980 to 843,800 in 1985, a 20 per cent drop in absolute terms. This fact has been interpreted as an incapacity of the economy of Mexico City to generate enough employment for the supply of labour (De Oliveira and García, 1986; Garza, 1990; Hiernaux, 1992; Rendón and Salas, 1992).

The ENEU survey, which captures all types of manufacturing activities, not only manufacturing activities carried out in specialised establishments, shows that employment in manufacturing between 1979 and 1986 declined only in relative terms, not in absolute terms. Employment grew during this period in manufacturing at a 1 per cent annual rate of growth (see table 5.A.2).[8] Nonetheless, in relative terms it decreased from 30.6 per cent to 25.5 per cent (table 5.6). The share of employment in manufacturing dropped dramatically, from 30.6 per cent to 21.3 per cent between 1979 and 1993 (see table 5.6).

Apparently, what happened, if both sets of evidence are put together, is that the crisis affected, to a much greater extent, manufacturing activities carried out in specialised establishments than manufacturing activities carried out in dwellings or on the street (e.g. handicrafts). Consequently, as a result of the crisis, in the manufacturing mix of the city, non-registered activities gained relative importance in employment terms. The most likely result of such a change was a drop in average earnings. Unfortunately, the evidence on income per hour is available only from 1986 onwards.

During the adjustment period as a whole (which, owing to problems with the data, I end here in 1993 instead of in 1994)[9] employment in manufacturing was stagnant (it grew at 0.6 per cent annually from 1986 to 1993, versus 3.2 per cent for employment as a whole in Mexico City). From 1989 to 1993, the sub-period of economic growth during adjustment, employment in manufacturing in Mexico City decreased at a rate of growth of -0.9 per cent annually (table 5.A.2). Paradoxically, during the 1986-1989 sub-period, when GDP per capita at the national level was stagnant, employment in manufacturing in Mexico City grew at 2.6 per cent annually. The loss of employment was not present during the 1989-1993 sub-period in all branches of manufacturing activities, as can be seen in table 5.A.2. This quite negative behaviour can be explained by two hypotheses: 1) liberalisation, which caused bankruptcy of many manufacturing enterprises; and 2) industrial geographical re-distribution, as the newly established enterprises, more oriented to foreign markets, did not establish themselves in Mexico City.

Between 1986 and 1994, income per hour in the manufacturing sector grew less than the average for all workers in Mexico City (1.2 per cent annually compared to 1.8 per cent). When this behaviour is broken down into the two sub-periods, it turns out, paradoxically, that during the 1986-1989 period (when employment grew) average income showed an important decline (-3 per cent annually) and during the sub-period 1989-1994 (when employment was stagnant), it showed an important increase. Nevertheless, during the 1989-1994 sub-period, in some industries (such as food, beverages and tobacco, and chemistry, oil and plastics), income per hour increased higher than the average for all activities (table 5.A.7). This paradox is not restricted to manufacturing, as employment in the city as a whole grew faster during the 1986-1989 period, when income per hour decreased, than during the 1989-1993 period, when income per hour increased (see tables 5.A.2 and 5.A.7).

That paradox may have resulted from two different processes. On the one hand, during the 1986-1989 period the consumer price index increased annually, on average, by 101 per cent, whereas during the 1989-1994 period average annual inflation was 15.6 per cent. In the face of such different rates of inflation and the same wage policy (signalled by the so-called "Pactos", which were agreements between the government and representatives of business groups and labour groups, and which meant controlling minimum and contractual wage increases below inflation), the impact on real wages was much larger during the 1986-1989 period (see chapter 2 for a detailed description of the "Pactos"). On the other hand, although the production process of some industries moved out of the city (e.g., chemistry, oil and plastics), managerial and administrative employees, who earn the highest salaries, remained in the city. As a result, average income per hour increased in some manufacturing activities. A similar mixed effect can be attributed to the bankruptcy of many enterprises, as, in general, these were the smallest enterprises that paid the lowest wages. If the lowest wages are eliminated, average income goes up (see Cortés, 1997: 10-11).

We may conclude that there is no evidence to support the view that the decline of employment in manufacturing generated, or was associated with, an overall decline in the demand for labour, since employment in other economic activities increased and, as can be seen in table 5.A.2, overall employment grew. For example, the most dynamic economic activity during the adjustment period was in services. Its contribution to the GDP of Mexico City rose from 34.1 per cent to 43.2 per cent between 1970 and 1990 (Garza and Rivera, 1994). Within the service sector, of all the groups in which services have been classified, between 1986 and 1993 employment in the producer services showed the highest rate of growth: 6.9 per cent annually. But it may be noted that this was entirely due to professional services, which grew at the very high rate of 10.3 per cent annually, while financial services[10] grew at only 0.9 per cent annually (table 5.A.2). This may have resulted from economic changes, which imply a greater demand for professional services. Of total employment in producer services in Mexico City, the share of professional services increased from 2.7 per cent in 1986 to 4.5 per cent in 1993, whereas that of financial services decreased from 3 per cent to 2.8 per cent (table 5.A.1). In terms of income per hour, in an apparent additional paradox, professional services grew very little (1.1 per cent annually from 1986 to 1994) while financial services had the highest rate of growth (6.4 per cent annually) (table 5.A.2). It is appropriate to remember that the banking system, which forms the main component of the "financial services and real estate" branch, was privatised during the 1989-1994 period.

The extraordinarily rapid growth of professional services (more than three times higher than the employment rate of growth for Mexico City during that period) may have resulted from the modernisation of economic activities, which might have increased the demand for legal, accountancy, advertising, computing, marketing, and research services.[11] By contrast, the decline in employment in financial activities and the rise in income per hour may be explained by the privatisation of the banking sector, which took place in the first half of the 1990s. It was followed by a huge restructuring, which involved the laying off of many people and, most certainly, high salary increases at the top.

Another consequence of Mexico City's economic transformation seems to have been the growth of distribution services.[12] This sector increased its share in Mexico City's total employment from 20.5 per cent in 1979 to 28.5 per cent in 1994 (table 5.A.1). This was most likely associated with the liberalisation of the Mexican economy, which led to a much larger share of exports and imports in GDP than before. For instance, between 1988 and 1994 the ratio of imports to GDP almost doubled (from 10.4 per cent to 18.2 per cent). Something similar, but not as dramatic, was experimented by exports. In relative terms, the growth of this sector was primarily associated with transport and wholesale activities, and, to a lesser degree, to retail commerce (see tables 5.A.1 and 5.A.2). These activities are directly connected to international as well as to domestic trade. For instance, taking into account the fact that Mexico's transport and warehouse network is heavily concentrated in Mexico City, the traffic of goods and people to and from the capital increased as the economy opened up to international markets. Moreover, the taxi and minibus ("pesera") systems expanded with the spatial extension of the city, and with the credit granted by the Mexican government in conjunction with the banks as part of the privatisation of the city's bus transportation system[13] during the first half of the 1990s.

Some activities that have been associated with the increase in labour supply are petty trade, street vending and personal services. Petty trade and street vending are included in the ENEU survey under retail trade activities. Given that, in 1979, employment in wholesale trade cannot be separated from retail trade, we can only analyse the evolution of the two taken together, which I will call commerce. Commerce (the sum of wholesale and retail trade) increased its share in total employment from 16.4 per cent in 1979 to 19.1 per cent in 1986 and to 21.3 per cent in 1993 (table 5.6 and 5.A.1). The rate of growth in the population involved in commerce was indeed very high in this period (5.9 per cent annually), well above the average rate of growth of employment in the city as a whole (3.7 per cent). Unfortunately there is no quantitative evidence on the composition of retail trade and wholesale trade. Neither is there the possibility of distinguishing, in this period, street vendors from established retail establishments. The very high rate of growth certainly lends support to the idea that there was a very high increase in the number of street vendors and similar marginal commercial activities. Nevertheless, one should remember that average weekly working hours decreased between 1979 and 1986. Thus, the rate of growth of equivalent workers in commerce, as in all other activities, might be lower. In sharp contrast with the 1989-1993 period, which saw an important increase in private consumption at the national level, the 1979-1986 period experience a growth in private consumption lower than the population growth rate, i.e. a decrease in private consumption per capita. Thus it is very likely that labour productivity decreased in commerce during this period.

From 1986 to 1993 the share of wholesale trade in employment increased rapidly; at the same time, the share of retail trade increased very slowly (table 5.A.1). A proportion of the increase in retail trade activities may have been associated with the development of a network of modern department stores, shopping mall complexes and large discount stores, which took place during the sub-period 1989-1994, when private consumption in the country grew at a very high rate, well above that of GDP (3.7 per cent versus 3 per cent annually). Average income per hour, for which I do not have information in the 1979-1986 period, increased at 3.2 per cent annually during the adjustment period (1986-1993), while income per hour in retail trade decreased very slightly (-0.2 per cent annually, see table 5.A.7). But this is explained completely by the behaviour of the latter variable during the 1986-1989 period, when it decreased −1.7 per cent annually. During the consumption boom of the sub-period 1989-1994 retail trade income per hour rose slowly at an annual rate of 0.7 per cent (table 5.A.7). In this period, therefore, in sharp contrast with the preceding one, there is no evidence that growth in employment in commerce was based on marginal activities. Nevertheless, as income per hour in retail trade deteriorated while it was increasing in most of the branches, the standard of living of persons engaged in that activity deteriorated in relative terms.

Another economic activity that the literature on the impact of adjustment has characterised as "marginal" is personal services. This sector is composed of a wide variety of activities — among others, domestic services, repair services, hotels, restaurants and entertainment activities. The share of personal services in the total labour force slightly increased during adjustment (see table 5.A.1). When the period is divided into two sub-periods (1986-1989 and 1989-1993), the surprising fact is that the rate of growth of employment in personal services in relation to overall growth in employment was higher in the first sub-period of stagnation, whereas in the second sub-period of moderate growth it was lower (tables 5.A.1 and 5.A.2). At the same time, income per hour deteriorated in the first sub-period and increased in the second sub-period (see table 5.A.7). Again, concerning personal services, there was an inverse relationship between overall growth of employment and overall income per hour. Income grew in this sector less during the second sub-period of adjustment than the average for all workers.

Within the sector of personal services, repair services showed the highest increase during adjustment (9.1 per cent annually) but had an increase in income slightly below the average of the sector. The supply of this activity, composed mainly of male workers, may have increased as some workers, after learning some skills or being fired, shifted from manufacturing to open small repair businesses of their own.

Construction is a sector deeply associated with poverty. Not so much because average earnings are below average, which, as can be seen in table 5.A.7 and 5.A.8 is frequently the case, but mainly because construction jobs are highly unstable, so that direct construction workers work only part of the year. It is a highly pro-cyclical activity, growing and falling very quickly. Construction workers decreased in the 1979-1986 period in absolute numbers in Mexico City (its share in employment fell from 5 per cent to 4 per cent); their numbers grew slowly during the 1986-1989 sub-period, and very fast during the 1989-1993 sub-period (tables 5.A.1 and 5.A.2). This was due to the fact that, from 1989 to 1994, all types of construction in Mexico City flourished. Building construction was associated with the creation of new business offices, department stores, shopping malls, new residential housing developments, etc. Income per hour also fluctuated sharply in this sector. In this case the association between growth in demand and rise in income per hour looks as expected: during the 1986-1989 sub-period, when employment grew slowly (2.1 per cent annually) income per hour fell quickly (-6.6 per cent annually); in the second sub-period, when employment grew quickly (7.1 per cent annually) income per hour grew very quickly (10.5 per cent annually). In this last case, a real shortage of construction workers might have pushed income well above the average increase.

There were some differences in terms of gender participation in economic activities. The employment rate of growth of female and male workers was the same in the 1986-1993 period (3.2 per cent annually). But, by sub-periods, male workers grew faster in the 1986-1989 sub-period than female workers (4 per cent versus 3.6 per cent), but slower in the 1989-1993 sub-period (2.6 per cent versus 2.8 per cent) (see tables 5.A.4 and 5.A.6).

The decline in the manufacturing sector affected mostly male workers. Between 1989 and 1993 the rate of growth of male employment in the manufacturing sector was negative (-1.6 per cent) and between 1986 and 1989 it grew below average. Indeed, in 1986 the manufacturing sector (with 28.4 per cent of the male population) was the main male employer; by 1993, however, it was displaced by distribution services (29.8 per cent versus 23.5 per cent in manufacturing). The very rapid growth of male employment in the distribution services sector (5.5 per cent annually in the 1986-1993 period) resulted from fast growth in all its branches comprising it, but especially from the fast growth of employment in wholesale distribution and in transport and communications (tables 5.A.3 and 5.A.4).

In the whole period of adjustment (1986-1993) employment in the manufacturing sector for female workers grew by 1.2 per cent annually (higher than the rate for men: 0.5 per cent). Nevertheless, this rate was much lower than the overall female employment growth rate (3.2 per cent, see table 5.A.6). In that same period, retail sales and domestic services, two categories that concentrate the highest percentage of female employment, grew by 3.9 per cent and 0.8 per cent, respectively, per annum. Although retail sales had been identified as a category that has grown as a result of women's survival strategies, employment did not grow uncontrollably considering that the average in that period was 3.2 per cent (see table 5.A.6).[14] Retail sales showed a female employment rate of growth slightly higher than the female overall rate of growth, and domestic services showed a much lower employment rate of growth. Table 5.A.6 shows that female employment grew faster in other economic activities; for example, in the producer service sector, especially in professional services, which showed the highest rate of growth between 1986 and 1993.

As can be seen in tables 5.A.8 and 5.A.9, income per hour for male workers grew faster than for female workers in the 1986-1994 period (1.8 per cent versus 1.6 per cent annually). This led to a widening gap in income per hour between male and female workers during the adjustment period (1986-1993). While it was 4.3 per cent higher in 1986, it had become 7.7 per cent by 1994. In that same period, while income per hour grew in most categories for both men and women, it is remarkable that female income per hour in retail sales trade decreased at a rate of -1.5 per cent annually. A plausible hypothesis is that retail trade was becoming, in Mexico City, an almost saturated activity. In that same period, the growth rate in income per hour in domestic services for female workers grew very little (0.3 per cent annually), having decreased steeply in the 1986-1989 sub-period. So these two activities, retail sales trade and personal services, might explain an important part of the overall difference by gender in the rate of growth in income per hour.

This evidence suggests that the increase in the number of men and women in the labour market is associated with the demand for labour (which, to be sure, is structurally different), rather than with survival strategies in the 1986-1993 period. Changes in the demand for labour began even before the 1982 economic crisis (e.g. the percentage decline of all workers, male and female, in the manufacturing sector), while other changes took place during the adjustment period of trade liberalisation.

2. XALPA: HOUSEHOLD MEMBERS PARTICIPATION IN THE LABOUR MARKETS

In this section I will analyse changes in the labour force participation of household members in Xalpa during the period 1982-1994. The discussion will be based on data collected for all adult members (For more detailed information on the methodology of the survey of this study, please refer to Damián, 1999, Methodological Appendix 1).

In Xalpa, the level of labour force participation in the labour market at the time of my fieldwork (July-September 1995) was higher than that for Mexico City. According to the sample results of my survey, 57.1 per cent of the population aged 12 and over was engaged in economic activities. This rate is 3 per cent higher than the labour force participation rate for Mexico City in that year. This difference was due to a greater proportion of working women in households included in my sample than in Mexico City (42.5 per cent compared to 37.1 per cent for Mexico City).

As noted, it has been suggested that more household members became economically active in response to the economic crisis. In her study of the impact of debt crisis and economic restructuring on Mexico City, Benería (1992:92) argues that the two groups most affected by this response were the following: teenagers and women.[15] These population groups (together with elderly persons) have been defined by some scholars as "secondary workers", that is, they are not the main breadwinners, as they only enter the labour market when the economic conditions of households become economically critical (see Jusidman, 1988:246). This definition assumes that work is always available for these population groups and that they are willing to work at any earnings level. Since my study is based on a retrospective survey, there are some difficulties in identifying whether all who needed to or were willing to work were able to find a job. Nonetheless, based on the data collected in my fieldwork, I found that, in 1995, 22 persons had either lost their job or stopped working for a period of up to six months (17 of them for up to three months and five of them for up to six months). The majority of those who lost their job were persons who were willing to work but were unable to find employment. For persons who stopped working, they stated that they had done so so because the payment rate was very low.

Table 5.8. Xalpa: Percentage of workers according to the period at which they entered the labour market

Household members	Before 1982	1982-1988	1989-1994	Total	Num. of cases
Fathers	78.0	11.0	11.0	100	74
Female household heads	84.2	10.6	5.3	100	19
Wives	70.6	11.7	17.7	100	34
Sons	11.8	26.4	61.8	100	34
Daughters	12.1	30.3	57.6	100	33
Other household members	53.2	22.6	24.2	100	62
Total	54.3	18.4	27.3	100	256

Source: Own survey.

My fieldwork data show that 54.3 per cent of household members began to work before 1982 (table 5.8), of which 62.5 per cent were household heads,[16] 16.3 per cent were wives, and 7.7 per cent were daughters and sons. The remaining percentage was composed of other relatives living in the same household. According to my survey, the households interviewed stated that, in 1982, few of the sons and daughters included in my sample were old enough to be considered part of the labour force (12 years of age and above). Nevertheless, in that year around 33 per cent of them were engaged in paid activities. At the time of the fieldwork (1995), 32.7 per cent of the the group of sons and daughters taken together were participating in the labour market (36.7 per cent of the sons, and 28.6 per cent of the daughters). A major percentage of the sons and daughters entered the labour market after 1982 (see table 5.8).

Between 1982 and 1988, the percentage of household members who entered the labour market was small (18.4 per cent), yet the majority of them were daughters and sons (52 per cent). In the period between 1989 and 1994, the percentage of labour market entries increased to 27.3 per cent, with daughters and sons still comprising the majority of this group (54.7 per cent). However, contrary to the idea that after the economic crisis of 1982 "secondary workers" were forced to engage in paid activities as a result of a deterioration in household living conditions, my fieldwork data indicate that new entries to the labour market were not associated with the crisis.[17] In effect, in Xalpa, it is not in the crisis period that the majority of the new entrances took place, but in the 1989-1994 period, as a result of the resumption of economic growth and increased income per hour of workers (see Section 1 of this chapter). Additionally, in Xalpa, improvements in certain areas of the living conditions of households were associated with more members participating in paid activities (see section 8, chapter 3). For instance, most dwelling improvements and expenditure on household appliances were observed during the second half of the 1980s and in the early 1990s,[18] that is, when the majority of household member's new entries into the labour market took place in Xalpa.

García and Oliveira (1994:227) have claimed that during the 1970s young women without small children and with no marital history were the predominant type of women entering the labour market. According to the authors, this trend changed after the 1982 economic crisis. García and Oliveira argue that the deterioration in household income led to an increase in the number of working women with small children, particularly among households in popular sectors with greatest deprivation levels (*Ibid.*: 228). Nevertheless, my fieldwork data point out that participation in paid activities was typically observed among women without children (83.5 per cent of working women), and that the proportion of mothers participating in the labour market increased less during the years of the economic crisis than in the years of economic recovery: 11.8 per cent between 1982 and 1988 compared to 17.7 per cent between 1989 and 1994. The higher increase in the later period might be associated to the fact that, as children grow older, and as they start working, mothers are liberated of part of their domestic burden and have a choice to work.

Another fact that has been associated with the deterioration of living conditions is the entry of teenagers into the labour market. In my fieldwork sample, although many daughters and sons entered the labour market when they were teenagers, their entry took place at an older age compared to the age at which their parents entered the labour market (see table 5.9). The majority of sons and daughters started working when they were between 16 and 20 years of age; their parents, for the most part, had entered the labour market when they were between 6 and 15 years old. In 1995, at a moment of severe crisis, when carrying out the interviews I identified only two children who had recently started working, one six years old and the other 11 years old. However, their entry into the labour market was not associated with the economic crisis, but, in one case, with the divorce of parents, and, in the other case, with the physical incapacity of the household's main breadwinner, who had recently suffered an accident.

Table 5.9. Xalpa: Age at which household members entered the labour market

Household members	6-15 years	16-20 years	21 years and more	Total
Fathers	65.3	29.3	5.4	100.0
Female household heads	63.2	21.1	15.7	100.0
Wives	41.7	27.8	30.5	100.0
Sons	22.2	69.4	8.4	100.0
Daughters	27.3	69.7	3.0	100.0
Total	44.8	41.0	14.2	100.0
Males	49.3	41.2	9.5	100.0
Females	39.2	40.8	20.0	100.0

Source: Own survey.

Gender plays an important role in differentiating labour market entry characteristics. In Xalpa, 61.1 per cent of household members who worked were males, and 38.9 per cent were females. Men were more likely to start work at an early age than women were. Hence, nearly 50 per cent of the men, as compared to 39.2 per cent of the women, began to work when they were between 6 and 15 years old. By contrast, 20 per cent of the women started to work when they were older than 20 years of age, whereas, for men, this percentage was 9.5 per cent (see table 5.9).

According to Benería (1992:93), given the duration of the crisis, interruptions in the schooling of teenagers are likely to be permanent, leaving a negative impact on the education of the population. My fieldwork data show some improvement in terms of the educational level of household workers (see table 5.10). Almost 7 per cent of household members who entered the labour market before 1982 were illiterate; 58.7 per cent had no more than primary school education (up to 6 years of schooling); and only 9.9 per cent had more than secondary education (up to 9 years of schooling). For household members who entered the labour market between 1982 and 1988: none were illiterate; 18.1 per cent had no more than primary school education; and 38.3 per cent had more than secondary school (more than 9 years of schooling). Finally, for household members who entered the labour market between 1990 and 1994, although there was a small percentage of illiterates (4.2 per cent), my sample results indicated a significant improvement in their overall educational level: 48.6 per cent had an educational level above secondary school

Table 5.10. Xalpa: Educational level of workers according to the period at which household members entered the labour market

Educational level	Before 1982	1982-1988	1989-1994
Illiterate	6.7	---	4.2
1 to 6 years of school	58.7	18.1	14.3
7 to 9 school	21.1	42.3	37.1
More than 9 years of school	9.9	38.3	48.6
Number of cases	139	47	70

Source: Own survey.

Improvements in educational levels were also reflected in schooling differences between parents and children (see table 5.11). None of the sons and daughters was illiterate, whereas a percentage of their parents were. Approximately 50 per cent of the parents included in my sample had completed no more than primary school, compared to slightly more than 10 per cent for the sons and daughters who were engaged in paid work. Considering the grouping of sons and daughters included in my sample as a whole, working women had made the most remarkable improvements in terms of educational levels: more than 50 per cent of the daughters had more than secondary school; the corresponding percentage for the sons was slightly more than 30 per cent. Therefore, my fieldwork data demonstrate that, in spite of the economic crisis, there was an inter-generational improvement in terms of educational level.

Table 5.11. Xalpa: Educational level of household workers

Educational level	Fathers	Female household heads	Wives	Sons	Daughters	Total
Illiterate	5.3	15.8	8.3	---	---	6.7
Up to 6 years of schooling	52.1	52.6	47.2	11.1	12.1	38.7
Up to 9 years of schooling	30.6	21.1	27.8	58.3	36.4	34.6
More than 9 years of schooling	17.3	10.5	16.7	30.6	51.5	20.0

Source: Own survey

Gender studies have documented women's disadvantaged position in the labour market. Such studies suggest that, as a result of gender-power relations, women were confined to unskilled activities and therefore occupied the lowest position in the labour market (Roldán, 1985; García and Oliveira, 1994). Aggregate data of my sample results support, in general, the proposition that a major proportion of women is concentrated in unskilled jobs and that men are concentrated more in semi-skilled jobs. Nevertheless, concerning intermediate and professional occupations, my survey indicated that women accounted for a higher proportion than men (see table 5.12).

Although it has also been said that during adjustment new entrants into the labour market went into jobs with very poor working conditions, especially for women (Benería, 1992:92-93), my fieldwork data indicate that the difference in job position achieved by daughters compared to their mothers is significant. While 55 per cent of mothers were in unskilled occupations, the percentage of daughters in this type of jobs was 36 per cent. At the other extreme, a significant percentage of daughters were working in intermediate or professional occupations as compared with 5 per cent of mothers in this category (see table 5.12). Despite this being a significant inter-generational change, it is less impressive than the one observed in educational levels.

Table 5.12. Xalpa: Skill qualifications of household workers in 1995

Skill Categories	Total	Male	Female	Father	Mother	Son	Daughter
Unskilled	38.6	34.7	44.3	31.0	55.0	41.4	36.4
Semi-skilled	38.6	44.1	30.4	47.9	22.5	37.9	45.5
Skilled	15.2	16.1	13.9	15.5	15.0	20.7	9.1
Intermediate & professional	7.1	5.0	10.2	5.6	5.0	----	9.0
Not specified	0.5	---	1.3	---	2.5	----	----
Total	100	100	100	100	100	100	100
Num. of cases	197	118	79	69	39	27	22

Source: Own survey

The positions of sons in the labour market in terms of skill are a complete surprise. Male children are in a worse position than their fathers and sisters. Despite the son's much higher level of education, the percentage of sons in unskilled jobs was higher than the percentage of fathers in this type of job — 41 per cent compared to 31 per cent, respectively (see table 5.12). In terms of more skilled jobs, sons also did not achieve a better position. While 5 per cent of fathers were in intermediate or professional jobs, none of the sons had this type of job. Based on this evidence, it can be said that the negative impact of the economic crisis affected most of all young males. These young males, with much higher levels of education than their fathers, were in less skilled positions at work.[19] This lack of improvement of sons in the labour market has to be explained by overall changes in the demand for labour in Mexico City. As noted in the previous chapter, the growth in the demand for labour seemed to have positively affected the working opportunities for women.

With regard to the position of workers in the labour market, my data indicate that the percentage of salaried workers was smaller than that observed in Mexico City. Salaried workers accounted for 62.3 per cent of my sample: self-employed workers, 30.6 per cent; and unpaid workers, 7 per cent (see table 5.13).

Table 5.13. Xalpa: Position of household members in the labour market in 1995

Position at work	Total	Fathers	Mothers	Sons	Daughters
Salaried worker	62.3	68.5	38.4	70.6	67.6
Self-employed	30.6	31.5	58.8	15.7	18.9
Unpaid worker	7.1	-----	2.9	13.7	13.5
Total	100.0	100.0	100.0	100.0	100.0

Source: Own survey.

As has been documented in many gender studies, the proportion of women in self-employment was higher than that of men. However, gender may not be the only factor that explains this situation. Age seems to be related also to the proportion of workers in self-employment. The percentage of workers in self-employment tends to increase with age. Male workers are predominantly salaried when they are between 16 and 50 years of age; however, from 51 years of age and older, self-employment seems to be the dominant option for them (more than 80 per cent of workers in this age group was working as a self-employee). Women are predominantly salaried when they are between 16 and 35 years of age; from 36 years onward, they tend to be concentrated in self-employment. This is partly explained by the fact that many enterprises do not hire persons over 40 years of age, especially for unskilled or semi-skilled jobs.

Inter-generational differences for women were remarkable in regard to their position in the labour market. While the percentage of fathers and sons working in salaried occupations was almost the same (68.5 per cent and 70.6 per cent, respectively), the percentage of daughters in salaried jobs was considerably higher compared to their mothers (67.6 per cent and 38.4 per cent, respectively) (see table 5.13). Another significant difference amongst women working in salaried activities was that 46.2 per cent of female household heads were working in this type of job, compared to 19.0 per cent of women living with their partners. Taking into consideration that salaried work has been identified as "formal" work, an important percentage of women entering the labour market have found employment in the "formal" sector.

3. SUMMARY

I have shown that changes in the structure of employment in Mexico City are highly associated with the performance of the economy in general. The proportion of salaried work seems to be determined by changes in GDP per capita. That is, it declines in recession and grows during economic recovery. It should be remembered that, in chapter 4, I also found that the labour force participation rate (LFPR) in Mexico City was pro-cyclical.

Despite, the increase in the proportion of self-employment during recession, the data presented in this chapter suggest that the existence of non-salaried work does not necessarily mean a lower level of income. Self-employment grew faster during the period in which average income per hour for these workers was higher than for waged workers.[20] In some aspects, people may have been better off working for themselves than by engaging in "formal" employment, and, therefore, this cannot be taken simply as a result of survival strategies. This was particularly true for women. Differences between the earnings of female self-employed workers and those of female salaried workers were higher than the differences observed for male workers. Nonetheless, according to the ENEU data, the "informalisation" of work affected male workers more than females, given that the self-employment share of the former grew more than that of the latter.

With regard to the transformation of Mexico City's economic structure by branch of activities, I confirmed the fact that employment in manufacturing declined in favour of employment in services and in commerce. Nevertheless, I also found that this process was also present in the sector recorded in the Economic Censuses, i.e., the 'formal' sector. Moreover, despite the fact that the service and the commercial activities (some time identified by some authors as "informal") have been growing faster than manufacturing, the former have provided the major proportion of new waged jobs, that is, the type of jobs considered to be a measure of economic success. Therefore, I may conclude that there is no clear evidence to confirm that the decline in manufacturing employment was associated with an overall decline in the demand for labour; rather, this decline was associated with a process of economic restructuring.

Employment data on Mexico City suggest that most of the changes in the composition of the labour force have paralleled the transformation of the economy of Mexico City. During adjustment, the most dynamic sectors were associated, on the one hand, with producer services (financial and professional services), which are economic activities that depend on overall economic growth, and, on the other hand, with distributive services (transport, and wholesale and retail sales activities), which are economic activities that depend on the economic transactions and the volume of goods and services traded at the national and the international levels.

Employment figures show that the growth in the number of female workers was highly favoured by the increase in service and commercial activities. Therefore, the increase in women's work may be explained by changes in the demand for labour at the national and city levels, rather than by the emergence of survival strategies. For instance, salaried employment for women grew faster than salaried employment for men in the recorded sector. Moreover, in Mexico City, income per hour also grew faster for women than it did for men between 1989 and 1994. The increase in jobs for women may represent an access to income over which they may have full control, an access which, at the same time, may allow them to reduce the degree of their dependency on other household members; it may not necessarily represent a deterioration in their living conditions.

Based on data collected in Xalpa I found that a major proportion of entrants of "secondary" workers took place in the 1989-1994 period, when the economy recovered and income per hour was growing in Mexico City. The incorporation of "secondary" workers may have also resulted from the ageing process of the households. However, my fieldwork data do not support the idea that there was an increase in the number of children engaged in paid activities, as suggested by studies on survival strategies, since the age at which sons and daughters entered the labour market has risen in comparison with their parents. Moreover, contrary to the idea that the need for income resulted in the abandonment of children and teenagers of school, my data suggest that the educational level of household members engaged in paid activities had improved, despite the economic crisis.

There seems to be some indication that changes in overall demand for female workers had some benefits for women in Xalpa. Skill qualification improvements have resulted in daughters having a better position at work than their mothers. In contrast, males seemed to have been negatively affected by changes in the Mexico City economy. This was shown by the fact that sons' position at work was worse than their fathers and sisters. In contrast, a greater proportion of daughters were in salaried jobs than their mothers; therefore, I may conclude that an important proportion of women entered "formal" sector activities.

Labour Markets in Mexico City and Xalpa 219

In summation, based on the evidence provided in this chapter, I can assume that in Mexico City, as well as in Xalpa, labour force participation was highly associated with labour demand, as it has been in other cities (see Pahl and Wallace, 1985; Chant, 1991; MacCrone, 1994); and this was not necessarily explained by household survival strategies.

Notes

[1] There is a notion that only certain activities or types of employment, such as manufacturing activities or waged employment, are relevant in explaining economic growth. Nonetheless, only since fairly recently (i.e., after the second world war) has wage labour been perceived as the only desirable form of work, the measure of economic success. Formerly, in the two centuries leading up to the second world war, waged labour was only one of a variety of forms of work. As a result of this perception, other forms of work have been considered as "unproductive", "informal" or traditional activities.

[2] It should be noted that earnings of self-employed workers may vary considerably since in this employment category we may find professional workers as well as unskilled workers.

[3] This conversion is made at the prevailing exchange rate which, as the December 1994 crisis showed, was highly overvalued. Accordingly, real earnings per hour in dollar terms was much lower.

[4] There is another reason for the non-comparability of salaried and self-employment income. This has to do with the fact that self-employed income is, quite frequently, a "gross income", in the sense that depreciation of capital is not deducted (e.g. a taxi driver who drives his own car and calculates his income without deducting the depreciation of the car).

[5] In order to compare the various surveys of different years, I classified piece-rate workers as salaried, as was done in the 1979 ECSO. Conceptually, their classification as self-employed or as salaried depends on the place and on the conditions of work. In the cases mentioned by Benería and Roldán, they are clearly closer to self-employed workers.

[6] The figures, which have been derived from economic censuses, have to be taken with care for three reasons. First, they represent a fragment of total employment in the economy. The total number of workers in the 'formal' sector identified by the economic censuses of 1994 (data for 1993) was 12.1 million, which is around 50 per cent of the total employed population in non-agricultural activities registered by the 1993 ENE. Second, as mentioned in chapter 4, is the fact that economic censuses have been expanding their coverage, so that part of the growth captured might be a statistical phenomenon and not a real one. Third, the figures have not been standardised and thus reflect heterogeneous workers in terms of their hours of work.

[7] Own calculations based on Garza and Rivera (1994, table 3.3:53).

[8] Tables numbered 5.A are included in the Statistical Appendix to this chapter.

[9] The composition by economic branches in 1994 seems to have uncontrolled changes. In effect, the proportion of employment in manufacturing grows suddenly from 21.3 per cent to 23.1 per cent and the proportions in services and in commerce fall. This is not very consistent with the previous trend and with what happened afterward. The 1994 ENEU data on composition by economic branches for Mexico City requires more

evaluation before it can be used safely. This is not the case with the other variable that will be analysed in this same section: income per hour.

[10] Includes "Banking, financial services and real estate."

[11] Part of this amazing growth in professional services might have resulted from the adoption of a strategy of sub-contracting these services instead of having them vertically integrated in the firm. The classification by economic activities is defined by the products or services sold by the firm. So an accountant in a chemical firm was an industrial worker in the chemical branch. But if accountancy services have been sub-contracted, this accountant will now work for an accountancy bureau, which is classified in producer services. The same can be said of legal services, transportation, etc.. This might be the explanation of employment growing very quickly and income per hour remaining stagnant in professional services.

[12] Distribution sector includes transportation and communications as well as wholesale and retail trade.

[13] Starting in 1982 public bus transportation in Mexico City was managed by one public enterprise (Ruta 100). This was left to stagnate and the government encouraged the expansion of services provided by a privately-owned mini-bus system which now covers almost 100 per cent of the bus transportation system. Increased employment in this sector is associated to technological change: big buses were substituted by microbuses, thus converting the system into a more labour intensive one.

[14] Again, the lack of detailed information for the period 1979-1986 prevents us from testing what happened directly owing to the effect of the crisis, where many scholars have held that female employment in retail trade grew without control.

[15] As noted in chapter 3 Benería's study of Mexico City is based on a non-representative sample of households of women working in industrial subcontracting. In her study comparability problems arise because: 1) conclusions were drawn based on two different non-random samples (see footnote 26, chapter 3); and 2) the effects of changes on the household demographic structure were not made explicit and, therefore, it is difficult to know whether changes in the labour force participation rate were the result of an ageing process of the population.

[16] The household head is the person identified by the respondents as such.

[17] As noted above, conclusions based on the Xalpa survey should be taken with caution, since they may be biased by the demographic characteristics of the sample, as well as by some selection problems derived from the retrospective analysis (for further discussion see Damián, 1999, Methodological Appendix 1).

[18] For further discussion on this issue, refer to chapter 3, section 8.

[19] This affords strong evidence against the simplistic human capital theory of development and of poverty. Educational improvement does not translate into different jobs for people (or better salaries), unless there is a change in the structure of demand. This evidence also reminds us that schooling is not the only human capital. Skilled industrial workers were (and some times still are) a product of in-work training and not of school years. The human capital of these fathers was larger than the corresponding level for their sons.

[20] As noted above (endnote 2), the income of self-employed workers may vary considerably, since this group is an heterogeneous one. Therefore, conclusions should be taken with caution.

Appendix 1. Labour Force and Income Data for Mexico City

Table 5.A.1. Mexico City: Percentage of workers by economic branch, 1979 and 1986-1993

Economic Branch	1979	1986	1989	1992	1993
Total	100.0	100.0	100.0	100.0	100.0
Manufacturing	31.0	25.5	24.6	22.0	21.3
Food, beverages and tobacco		3.1	3.8	3.6	3.6
Textile clothing and footwear		5.2	4.9	3.9	4.0
Paper, wooden goods, printing and publishing		3.5	3.8	3.5	3.5
Chemistry, oil and plastics		5.3	4.1	4.5	3.7
Metal, machinery and vehicles		6.7	5.8	4.9	4.6
Other manufacturing		1.7	2.2	1.6	1.9
Construction	5.0	4.0	3.8	3.5	4.5
Sum other services (1979 definition)[a]	33.0	34.9	36.3	37.0	36.9
Producer Services		5.7	6.5	7.0	7.3
Banking, financial services and real estate		3.0	2.9	2.8	2.8
Professional services		2.7	3.6	4.2	4.5
Social services and public administration and defence		18.8	18.2	17.9	17.9
Education		5.8	5.7	6.4	6.4
Health		4.2	4.4	3.8	3.7
Public administration and defence	7.8	8.8	8.1	7.7	7.8
Distribution services	20.5	24.9	25.2	28.2	28.2
Transport and communications	4.1	5.8	5.7	7.2	6.9
Commerce[b]	16.4	19.1	19.5	21.0	21.3
Wholesales		2.9	3.4	3.8	3.8
Retail sales		16.2	16.1	17.2	17.5
Personal services		19.2	19.7	19.8	19.5
Domestic services		6.5	6.3	6.3	6.0
Repair services		4.2	4.3	6.5	6.2
Hotel, restaurants, and entertainment		6	6.3	5.9	6.2
Other services		2.5	2.8	1.1	1.1
Other activities and not specified	2.2	1.7	2.1	1.6	1.4

Sources: Own calculations base on 1979, ECSO; 1986, 1989, 1992 and 1993, ENEU databases.
[a] Except public administration and defence, and distribution services, this item includes all services
[b] Includes wholesales and retail sales.

Table 5.A.2 Mexico City: Rate of growth in occupation by economic branch, 1979-1986, 1986-1994

Economic Branch	1979-1986	1986-1989	1989-1993	1986-1993
Total	3.7	3.9	2.7	3.2
Manufacturing	1.0	2.6	-0.9	0.6
Food, beverages and tobacco		11.2	1.3	5.4
Textile clothing and footwear		1.8	-2.4	-0.6
Paper, wooden goods, printing and publishing		6.8	0.6	3.2
Chemistry, oil and plastics		-4.6	0.1	-2.0
Metal, machinery and vehicles		-1.0	-3.1	-2.2
Other manufacturing		13.2	-1.0	4.9
Construction	-0.9	2.1	7.1	5.0
Sum other services (1979 definition)[a]	4.4	5.3	3.1	4.0
Producer Services		8.5	5.7	6.9
Banking, financial services and real estate		2.7	1.8	2.2
Professional services		14.3	8.6	11.0
Social services and public administration and defence		2.8	2.3	2.5
Education		3.3	5.7	4.7
Health		5.5	-1.7	1.4
Public administration and defence	5.4	1.1	1.7	1.4
Distribution services	6.6	4.3	5.6	5.1
Transport and communications	8.8	3.3	7.7	5.8
Commerce [b]	5.9	4.6	5.0	4.8
Wholesale distribution		9.5	5.6	7.3
Retail sales trade		3.7	4.9	4.3
Personal services		4.8	2.4	3.4
Domestic services		2.8	1.5	2.0
Repair services		4.7	12.5	9.1
Hotel, restaurants, and entertainment		5.6	2.3	3.7
Other services		7.9	-18.7	-8.2
Other activities and not specified	-0.4	11.5	-7.2	0.4

Sources: Own calculations base on 1979, ECSO; 1986, 1989, 1992 and 1993, ENEU databases.

[a] Except public administration and defence, and distribution services, this item includes all services.

[b] Includes wholesales and retail sales.

Table 5.A.3. Mexico City: Percentage of male workers by economic activity, 1986-1994 (per cent)

Economic Branch	1986	1989	1992	1993
Total all economic activities	100.0	100.0	100.0	100.0
Manufacturing	28.4	27.8	24.5	23.5
Food, beverages and tobacco	3.4	4.1	4.2	3.9
Textile clothing and footwear	4.2	4.3	3.1	3.4
Paper, wooden goods, printing and publishing	4.5	4.9	4.4	4.3
Chemistry, oil and plastics	5.7	4.4	4.6	3.9
Metal, machinery and vehicles	8.6	7.4	6.4	5.7
Other manufacturing	2.0	2.7	1.8	2.3
Construction	5.7	5.6	5.1	6.4
Producer Services	5.4	6.3	6.5	6.7
Banking, financial services and real estate	2.6	2.6	2.4	2.8
Professional services	2.8	3.7	4.1	3.9
Social services, public administration and defence	16.0	14.9	13.8	13.7
Education	3.4	3.2	3.4	3.5
Health services	2.7	2.6	2.1	2.1
Public administration and defence	9.9	9.1	8.3	8.1
Distribution services	25.6	25.7	29.5	29.8
Transport and communications	7.9	7.8	9.8	9.6
Wholesale distribution	3.3	3.8	4.4	4.2
Retail sales trade	14.4	14.1	15.3	16.0
Personal services	16.5	17.3	18.2	18.1
Domestic services	1.7	1.8	2.1	2.1
Repair services	6.1	6.1	9.6	9.0
Hotels, restaurants, and entertainment	5.3	5.4	5.2	5.8
Other services	3.4	4.0	1.3	1.2
Other activities and not specified	2.2	2.4	2.4	1.8

Source: Own calculations based on ENEU, databases 1986-1994, INEGI.

Table 5.A.4. Mexico City: Employment growth rate of male workers by economic branch, 1986-1993 (per cent)

Economic Branch	1986-1989	1989-1993	1986-1993
Total	4.0	2.6	3.2
Manufacturing	3.3	-1.6	0.5
Food, beverages and tobacco	10.7	1.4	5.3
Textile clothing and footwear	4.8	-3.2	0.2
Paper, wooden goods, printing and publishing	7.0	-0.7	2.6
Chemistry, oil and plastics	-4.6	-0.4	-2.2
Metal, machinery and vehicles	-1.1	-3.8	-2.7
Other manufacturing	15.0	-1.4	5.3
Construction	3.4	6.1	5.0
Producer Services	9.5	4.2	6.5
Banking, financial services and real estate	4.0	4.6	4.3
Professional services	14.1	4.0	8.2
Social services, public administration and defence	1.6	0.5	1.0
Education	1.9	5.0	3.7
Health services	2.7	-2.7	-0.4
Public administration and defence	1.1	-0.3	0.3
Distribution services	4.2	6.5	5.5
Transport and communications	3.6	8.1	6.1
Wholesale distribution	9.0	5.2	6.8
Retail sales trade	3.3	5.9	4.8
Personal services	5.7	3.8	4.6
Domestic services	6.0	6.7	6.4
Repair services	4.0	13.1	9.1
Hotels, restaurants, and entertainment	4.7	4.5	4.6
Other services	9.8	-24.0	-11.0
Other activities and not specified	7.1	-4.5	0.3

Source: Own calculations based on ENEU databases.

Table 5.A.5. Mexico City: Percentage of female workers by economic activity, 1986-1994 (per cent)

Economic Branch	1986	1989	1992	1993
Total	100.0	100.0	100.0	100.0
Manufacturing	20.0	18.7	17.1	17.5
Food, beverages and tobacco	2.4	3.2	2.5	3.0
Textile clothing and footwear	7.1	6.1	5.1	5.3
Paper, wooden goods, printing and publishing	1.7	1.7	1.8	1.9
Chemistry, oil and plastics	4.6	3.6	4.3	3.4
Metal, machinery and vehicles	3.0	2.9	2.2	2.7
Other manufacturing	1.2	1.2	1.2	1.2
Construction	0.8	0.6	0.6	0.9
Producer Services	6.4	6.7	7.9	8.4
Banking, financial services and real estate	3.9	3.3	3.6	2.9
Professional services	2.5	3.4	4.3	5.5
Social services, public administration and defence	23.9	24.3	25.4	25.6
Education	10.2	10.2	11.8	11.7
Health services	7.0	7.7	6.8	6.7
Public administration and defence	6.7	6.4	6.8	7.2
Distribution services	23.6	24.1	26.0	25.2
Transport and communications	1.9	1.9	2.4	1.9
Wholesale distribution	2.3	2.5	2.9	2.9
Retail sales trade	19.4	19.7	20.7	20.4
Personal services	24.4	24.1	22.7	21.7
Domestic services	15.4	14.7	13.8	13.1
Repair services	0.7	0.9	1.0	0.9
Hotels, restaurants, and entertainment	7.4	8.0	7.1	6.8
Other services	0.9	0.5	0.8	0.9
Other activities and not specified	1.0	1.5	0.2	0.7

Source: Own calculations based on ENEU, databases 1986-1994, INEGI.

Table 5.A.6. Mexico City: Employment growth rate of female workers by economic branch 1986-1993 (per cent)

Economic Branch	1986-1989	1989-1993	1986-1993
Total	3.6	2.8	3.2
Manufacturing	1.3	1.1	1.2
Food, beverages and tobacco	14.1	1.1	6.5
Textile clothing and footwear	-1.5	-0.8	-1.1
Paper, wooden goods, printing and publishing	3.6	5.7	4.8
Chemistry, oil and plastics	-4.5	1.3	-1.2
Metal, machinery and vehicles	2.5	1.0	1.6
Other manufacturing	3.6	2.8	3.2
Construction	-5.8	13.8	4.9
Producer Services	5.2	8.8	7.2
Banking, financial services and real estate	-2.0	-0.5	-1.1
Professional services	14.8	15.9	15.4
Social services, public administration and defence	4.2	4.1	4.2
Education	3.6	6.4	5.2
Health services	7.0	-0.7	2.5
Public Administration and Defence	2.1	5.9	4.2
Distribution services	4.4	3.9	4.1
Transport and communications	3.6	2.8	3.2
Wholesale distribution	6.6	6.7	6.6
Retail sales trade	4.2	3.7	3.9
Personal services	3.2	0.1	1.4
Domestic services	2.0	-0.1	0.8
Repair services	12.7	2.8	6.9
Hotels, restaurants, and entertainment	6.4	-1.3	1.9
Other services	-14.8	19.1	3.2
Other activities and not specified	18.6	-15.0	-2.0

Source: Own calculations based on ENEU databases 1986-1993, INEGI.

Appendix 1. Labour Force and Income Data for Mexico City   227

Table 5.A.7. Mexico City: Average income per hour by economic activity and rate of growth, 1986-1994

Economic activity	Average income per hour (Pesos of 1994)					Annual growth rate		
	1986	1989	1992	1993	1994	1986-1989	1989-1994	1986-1994
Average income per hour	7.1	6.8	7.5	7.8	8.2	-1.5	3.8	1.8
Manufacturing	6.9	6.3	7.0	7.0	7.6	-3.0	3.7	1.2
Food, beverages, and tobacco	5.5	6.0	6.0	5.6	6.6	2.9	1.9	2.3
Textile clothing and footwear	6.1	5.6	5.9	5.9	5.8	-2.7	0.8	-0.5
Paper, wooden goods, printing and publishing	7.0	6.4	7.5	7.2	8.1	-3.0	4.8	1.8
Chemistry, oil and plastics	6.8	7.8	7.7	8.0	9.0	4.7	3.0	3.6
Metal, machinery and vehicles	6.6	5.8	7.7	7.2	7.7	-4.0	5.7	1.9
Other manufacturing	7.6	6.6	7.5	9.0	8.4	-4.6	4.7	1.1
Construction	6.6	5.4	7.3	6.9	8.9	-6.6	10.5	3.7
Producer Services	11.0	10.8	12.5	12.9	14.1	-0.7	5.4	3.1
Banking, financial services and real estate	11.6	10.1	13.9	14.4	19.1	-4.6	13.6	6.4
Professional services	10.3	11.3	11.5	12.0	11.3	3.1	0.0	1.1
Social services, public administration and defence	8.4	7.4	8.4	9.4	10.3	-4.1	6.8	2.6
Education	10.0	8.8	9.6	10.5	11.3	-4.1	5.2	1.6
Health services	9.8	7.9	8.7	9.9	11.0	-6.8	6.8	1.5
Public administration and defence	6.7	6.2	7.4	8.3	9.1	-2.9	8.0	3.8
Distribution services	6.7	6.8	7.1	7.1	7.2	0.5	1.2	1.0
Transport and communications	7.6	7.7	8.4	7.3	7.5	0.2	-0.3	-0.1
Wholesale distribution	7.5	8.2	9.0	8.4	9.7	3.0	3.3	3.2
Retail sales trade	6.3	6.0	5.9	6.7	6.2	-1.7	0.7	-0.2
Personal services	6.0	5.6	6.3	6.5	6.5	-2.3	3.2	1.1
Domestic services	4.7	3.6	4.8	5.0	4.9	-8.9	6.6	0.5
Repair services	5.8	5.9	6.2	7.1	6.3	0.7	1.1	1.0
Hotels, restaurants, and entertainment	7.2	7.4	7.9	7.8	8.6	0.7	3.1	2.2
Other services	7.1	6.4	8.4	5.1	5.9	-3.6	-1.4	-2.3

Source: Own calculations based on ENEU, databases 1986-1994, INEGI.

Table 5.A 8. Mexico City: Income per hour and employment growth rate of male workers by economic activity, 1986-1994

Economic activity	Average income per hour (Pesos of 1994)					Annual growth rate		
	1986	1989	1992	1993	1994	1986-1989	1989-1994	1986-1994
Total average income per hour	7.2	7.0	7.8	7.9	8.4	-1.2	3.7	1.8
Manufacturing	6.7	6.5	7.45	7.6	8.1	-0.7	4.4	2.4
Food, beverages and tobacco	5.6	6.0	6.1	5.9	6.8	2.4	2.2	2.3
Textile clothing and footwear	6.7	6.5	6.8	7.3	6.6	-1.0	0.2	-0.3
Paper, wooden goods, printing and publishing	6.5	6.3	7.4	7.3	8.9	-1.1	7.2	4.0
Chemistry, oil and plastics	6.7	7.6	8.0	8.1	9.4	4.5	4.3	4.4
Metal, machinery and vehicles	6.8	6.1	8.3	8.0	7.7	-3.6	4.7	1.5
Other manufacturing	7.7	7.1	7.3	9.7	9.4	-2.7	5.7	2.5
Construction	6.7	5.4	7.3	6.6	8.6	-7.3	9.9	3.1
Producer Services	12.2	11.7	13.9	14.6	14.9	-1.5	5.0	2.6
Banking, financial services, and real estate	13.6	11.2	16.1	14.8	22.9	-6.2	15.4	6.8
Professional services	10.8	12.0	12.6	14.5	10.7	3.4	-2.2	-0.1
Social services, public administration and defence	8.3	7.2	8.1	9.2	10.3	-4.6	7.5	2.8
Education	10.1	9.1	9.7	10.6	12.6	-3.5	3.9	0.7
Health services	11.9	9.4	9.5	12.8	12.9	-7.9	7.8	1.0
Public administration and defence	6.7	5.9	7.0	7.8	8.8	-4.0	6.9	2.2
Distribution services	6.9	6.8	7.4	6.9	7.2	0.0	0.9	0.5
Transport and communications	7.6	7.7	8.4	7.0	7.2	0.2	-2.4	-1.3
Wholesale distribution	7.9	8.4	9.7	8.4	9.1	1.7	0.1	0.8
Retail sales trade	6.1	5.9	6.1	6.5	6.4	-1.1	2.5	1.0
Personal services	6.5	6.6	6.7	7.2	7.0	0.5	1.0	0.8
Domestic services	5.2	5.9	6.1	5.2	5.7	4.1	-2.9	0.1
Repair services	5.9	5.8	6.2	7.1	6.1	-0.1	5.0	2.8
Hotels, restaurants, and entertainment	7.4	8.3	8.6	8.5	8.7	4.0	0.6	2.1
Other services	7.2	5.9	7.8	5.2	6.1	-6.3	-3.2	-4.5

Source: Own calculations based on ENEU, databases 1986-1994, INEGI.

Appendix 1. Labour Force and Income Data for Mexico City   229

Table 5.A.9. Mexico City: Income per hour and employment growth rate of female workers by economic activity, 1986-1994

Economic activity	Average income per hour (Pesos of 1994)					Annual growth rate		
	1986	1989	1992	1993	1994	1986-1989	1989-1994	1986-1994
Average income per hour	6.9	6.3	7.0	7.5	7.8	-2.9	4.5	1.6
Manufacturing	6.2	5.6	5.9	5.5	6.2	-3.4	2.2	0.1
Food, beverages and tobacco	5.1	5.8	5.5	4.7	5.9	4.5	0.4	2.0
Textile clothing and footwear	5.4	4.3	4.7	4.4	4.9	-7.0	2.6	-1.1
Paper, wooden goods, printing and publishing	5.3	7.0	8.2	7.0	5.5	9.6	-4.8	0.3
Chemistry, oil and plastics	7.0	8.2	7.0	8.0	8.2	5.3	0.0	2.0
Metal, machinery and vehicles	5.2	4.5	4.8	4.1	7.6	-4.9	11.2	4.8
Other manufacturing	7.5	4.8	7.8	6.8	5.7	-14.2	3.8	-3.3
Construction	5.4	6.3	6.4	10.0	13.8	4.9	17.0	12.3
Producer Services	9.1	9.3	10.4	10.5	12.5	0.7	6.1	4.0
Banking, financial services and real estate	9.1	8.5	11.3	13.5	12.3	-2.4	7.7	3.8
Professional services	9.1	10.0	9.6	9.0	12.6	3.2	4.7	4.1
Social services, public administration and defence	8.6	7.6	8.8	9.6	10.2	-4.1	6.2	2.2
Education	9.9	8.6	9.5	10.5	10.8	-4.5	4.6	1.1
Health services	8.2	6.9	8.2	8.1	9.8	-5.5	7.1	2.2
Public administration and defence	6.9	6.8	8.1	9.4	9.8	-0.3	7.5	4.5
Distribution services	6.6	6.7	6.1	7.5	7.2	0.6	1.4	1.1
Transport and communications	7.1	7.7	8.2	10.2	10.3	2.6	6.0	4.7
Wholesale distribution	6.3	10.0	7.3	8.4	11.1	16.8	2.2	7.4
Retail sales trade	6.5	6.1	5.6	7.0	5.8	-2.1	-1.1	-1.5
Personal services	5.4	4.3	5.4	5.4	6.0	-7.5	6.8	1.2
Domestic services	4.6	3.1	4.5	4.9	4.8	-12.7	9.0	0.3
Repair services	4.9	7.1	7.1	6.4	8.8	13.2	4.5	7.7
Hotels, restaurants, and entertainment	6.9	6.0	6.8	6.5	8.3	-4.6	6.7	2.3
Other services	6.8	11.9	10.4	4.8	5.8	20.6	-13.4	-2.0

Source: Own calculations based on ENEU, databases 1986-1994, INEGI.

6 Conclusions

1. INTRODUCTION

There is a consensus among scholars that the serious economic problems that Latin American countries were suffering during the 1980s were the precipitating factor of the economic reforms implemented in these countries, not the IMF/World Bank adjustment policy package. The worldwide economic conditions of the 1980s made unsustainable the previous economic development strategy (i.e., import substitution). Governments of developing countries, among them the Mexican government, were forced to adjust their economies in order to compete in a globalised world. In a context of severe financial restrictions, the approval of stabilisation and adjustment programmes by the IMF/World Bank became a precondition for refinancing the debts of developing countries.[1]

When structural reform policies were first introduced, governments seemed to be able to negotiate with the IMF/World Bank some changes in the policy conditions. Apparently, governments had some scope to negotiate policy reform, including protection for the poor. However, as national economies became more dependent on international financial markets, governments have had a much more reduced margin to act upon their national economies (Stewart, 1998:41). Economic reforms and higher interest rates became a precondition to attract external capital and private investment.

Nevertheless, criticism has been raised on the theoretical shortcomings of the Washington Consensus approach to policy reform. First, this approach has been criticised on the grounds that the neoclassical orthodoxy in aid referred to the economic success of the East Asian region to vindicate the promotion of free-market economies, failing to acknowledge the role of the State in the growth of these countries. The role of the State in promoting and protecting the economy of East Asian countries was crucial (Stewart, 1998: 52). Most of these countries did not adopt the reform package proposed by the Washington Consensus. On the contrary, they implemented an interventionist industrial policy. For instance, the Korean government selectively subsidised some industries in order to modify relative prices and stimulate economic activities. To achieve export goals, this government also set discriminatory interest rates, regulated credit allocations as well as prices, and set in place controls on capital outflows. Other governments of East Asian countries (e.g. Taiwan) also invested in economic activities, granted cheap credit, and guaranteed the demand for new industrial products (Stewart, 1998: 49-50). Nevertheless, all these policies were not included in the Washington Consensus because they involve subsidised credit, import protection, and state ownership. Although this economic success took place in particular historical circumstances (e.g. commodity composition of output at the starting-point of development and external conditions), it is clear that the East Asian "miracle" did not result from the application of a policy reform similar to the one dictated by the Washington Consensus.

2. CRITICISMS OF THE WASHINGTON CONSENSUS AND THE MEXICAN CASE

Despite the presence of several methodological difficulties in determining whether a deterioration in the living conditions of the population was due to policy reform, there is a growing concern among scholars on whether the economic reforms proposed by the IMF/World Bank are conducive to economic growth.

The 1998 World Bank Country Report on Mexico recognised that, although many far-reaching economic reforms were implemented, "... Mexico was unable to repeat the growth performance achieved in the earlier decades, and in 1995 became immersed in another very sharp recession" (*Ibid.*). Based on these events, the Bank poses the following questions: "... why growth took so long to recover from the 1982 crisis ... [and] ... why the country's economic growth in the early 1990s remained so far below the rates achieved in earlier decades in spite of the many reforms that were implemented" (*Ibid.*).

The World Bank (1998:v) answers these questions by explaining that the slow economic recovery in Mexico was a result of the incompleteness of policy reforms.[2] According to the Bank, the past policy reforms have been effective in the areas where they were implemented and the reform process is pointing in the right direction.

However, while the Bank recommends the deepening of policy reforms, some scholars (e.g. Stewart, 1995 and 1998; and Stiglitz, 1998), based on the difficulties observed in restoring economic growth in many adjusting countries, began to dispute whether the prescribed reform policies were the appropriate policies for these countries. According to Stewart (1998:42) the need for developing countries to carry out economic reform is not in question. However, the effectiveness of the prescribed policy reforms of the Washington Consensus is in doubt.

In the case of Mexico, the performance of the economy during the stabilisation and adjustment periods (1982-1985 and 1986-1994) was negative. Although some macroeconomic variables improved during the period of 1989-1994, GDP per capita in 1994 was lower than the 1982 level. Therefore, we may conclude that adjustment was not effective in spurring rapid economic growth. This was confirmed in December 1994. Although it seemed that economic recovery in Mexico was marching swiftly, the 1994-1995 financial crisis showed that economic growth was very fragile and highly dependent on capital inflow. In the aftermath of the 1994 financial crisis, capital inflows declined from 7.8% of GDP in 1994 to 0.3% in 1995, the annual inflation rate reached 50%, and GDP declined by –6.5% in that year. The Mexican economy recovered much faster than after the 1982 crisis. An important element to explain this quick recovery was that, in sharp contrast to what happened after 1982, there was an important financial support from the U.S. government together with IMF/World Bank loans. In 1996, the economy returned to a positive economic rate of growth; by 1997, GDP per capita had reached the 1994 level. However, as we will see below, this crisis severely affected the level of poverty in Mexico.

One of the main criticisms of the policy reform package advocated by the Washington Consensus is the "...use of a small set of instruments (including macroeconomic stability, liberalised trade and privatisation) to achieve a relatively narrow goal (economic growth)" (Stiglitz, 1998:31).[3] Stiglitz argues that a broader set of instruments is necessary to achieve a much broader goal (i.e. higher living standards). The author suggests that:

> [the] focus on inflation –the central malady of the Latin American countries, which provided the backdrop for the Washington Consensus– has led to macroeconomic policies that may not be the most conducive for long-term economic growth (Stiglitz, 1998:5).

Stiglitz argues that the policy prescription of aggressive, preemptive strikes against inflation is based on the assumptions that: 1) inflation is costly; 2) once it starts to rise, inflation has a tendency to accelerate out of control; and 3) increases in inflation are very costly to reverse.

Based on empirical studies, which analyse the cost of inflation for economic growth, Stiglitz (1998:8) has pointed out that there is little evidence to suggest that an inflation rate of up to 40% is costly in terms of growth. This author holds that "controlling high and medium rate inflation should be a fundamental policy priority but pushing even lower is not likely to significantly improve the functioning of markets" (Stiglitz, 1998:8).

In the case of Mexico, the inflation rate remained well above 40% during the period of 1982-1988. Therefore, it seems that controlling inflation was an appropriate policy at the time. From 1989 on, with the exception of 1995 and 1996, the inflation level has stayed below 20%. Nevertheless, the Mexican government continues to consider reducing inflation as one of its most important, if not the most important, economic target.[4] Accordingly, one question that arises is, How costly has it been for economic growth and poverty reduction to maintain the inflation rate far below 40%?[5]

Inflation control, as it has been implemented in Mexico, has had some direct impact on the wellbeing of the population. In the first place, a central instrument in the attempt to curb inflation has been wage control. The government has justified this policy by arguing that its aim was to "avoid massive company shutdowns and the uncontrollable growth of unemployment" (Aspe, 1993:18). Nevertheless, it has been argued that wage controls were unnecessary, for fiscal and monetary austerity were sufficient to stop inflation (Gould, 1996:27). As a result of the wage control policy, average earnings declined sharply, reaching their lowest level in 1988 compared with that of 1981; by 1994, average earnings were nearly 20% below the 1981 level. Therefore, in terms of living standards, the wage control policy clearly pushed poverty incidence upwards.

To achieve macroeconomic stability, the IMF/World Bank recommended management of the budget deficit. As part of this policy, the Mexican government reduced the amount of subsidies on basic foodstuff products and increased the prices of public sector goods. I analysed the case of the general subsidy on tortilla, which was replaced with a targeted subsidy, without this representing any improvement in terms of economic efficiency. Nevertheless, as noted in chapter 2, the implementation of a targeted subsidy had a negative impact on the wellbeing of the poor, particularly the urban poor.

Another policy reform that may have discouraged productive investment was the policy of maintaining high real interest rates. However, as has been pointed out by Stewart (1998: 43-44), the Washington Consensus recommendations failed to promote an increase in domestic savings, despite high real interest rates. This policy was followed in the belief that high real interest rates will attract foreign savings and foreign investment. In Mexico it was not until 1991 when foreign savings and foreign investment began to increase, representing 5% to 7% of GDP during the period of 1991-1994 (Zedillo, 1998:35). However, a very high percentage of such inflow of foreign savings, the percentage attracted by high real interest rates, was composed of short term, volatile flows of portfolio investment in government securities.

High real interest rates represent the price of capital. Policies which promote the rise of real interest rates and which bring about a decrease in real wages imply a redistribution of income in favour of capital and against workers. This is what happened in Mexico. Real interest rates –with some ups and downs- were maintained high; at the same time, real wages declined. In consequence, the functional distribution of income experienced a pronounced shift: the share of wages in GDP, which was 37.5% in 1981, fell dramatically so that, in 1993, after some recovery, its share of GDP was 28%. Household income distribution also became more unequal, as was shown in chapter 2. Slow and irregular growth and increased income inequality cannot result in anything other than an increase in poverty (as I showed in chapter 3).

Another aspect of the IMF/World Bank approach to policy reform that has been challenged is that their recommended policies are "...based on a rejection of the State's activist role and the promotion of a minimalist non-interventionist State. The unspoken premise is that governments are worse than markets. Therefore, the smaller the State the better the State" (Stiglitz, 1998: 24-25). During the Salinas administration there was a strong emphasis on the privatisation of state-owned firms. According to Stiglitz (1998:20-1), "the advocates of privatisation may have overestimated the benefits of privatisation and underestimated the cost ... If, for instance, competition is lacking, creating a private, unregulated monopoly will likely result in even higher prices for consumers." One of the most striking examples of this type of unaccounted costs was the privatisation of Teléfonos de México (the Mexican Telephone Company – TELMEX, for its Spanish acronym). Once TELMEX was privatised, the government granted a five-year "transition" period in which no other telephone company would be allowed to operate in Mexico. As a result, TELMEX was in effect transformed from a public monopoly into a private monopoly. Although the government formally controlled phone rates, they increased faster than the general inflation rate. In this case, monopolistic rents (which were previously transferred to telephone users) were now additionally transferred to the privately-owned telephone company monopoly, thereby continuing to deteriorate telephone users' real income.

3. STABILISATION, ADJUSTMENT AND POVERTY

A few years after the implementation of stabilisation and adjustment programmes, there began a debate on the cost of these policy reforms for the population in general, and for the poor in particular. Supporters of policy reform claim that a more open world economy will enhance economic growth. This, in turn, will expand employment, and, therefore, poverty will be reduced. Critics of adjustment claim that this promise is still a distant prospect for the poor in many developing countries, and that, on the contrary, adjustment has had adverse consequences for the poor.

Concerning poverty reduction in Mexico, we have seen that there is no consensus among scholars about the changes in the level of poverty during the years that followed the 1982 economic crisis. Differences in conclusions arise mainly from the application of different definitions of poverty thresholds and, secondarily, from the way data are handled and from the different methodologies that have been used to measure poverty. From the point of view of the evolution, since the 1982 crisis, of income poverty at the national level, we found three main views held by researchers: 1) poverty grew and attained its highest level in 1989, thereafter declining slightly; 2) poverty increased until 1992 (though at a slower pace between 1989-1992 than during the 1984-1989 period), and thereafter it remained at the same level from 1992 to 1994; and 3) the incidence of poverty did not increase in the period of 1984-1992, remaining virtually at the same level during the entire period. I have already pointed out (chapter 3) that the last proposition is difficult to uphold, since most evidence points to a deterioration in GDP per capita, in wages, and in income distribution.

Despite disagreements between the two first-mentioned views regarding the year at which poverty reached its peak, both agree that during the period 1984-1992 poverty increased in Mexico. Nevertheless, as I noted in chapter 3, the proposition that poverty began to decrease in 1989 implies that the policy reform was effective, since eventually poverty declined. In contrast, the proposition that poverty did not decline in the period of 1989-1992 implies that the stabilisation and adjustment policies were ineffective, since poverty was not reduced. In the latter view, the increase in poverty has been attributed to the fact that, although the Mexican economy recovered from 1989 onwards, income distribution worsened, and, therefore, the benefits of this recovery were concentrated on the richest segments of society. My own poverty estimates also support the proposition that poverty increased in Mexico City during the period of stabilisation and adjustment.

Although the first years of the 1990s were characterised by improvements in some macroeconomic variables and in wages, the financial crisis of December 1994 has raised questions as to whether stabilisation policies and adjustment reforms were appropriate for promoting sustained growth. As mentioned before, GDP in 1995 experienced a negative growth rate of −6.5%, which in per capita terms represents a negative growth rate of about −8.5%. Moreover, private consumption experienced an even higher negative growth rate, −12.5% (−14.5% in per capita terms), and inflation rose to more than 50%. The 1994-1995 financial crisis seems to have had serious consequence for the population. The results of the ENIGH 1996 (INEGI, 1998) reflect a drastic decline in income in all segments of the population. If the figures are corrected, overall per capita household income declined nearly 25% between 1994-1996 (without adjusting the data to national accounts). Accordingly, there was a sharp increase in the level of extreme poverty, from 40.5% of households in 1994 to 55.0% of households in 1996.[6] Although these estimates are preliminary (as adjustment of income to national accounts has not been performed), it seems that the 1994 economic crisis led to the highest increase in income poverty in Mexico since the 1982 economic crisis (Boltvinik, 1998b), despite economic reform.

In conclusion, it seems that policy reform was not able to prevent a deep deterioration in household income. Therefore, we may say that, in general, the IMF/World Bank (i.e. Washington Consensus) policies were not able to achieve a reduction in poverty and in income inequality in Mexico. From the point of view of income poverty, the experience of adjustment in Mexico has been negative.

Despite the increase in income poverty in Mexico and Mexico City, some social indicators show improvements in particular areas of welfare. For instance, life expectancy increased by more than four years between 1980 and 1992; infant mortality continued to decline; and access to education and health services improved. With regard to the paradox of income declining and improvements in some social indicators, I pointed out that many major studies on poverty have found a very weak correlation between current disposable household income and direct measures of deprivation, not only in Latin American countries, but also in several Anglo Saxon countries (see Beccaria, *et al.*, 1992; Boltvinik, 1998a; and Nolan and Whelan, 1996). I stated that this paradox might be explained by the following factors. First, social indicators may have continued to improve despite the economic crisis because the satisfaction of some needs (e.g. education or health care) are largely organised outside the market — that is, the government provides them. Therefore, because social spending in real terms was not reduced in Mexico, the population did not lose the opportunity to satisfy these needs, despite a reduction in income. Although the Mexican government allocated a higher share of the public budget to debt servicing, social expenditure as a percentage of GDP was protected; in some areas, social expenditure actually increased in real terms. As a result, health care coverage and educational levels rose. Moreover, the Mexican government was able to continue to investing in other services supplied by the public sector — e.g., piped water or sewerage — that have a positive impact on welfare indices.[7]

Additionally, there were improvements in the material conditions of households, particularly those related to dwelling characteristics. This could be interpreted as clear evidence of a betterment in household income, raising the question of whether income figures in Mexico are reliable at all. This paradox might be explained, as I have argued, by the fact that flow variables (e.g. income) may change easily from one period to the next, whereas stock variables (e.g. dwelling) experience only marginal changes, so that the characteristics observed today are determined, to a great extent, by the characteristics which prevailed yesterday. Therefore, a deterioration in certain areas of the welfare (e.g. housing conditions) may not be apparent in a relative short period of time.

Moreover, as we saw in Xalpa, there seems to be a correlation between public service infrastructure supply (e.g. piped water and sewerage) and improvements in housing. I explained that, when public infrastructure is supplied, there is an implicit recognition by local authorities of people's land tenure rights, and, consequently, people feel confident to invest in their dwellings. Therefore, as the government continued to increase its coverage of this type of services despite adjustment, this may have led to improvements in housing conditions. Another hypothesis is that the use of concrete brick, which is a much cheaper construction material than the traditional brick, became generalised in this period, making it possible for households to improve their dwellings with low-cost materials. In addition, I also mentioned that the prices of some household appliances were reduced as a consequence of the implementation of trade liberalisation measures in Mexico. In this case, households, in their role as consumers, benefited from the government's trade liberalisation policy.

It should be noted that, although my data suggest that households in Xalpa were able to continue to improve their living conditions over time, the households included in my sample reduced expenses associated both with dwelling improvements and with the purchase of household basic appliances during the years that followed the 1982 economic crisis (1983-1985). It was not until 1991-1994 when there were clear signs of real improvements in the economic conditions of the households, as signalled by the fact that the proportion of households reporting improvements in these areas increased considerably. This fact confirms the proposition that income restrictions were more severe after the 1982 crisis than during the period of 1990-1994.

4. POVERTY AND THE LABOUR MARKET

As we saw, many scholars have claimed that after the 1982 economic crisis a decline in income was shown by the increase in the number of members of poor households, particularly children and women, being obliged to work in order to counteract the deterioration in living conditions (see Rendón and Salas, 1990; Tuirán, 1992; Jusidman, 1989; González de la Rocha, 1993). The propositions suggested by the survival strategies current of thought were based on aggregate data on Mexico, derived from employment and household income surveys; they were also based on some micro-social studies, which showed a tendency for employment to increase as income deteriorated.

In chapter 4 I stressed the difficulties encountered when analysing employment data on Mexico. Statistical employment material was barely produced in Mexico in the 1970s and in the 1980s. At the national level, there is no available data on the labour force for the 1980s. Therefore, it is not possible to build an employment time series at the national level corresponding to homogeneous periods of economic growth and of recession, whereby the association between labour force and GDP growth could be established. Nevertheless, for Mexico City there are some labour force figures for the eighties on which I relied to test this association.

Comparing data on Mexico and on Mexico City for the 1979-1991 period, for which national employment data are available, we may be tempted to conclude, as many scholars have done, that the labour force participation rate increased despite the economic crisis. We might then derive the corollary that labour force participation is counter-cyclical and is explained by labour survival strategies. However, by looking at available employment data for the city in the 1980s, I concluded that, in the aftermath of the 1982 economic crisis (1983-1984), labour force participation rates declined as GDP per capita contracted. This evidence showed that the economically active population (EAP) for the city did not behave counter-cyclically, as has been suggested by the labour survival strategies current of thought. Based on these findings we may assume that, after the 1982 economic crisis, employment at the national level may have also declined. Nevertheless, I cannot verify this assumption since national EAP data for the 1980s are not available.

I also pointed out the relevance of standardising employment indicators in order to compare them over time. First, I showed that, although at the national level the uncorrected labour force grew at a rate of almost 4% annually during the period 1979-1991, the standardised labour force grew at 3% annually, that is, 25% lower than the uncorrected labour figures. Moreover, conclusions concerning labour force trends may be completely altered after standardisation is performed. In effect, when comparing uncorrected labour data between 1979 and 1987, I found that the male labour force participation rate in Mexico City remained almost constant (70.5% and 70.8%) whereas the female rate increased (from 32.5% to 34%). But the equivalent calculations show that the male LFPR in fact declined while the female rate remained constant. That is, by means of the equivalent LFPR we arrived at an opposite conclusion to the one derived from uncorrected labour force participation rates. The reason behind these apparently contradictory results is that at the same time that the number of persons involved in the labour market increased very quickly, the average hours of weekly work decreased. The standardisation performed shows that there are alternative employment indicators which may be used in order to clarify contradictory trends in the labour market.

After employment figures were standardised and the employment trends were analysed by different periods, we arrived at the conclusion that the data derived from employment surveys at the national level are not conclusive with regard to the association between changes in the level of the labour force and economic growth. In the case of Mexico City, the evidence I presented challenges the idea that labour force growth is counter-cyclical.

In chapter 5 I analysed some changes in Mexico City's economy. I found that, as in the case of overall labour force participation, the growth of salaried work (and of its percentage share in total occupation) was highly associated with changes in GDP per capita. Nevertheless, the fact that self-employment showed a tendency to increase during recession seemed to support the idea that some "informal" activities grew in response to the income deterioration of households. But, surprisingly, data on Mexico City show that during the recessionary period (1986-1989) income per hour of work of the self-employed was substantially higher than that of salaried workers. Therefore, the increase in self-employment cannot be simply taken as a result of surviving strategies. This was particularly true for women. In effect, earnings per hour of female self-employed workers were much higher than those of female salaried workers.

With regard to the increase in the number of women and adolescents participating in the labour market I found that, upon performing the appropriate analysis, the increase in their participation did not have a counter-cyclical trend, and that, at least in the case of women, this increase may have resulted partially from changes in the demand for labour in Mexico in general and in Mexico City in particular, as well as from a secular trend of women entering the labour market.

The incorporation of women into the labour market in Mexico City was favoured by changes in the structure of labour demand. The increase in the share of services and commercial activities (which also generated a major proportion of salaried jobs) benefited the demand for female labour. Data on Mexico City suggest that women's participation in paid activities may be explained by changes in the demand for labour, rather than by survival strategies. It can be suggested that women, who may have responded to household income losses, would not have succeed if the demand for their labour had not favoured them.

Data derived from my fieldwork also support the idea of an increase in the demand for female labour. Inter-generational comparisons showed that daughters had a better educational level, skill qualification and position at work than their mother's had. In contrast, young male workers had a worse position at work compared with their fathers and sisters, despite their much higher level of education. This micro-contradiction — higher educational levels and lower skilled jobs for the new generation — points out a macro-contradiction: the imbalance between economic stagnation and continued educational improvement. This, in turn, implies a severe criticism of the simplistic theory of human capital which does not take into account that education per se becomes useless unless working opportunities change accordingly.

Moreover, I found that, in general, in Xalpa, children had better educational levels than their parents. This, together with the fact that they entered into the labour market at an older age than their parents, contradicts the perception that children were forced to engage in paid activities as household income declined.[8]

Another piece of evidence that has been used by the labour survival strategies current of thought is the increase in the number of household "earners" derived from the ENIGH surveys. In this case, I also highlighted the difficulties imposed by the limited sources of data. My first conclusion with regard to this issue was that the evidence on changes in income (and thus in income poverty) for the 1977-1984 period is not conclusive. I pointed out in chapter 4 that there remain too many areas of uncertainty regarding this period: uncertainty as to whether this period can be considered a period of crisis; uncertainty as to the evolution of household income; and uncertainty as to the evolution of household earners.

For the 1984-1989 and 1989-1992 periods, the number of earners increased, regardless of changes in GDP per capita and in consumption per capita. This means that this indicator grew during recession as well as during economic growth. Therefore, I concluded that there is no positive correlation between changes in the number of household earners and changes in economic performance or in household income. This same conclusion was maintained when I used a different, more appropriate, indicator to measure household working effort.

Based on the Integrated Poverty Measurement Method (IPMM) — which measures, among other indices, an Excess Working Time index (EWT) — I analysed the relationship between income poverty and time poverty for Mexico City. Time-poor households are households whose EWT is greater than 1. Intuitively, being time-poor means that a person is deprived of free time and/or time for education and, in extreme cases, even lacks time for domestic work. As in all poverty measurements, deprivation is measured against a social standard. Free time is measured indirectly, by time devoted to extra-domestic work.[9]

Based on the EWT index, I found that during the 1984-1989 period, although household real income declined abruptly and income-poverty increased markedly, there was only a slight rise in the extra-domestic work of households, as measured by hours of work (i.e. in time-poverty). My findings show that a major proportion (nearly two thirds) of the income-poor households were time-non-poor. This means that, although their income was insufficient, their available human resources for extra-domestic work were not fully mobilised to that purpose, that is, to increase household income. I also found that the proportion of income-poor, time-non-poor households increased considerably between 1984 and 1989. These two facts mean that income-poor households were unable either to increase the number of household members engaged in the labour market or to increase the hours worked by previously engaged members. The mere existence of this group, and its steep increase in the period 1984-

1989, suggests that, although as income declined some households may have responded by increasing the number of household members engaged in economic activities, this strategy was either not successful or it did not compensate the overall reduction of extra-domestic work performed by other households members of the above-mentioned group. My findings enabled me to assess the Mexican economy's incapacity to absorb, in real terms, this additional work effort. Based on these findings, despite the idea that "the actions and reactions of the poor ... may impact on the national economic structure" (Escobar, 1996: 540), my data suggest, as Chant (1994:220) observed for Puerto Vallarta, Mexico, that "no matter how much people may wish to protect incomes, the growing scarcity of viable employment options makes it difficult for them to do so."

The evidence presented in this book has led to the following central conclusions:

1) Some structural reform policies had a negative impact on household income, particularly household income subject to wage controls.
2) Despite the fact that household income declined and that income poverty increased, other welfare indicators improved for two main reasons. On the one hand, social public spending was protected during the period 1982-1994. This allowed an increase in health care coverage, a rise in educational resource indices (an indicator of quality improvement in education), and an expanded coverage of public infrastructure (piped water, sewerage and home electricity). On the other hand, some policy reforms, such as trade liberalisation, may have had a positive impact on household consumption, by reducing the prices of some household appliances. Additionally, dwelling improvements might have been induced by the expansion in the coverage of public infrastructure. Therefore, apparently, the paradox of improvement in welfare indicators and a decline in income has thus been solved.
3) Although it has been said that, after the 1982 economic crisis, households set in motion labour survival strategies, I have found that this proposition does not seem to hold true, if work effort is measured by hours of work. When analysis is conducted with the pertinent, comparable and standardised labour data, and these are linked with the corresponding changes in Mexico's economic performance, it becomes clear that the increases in the labour force are not counter-cyclical, as proposed by the labour survival strategies current of thought. This finding is supported by the lack

of evidence that households increase their extra-domestic work effort when their income declines. This also means that there is no evidence to believe that the level of employment in Mexico is determined by the supply of labour. On the contrary, the evidence suggests that employment is highly determined by the demand for labour.

These conclusions (and the growing criticism of the policy package of the Washington Consensus) have some important policy implications. In the first place, inflation control should cease to be the highest priority of economic policy in Mexico. Instead, as stated by Stiglitz, poverty reduction or population wellbeing should be the central goal. In the second place, wage control, as an instrument for controlling inflation, should be abandoned. In the third place, the importance of public social expenditure should be enhanced, especially in the light of the protective role it played during the eighties. Universal, non-targeted programmes of subsidies, which, under the Washington Consensus, are increasingly under attack, performed this protective role. In the fourth place, my conclusion regarding the dominant role of the demand for labour in the evolution of employment highlights the role of economic growth in the reduction of poverty. This, in turn, brings us back to the fact that the policy package of the Washington Consensus was unable, in the case of Mexico, to promote a steady process of growth. An alternative is required.

Notes

[1] As noted previously, the IMF/World Bank policy reform packages see trade liberalisation, macroeconomic stability, getting prices right, and the reduction of State intervention as preconditions for a good economic performance.

[2] The Bank holds that there are other two factors that explain Mexico's slow economic recovery: " ... (i) the obsolescence of old capital in the wake of reforms, ... [and] ... (ii) the existence of long lags in the impact of reforms ..." (World Bank, 1998: v). However, according to the Bank, these other two factors do not appear to have been quantitatively significant in explaining Mexico's slow recovery.

[3] Senior Vice President, Development Economics, and Chief Economist of the World Bank.

[4] Stiglitz also points out that it has been found that low levels of inflation may even improve economic performance relative to what it would have been with zero inflation (*Ibid.*:8).

[5] It should be noted that at present, in 1999, the Mexican government still considers a major priority the control of inflation. It has set a goal of no more than an annual rate of 13.5% in consumer price increases for 1999, for which it has implemented restrictive

monetary and fiscal policies, despite the fact that the inflation rate in 1998 was around 18%.
6 Extreme poverty was calculated with the COPLAMAR (1983) poverty line at 1996 prices.
7 Nonetheless, there is some evidence that indicates that infant mortality related to undernutrition increased during stabilisation and adjustment. This may indicate a deterioration in household income. More empirical research should be done in order to clarify whether the nutritional status of the population was negatively affected during the stabilisation and adjustment periods.
8 This conclusion has to be taken with caution since it is based on Xalpa findings. For the methodological problems related to the Xalpa survey, refer to the Methodological Appendix 1
9 This time devoted to extra-domestic work is compared against two standards. One, derived from the Mexican Constitution, is that persons who work (extra-domestically) should work no more than 48 hours a week. The other norm is the definition of how many persons should work (extra-domestically) in a given household. This is household specific. The methodology followed makes this depend on two things. On the one hand, the methodology excludes the persons who for diverse reasons are not performing extra-domestic work (handicapped, retired, part of the time of students). On the other hand, it takes into consideration the requirements of domestic work, which in turn depend on size and age structure of the household, on the availability of labour saving domestic appliances and equipment, on access to day-care for children, on disposition of running water within the household, and on the access of the household to paid domestic help. Both excluded persons and domestic labour requirements are expressed in number (or fractions) of persons-time (workweeks). Both of these quantities are subtracted from the number of members in the age range from 15 to 69 years old. This gives the number of persons who should work. Thus, the members of a household will be time-poor if the effective hours of weekly extra-domestic work outnumber the normative hours of extra-domestic work (the product of the number of persons who should work extra-domestically by 48 hours for each one).

Appendix: The Methodology for Measuring Poverty[1]

1. THE INTEGRATED POVERTY MEASUREMENT METHOD (IPMM)

The IPMM (Boltvinik, 1992 and 1994b) combines two methodologies. On the one hand, a poverty line-time procedure based on the Normative Basket of Essential Satisfiers (NBES). On the other hand, what Boltvinik calls the improved version of the Unsatisfied Basic Needs (UBN) method (Boltvinik, 1992 and 1998b).

Its foundation is the following conception of a household's sources of welfare and the consequent critique of the PL and the UBN methodologies (Boltvinik, 1992: 355-356):

> The satisfaction of needs at the household or the personal level depends on the following six welfare sources: (*a*) current income; (*b*) rights of access to free (or subsidised) goods and services; (*c*) property (or rights of use) of durable goods that provide basic services (basic accumulated patrimony); (*d*) knowledge and skills, conceived not as a means to income but as an expressions of a person's capabilities for understanding and for doing; (*e*) available time for education, for recreation and for domestic tasks; and (*f*) non-basic asset holdings and borrowing capability.
>
> There is a certain degree of substitution possibilities between some of these sources. With a higher income one can substitute some rights of access, by meeting educational and health requirements through the market. Lack of property of some durable goods (especially housing) can also be substituted by renting them. These substitution possibilities are not unlimited, however. Additional income cannot substitute educational deprivation or the lack of available time. If water and sewerage networks have not been built, it might not be possible on an individual basis to have access to such services.
>
> The main limitation of both the PL and the UBN methodologies — in terms of how the latter has been applied in Latin America — is that both methodologies proceed as if satisfaction of basic needs depended only on a couple of those welfare sources: the PL methodology, as if satisfaction depended only on current income or only on current income

and non-basic assets; the UBN methodology, in its usual applications in Latin America, as if need satisfaction depended only on basic asset holdings or on rights of access to free or subsidised services (as UBN indicators refer mostly to housing, water, sewerage, and child attendance at a primary school).

In other words, the PL methodology does not consider sources (*b*) to (*f*) when comparing the poverty line with household income, or sources (*b*) to (*e*) when comparing the poverty line it with household consumption expenditures. The usual applications of the UBN in Latin America disregard current income and sources (*d*) to (*f*). Both methods thus have a partial view of poverty and tend to underestimate its incidence. To the extent that the welfare sources considered by both methods are different, we can conclude that, rather than being alternative procedures, as they are usually considered, the two are complementary methodologies.

The IPMM was developed to account fully for the six welfare sources. In order to achieve full complementarity of the two methods on which the IPMM rests, it is necessary to specify which needs are to be assessed by UBN and which by PL. In other words, it is necessary to specify the satisfaction of which needs is to be assessed directly and which is to be assessed indirectly by income. In principle, all needs the satisfaction of which depends predominantly — for most households — on public expenditure, on household patrimony (accumulated assets) and on available time should be assessed directly (UBN). Accordingly, the satisfaction of the following needs should be assessed directly:

1. Water and sewerage.
2. Educational level and school attendance.
3. Electricity.
4. Housing.
5. Household furniture and basic appliances.
6. Free time.

Information on free time and on household furniture and basic appliances is not generally available, although the survey, on which the calculations presented in this book are based,[2] included questions on basic appliances and on working hours. However incomplete these may be, they provide a good proxy and they were thus used.

The indirect satisfaction of the following needs should be assessed by PL:

7. Food.
8. Clothing, shoes and personal care.
9. Hygiene (personal and household).
10. Transport and communications.
11. Recreation, information and culture. Income devoted to expenditures on this need is, nevertheless, not enough. Free time, included in item 6, is also required. The best alternate procedure, which would require specialised questions in surveys, would be to identify its level of satisfaction directly (thus making it a UBN need).
12. Additionally, almost all needs identified by UBN imply household current expenditures, which ought to be considered in calculating the poverty line.
13. Health care and social security. Health care and social security can be met through rights of access to free services — welfare source (*b*) — or through the market. This is especially important in countries that lack a National Health Service embracing all the population. Thus a mixed procedure should be followed, under which if individuals (households) lack rights of access to these services, their income is assessed to see if they can afford, besides items 7-12, private insurance for health care and for old age and other risks.

The specific application, the results of which were presented in chapters 3 and 4, considered five dimensions by UBN, one by a mixed UBN-PL procedure (health and social security), and one UBN indicator (working hours) which, combined with income to conform the income-time dimension, was designated as PLT. The five UBN dimensions and the mixed UBN-PL procedure are the following (worded as deprivation indicators)[3]:

1. Housing quality and quantity inadequacy, which is formed by two components: 1.1. Building materials inadequacy (as used in walls); 1.2. Insufficiency of housing space per dweller, i.e. overcrowding, as measured by the relation between total rooms and total number of dwellers. The indicator for the dimension is *the product* of the indicators of the components inasmuch as they are judged to be strictly complementary.

2. Inadequacy of sanitary conditions, integrated as a weighted average (using relative costs as weights) of three specific indicators: water supply, sewerage (or similar) and exclusive toilet.
3. Inadequacy of other services is the weighted average (again using relative costs as weights) of electricity and telephone indicators in metropolitan areas. In non-metropolitan areas, Boltvinik reduces this dimension only to electricity.
4. Inadequacy of basic household appliances. In the normative level, appliances included are those associated with food preparation and conservation, hygiene and recreation (e.g., stove, refrigerator, iron, washing machine, TV set, etc.).
5. Educational insufficiency, which is measured by educational levels, where literacy acts as a controlling element.
6. Inadequate access to health care and social security (mixed UBN-PL dimension).

The PLT index (income-time poverty) was built first by dividing household income per equivalent adult by an indicator of excess working time (EWT)[4] and then dividing this result by PL or by the Extreme Poverty Line (EPL). The EPL is based on a Normative Basket of Subsistence Satisfiers (NBSS), which was built by deducting from the NBES all items not strictly required for dignified subsistence in Mexican society.

The procedure of the improved UBN methodology starts by building an achievement indicator that results from dividing the household score by the normative score. In some indicators the scores have to be imputed to qualitatively different optional solutions (e.g., sanitary conditions, building materials). By dividing by the normative score, the achievement indicator loses any specific dimension it might have had and becomes a standardised pure number. The next step is to uniform, as far as possible, the range of variation of the standardised pure number by re-scaling all values above one (above the normative score) when there are values above two, so that these values will range from more than one to two. The idea is to get all indicators to vary from 0 to 2, with 1 as the normative value. The last step is to transform this achievement indicator into a deprivation indicator, which is done by subtracting its value from one. Deprivation indicators will thus vary from +1 to -1, with 0 as the normative value. It follows that positive values express deprivation and negative values express welfare. Unfortunately, it was not possible to achieve the complete range for all indicators. Some are truncated indicators whose range shows only normative and deprivation values (0 to

+1) but is unable to show welfare values, due to the limited options built in questionnaires.

The six UBN indicators, including the mixed one, are combined, through a weighted average, into the UBN integrated indicator for each household, which indicates UBN poverty intensity for household j: $I(UBN)_j$. On the other hand, the above described PLT combination of income and time yields PLT poverty intensity for each household: $I(PLT)_j$. The weighted average of both intensity measures yields poverty intensity by the Integrated Poverty Measurement Method: $I(IPMM)_j$, which shows both if the household is poor/non-poor and its degree of intensity of poverty/welfare. Both for weighting UBN dimensions between them and for combining PLT and UBN, the cost structure provided by COPLAMAR's NBES is used (COPLAMAR, 1982 and 1983).

Once the three poverty-intensity measures have been calculated for each household, each household is classified — both for the partial PLT and the UBN methods as well as for the IPMM — into one of six strata, three for poor and three for non poor.

2. THE POVERTY LINE (PL) METHOD BASED ON A NORMATIVE BASKET OF ESSENTIAL SATISFIERS (NBES)

The first step in the PL-NBES methodology (COPLAMAR, 1982 and 1983) is the determination of the basket of goods and services required by a household of a given size during a given period (e.g. a year). The quantities required, in the case of consumer durables, are different (larger) than their annual use. For instance, a household requires a stove but uses, consumes or depreciates only 0.10 stoves each year. In non-durable goods (and in services) both quantities are equal. It is the vector of annual use that constitutes the Normative Basket of Essential Satisfiers. Besides the economies of scale associated with household size, an issue that the NBES did not solve, there are two main additional problems in calculating normative requirements that COPLAMAR's NBES did solve. First, what are the foundations for those normative requirements? This is the most complex problem in poverty studies and where fewer consensuses prevail. COPLAMAR's NBES departed from two criteria: 1) Mexico's reality as reflected in the list of goods and services frequently consumed by households; and 2) Mexican law, which reflects a mixture of reality and goals. Operationalisation of the first criterion began with the identification of what COPLAMAR called socially generalised consumption goods and services. Starting with the list of goods and services included in the consumption budget of the seventh decile of income distribution, and selecting only those that constituted socially generalised consumption items,[5] a second and more reduced list was produced. This second list was then subjected to a process of elimination of luxury goods, arriving thus at a third list, which could be called *socially generalised basic goods and services*. The second criterion considered rights, both social rights, which the law establishes for all inhabitants, and a specific class of rights, which the law establishes for people working for a wage or a salary. These rights were expressed into goods and services and were added to the third list, arriving thus at a fourth and final list of goods and services, which might be called *socially generalised and entitled goods and services*.

The goods and services in this fourth list were classified into two groups. On the one hand, those satisfiers that have to be met through private consumption, i.e., whose cost must be paid (or produced) by households. On the other hand, those satisfiers that are to be met through public expenditures. *Only satisfiers in the first group should form part of the poverty line,* as this is what one compares with household's current income or private consumption expenditures. Two possibilities are open here. The simplest one consists in defining a unique classification of satisfiers in both groups, which is then applied to all households. The second possibility consists in specifying for each household a classification according to its particular circumstances (e.g., for a household lacking access to governmental health services, one would include the cost of private health-care in its poverty line). In COPLAMAR NBES the first approach was adopted, which simplifies things but implies loosing precision. The following were defined as satisfiers to be met by public expenditures for all households: primary and secondary education (nine years of schooling), health services, and water and sewerage infrastructure. COPLAMAR assumed, for the purposes of measurement, that households would have free access to these services and would have to pay (purchase) or produce all other satisfiers. This simplified solution underestimates the poverty line — and thus poverty as well — for all those households that have no opportunity of access to these governmental services.

The resulting poverty line is then compared (when PL is applied by itself) with household income. Here again COPLAMAR's procedure was a simplified one. The poverty line was defined for the national average household size and age structure. The alternative, and a seemingly better procedure, would be to define a poverty line for each household according to the number, age and sex of its members. An intermediate procedure would be to calculate a per capita or per equivalent adult poverty line and to compare it with the corresponding concept for each household.[6] This is the procedure adopted by Boltvinik (1998b) and the one I have used for Mexico City.

When the poverty line methodology is applied as part of the IPMM, as is the case here, in calculating income poverty one has to subtract the cost of those items verified by the UBN methodology from the cost of the NBES, whereupon the resulting poverty line expresses only the cost of those items whose satisfaction is verified indirectly through income and which have been listed in the previous Section. This PL, which could be called the IPMM PL, is then compared not with household income but with household disposable income after subtracting from the first the amounts spent on the UBN goods and services.

3. ADJUSTING HOUSEHOLD INCOME TO NATIONAL ACCOUNTS (NA)

Cortés (1997, pp. 133-142) defined a procedure by which household income can be adjusted to National Accounts. This procedure was followed by Boltvinik (1998b) and I have also followed it here.

I will not describe in great detail the procedure followed but limit the exposition to show the main steps and the final result: the coefficients by which each source of household income has to be multiplied in order to arrive at figures which are compatible with National Accounts.

National Accounts (NA) cannot be regarded as a very accurate source of information. National Accounts have frequently been regarded as underestimating income derived from some informal activities. Nevertheless, NA have never been, as far as I know, criticised for overestimating income. Given this fact and given the fact that the estimation provided by Household Income and Expenditure Surveys of household national income and expenditure is lower than the same totals estimated by National Accounts, it seems necessary to adjust the survey figures to National Accounts, which are regarded at least to provide a minimum correct estimate for these magnitudes.

Mexican National Accounts do not calculate the household account, whereupon household income in National Accounts has to be estimated first. This is done by adding an estimation of savings by households to the amount of private consumption (from which a small proportion is subtracted which is regarded as consumption by non-profit organisations) provided by National Accounts. That estimation is obtained, paradoxically, from the percentage this consumption represents from expenditure in the income and expenditure surveys themselves.

Once this is done, the next step, which is not straightforward, is decomposing household income (NA) into its main sources: wages, entrepreneurial rent, and property rent, the latter item being subdivided into property rent and interest from capital. The income sources that are explicitly provided by NA are wages and real estate property rentals (this last is a branch of production, including owner-occupied imputed rents). The rest have to be estimated from external sources. This is done in great detail by Cortés. But before this is done, wages have to be made comparable in both sources. In their original presentation, they are not. In the ENIGH Surveys all income concepts are net of taxes and social security payments, whereas the income concepts presented in National Accounts include the full cost of labour from the entrepreneurial point of view. Cortés applied the income tax rates and social security rates to wage income in ENIGH and transformed them into figures comparable with NA. To estimate entrepreneurial rent and interest payments this author resorted to the official economic censuses.

Table M.1. Adjustment coefficients for income sources in the ENIGH surveys to make them equal to National Accounts estimates

Concept	1984	1989	1992
Wages	1.343	1.029	0.942 =1.0*
Entrepreneurial rents	5.634	4.975	4.598
Property rent			
Real estate rentals	1.687	1.310	1.123
Interests	22.028	8.194	44.442

Source: Cortés (1997), table 4.22: 137.
*The generally accepted procedure is that when ENIGH estimates are larger than NA no adjustment is performed

Once household income and its decomposition amongst income sources in NA are ready, the next step is to compare the resulting totals with the corresponding figures in ENIGH. This comparison provides the coefficients with which each income source, household by household, is to be multiplied in ENIGH, in each year, to obtain expanded income figures which can then be used to estimate poverty. The results are summarised in the table above.

As can be seen, except for coefficients of wages and real estate rentals, the other two coefficients are so huge that the appropriateness of performing the adjustment is brought into doubt. Unfortunately, the coefficient of entrepreneurial rent, which is so absurdly big, is applied both to income derived from large enterprises and from self-employment. This results in a very untidy estimate of poverty.

This is the reason why Cortés (1997, Appendix 4.6: 267-289) developed a more refined method for adjusting income data to National Accounts, which unfortunately depends on one question (the size of the enterprise the interviewed person is working in), which was not asked in 1984 or in 1989, but only in 1992. This refined procedure yields coefficients of adjustment of entrepreneurial rent according to the size of the enterprise. These coefficients in 1992 go from 1.669 in the micro-enterprises (1 to 5 workers) to, by way of example, 7.6 in those ranging from 51 to 100 workers, to 58.349 in those with 101 to 250 workers, and up to 271.455 in the larger ones (251 workers and more). This shows that the most important underestimation of entrepreneurial rent is to be found in the large enterprises, showing that this type of income is practically not captured by the ENIGH Surveys. Knowing this, but being unable to solve it, as occupied population in 1984 and 1989 cannot be identified by size of enterprise, makes one conclude that the results presented in the text underestimate, to an important degree, the level of poverty of all self-employed workers or of persons working in small enterprises.

Adjusting income data for the Metropolitan Area of Mexico City with the same coefficients of adjustment used for the national level, a procedure which no doubt is very easy to criticise, is the standard procedure employed by most researchers, who do some times disaggregate their results, at least by rural and urban areas. This is the procedure adopted by Boltvinik (1998), by INEGI-CEPAL (1993) and by many others. An alternative procedure, which is sometimes used, is to distinguish agricultural and non-agricultural income and to calculate correction coefficients for each one of these concepts.

Notes

[1] The text of this Appendix has been translated and adapted freely from Boltvinik (1998b).

2   Encuesta Nacional de Ingresos y Gastos de los Hogares (ENIGH) –National Income and Expenditure Household Survey (see INEGI, 1989b,1992b, 1993c).
3   The methodology used here, for the purpose of measuring the 1984-1989-1992 evolution of poverty in Mexico City, which is the same Boltvinik uses for the same purpose at the national level, is a somewhat simplified version of the methodology used by him for measuring poverty in 1992, as a consequence of the more limited scope of the 1984 questionnaire, and, in some respects, also of the 1989 questionnaire. The main simplifications in the methodology are: a) only materials used on walls, but not on roofs and floors, are used for qualifying housing quality; b) a simplified crowding indicator is used because of the lack of the number of dormitories; c) the sanitary indicator is simplified, since the only quality of the bathroom which can be taken into account is its exclusivity for the household members (and does not consider if the toilet has running water and if there is running water in other water taps); and d) the educational indicator has to be constructed only with educational levels attained and literacy (as school attendance was not registered).
4   EWT is equal to 1.00 when there is no excess of working time. Thus dividing by 1.00 leaves income unmodified. If there is excess of working time, EWT becomes larger than 1.00, whereupon dividing by EWT is equivalent to calculating what the income of the household would be if they had worked only the standard hours. When EWT is less than 1.00, the division is performed only for households whose income is above PL before the division, but not for households whose income is below PL, on the assumption that working below the weekly standard hours can be a choice for income non-poor households, but is a forced situation for the income-poor.
5   The operational definition of a socially generalised consumption item, for a given population group, is that expenditure was reported at least by a proportion of households that is 50% or more of the proportion of households which reported this expenditure in the ninth decile of income distribution.
6   There is, nonetheless, a somewhat strong counter argument for using the national average poverty line, as households can be regarded as being poor or not according to average demography and labour market participation rates, introducing a concept of potentially poor if households had this national average household size and structure. Perhaps an example will clarify this. A household, composed of a couple with no children, might be classified as non-poor. But the couple might be restrained from having children because they are afraid of being unable to cope with expenditures, not only because monetary needs would be larger, but because the woman might have to discontinue her job in order to take care of the children. Are they really non-poor?

Bibliography

Ajayi, Simeon Ibi (1995), "The State of Research on the Macroeconomic Effectiveness of Structural Adjustment Programmes in Sub-Saharan Africa", in Van Der Hoeven, Rolph and Fred Van Der Kraaij (eds.), pp. 54-69.

Anderson, Michel; Frank Bechhofer and Jonathan Gershuny (eds.), (1994), *The Social and Political Economy of the Household*, The Social Change and Economic Life Initiative Series, Oxford University Press.

Anderson, Michel; Frank Bechhofer and Stephen Kendrick (1994), "Individual and Household Strategies", in Anderson, *et al.* (eds.), pp. 19-67.

Aspe, Pedro (1993), *Economic Transformation, the Mexican Way*, The MIT Press, Cambridge, Massachusetts, London, England.

Azam, Jean-Paul (1995), "The Uncertain Distributional Impact of Structural Adjustment in Sub-Saharan Africa", in Van Der Hoeven, Rolph and Fred Van Der Kraaij (eds.), pp. 100-113.

Banco de Mexico, *The Mexican Economy*, Mexico, several years.

Bassols Batalla, Angel; Carlos Bustamante Lemus; Javier Delgadillo Macias and Gloria González (1992) (coord.), *México, Planeación Urbana, Procesos Políticos y Realidad*, Universidad Nacional Autónoma de México, Instituto de Investigaciones Económicas, Mexico.

Bazdresch, Carlos; Nisso Bucay; Soledad Loaeza; and Nora Lustig (1993), *México Auge, Crisis y Ajuste*, El Trimestre Económico, Num. 73, Fondo de Cultura Económica, Mexico.

Beccaria, Luis; Julio Boltvinik; Juan Carlos Feres; Oscar Fresneda; Arturo León and Amartya Sen (1992), *América Latina: El Reto de la Pobreza, Características, Evolución y Perspectivas*, Proyecto Regional Para la Superación de la Pobreza, United Nations Development Programme, Bogota.

Benería, Lourdes (1992), "The Mexican Debt Crisis: Restructuring the Economy and the Household", in Benería, Lourdes and Shelley Feldman, pp. 81-104.

Benería, Lourdes and Shelley Feldman (1992), *Unequal Burden, Economic Crises, Persistent Poverty, and Women's Work*, Westview Press, Boulder, San Francisco and Oxford.

Benería, Lourdes and Martha Roldán (1987), *The Crossroads of Class & Gender, Industrial Homework, Subcontracting, and Household Dynamics in Mexico City*, The University of Chicago Press, Chicago, London.

Blanco, Mercedes (1996), "Women's Employment and Careers in Mexico", in Randall, Laura (ed.), pp. 315-322.

Bolívar, Rene Coulomb and Carmen Muñoz B. (coords.), *Metrópoli, Globalidad y Modernización*, Programa Reencuentro de 2 Ciudades, México, Santiago de Chile, Universidad Autónoma Metropolitana, Unidad Azcapotzalco.

Boltvinik, Julio (1994a), *Pobreza y Estratificación Social en México*, Instituto Nacional de Estadística, Geografía e Informática, El Colegio de México, Universidad Nacional Autónoma de México, Mexico.
——— (1994b), "Poverty Measurement and Alternative Indicators of Development", in Van der Hoeven and Anker (ed.), pp. 57-83.
——— (1994c), "La Satisfacción de las Necesidades Esenciales en México en los Setenta y Ochenta", in Moncayo and Woldenberg (coords.), pp. 99-75.
——— (1995a), "La Evolución de la Pobreza en México, Entre 1984 y 1992, Según CEPAL-INEGI", in *Sociológica*, Universidad Autónoma Metropolina-Azcapotzalco, September-December, pp.11-40.
——— (1996), "Poverty in Latin America: a Critical Analysis of Three Studies", in *International Social Science Journal*, Num. 148, June, Blackwell Publishers, UNESCO, pp. 245-260.
——— (1997a), "La Magnitud y Características de la Pobreza en las Colonias", in Schteingart (coord.), pp. 427-478.
——— (1997b), "Diversas Visiones Sobre Pobreza en México. Factores Determinantes", in *Política y Cultura*, Spring 97, Num. 8, Universidad Autónoma Metropolitana-Xochimilco, Mexico, pp.115-135.
——— (1998a), "Condiciones de Vida y Niveles de Ingreso en México, 1970-95", in Ibáñez Aguirre, José Antonio (coord.), pp. 251-395.
——— (1998b), *Evolución y Características de la Pobreza en México. Una Visión Integrada*, Ph.D. Thesis Draft, CIESAS Occidente, Guadalajara, Mexico.
——— (1999) "Ensayo sobre las consecuencias de las políticas económica y social. México 1979-1995", (unpublished).
Boltvinik, Julio and Carlos Echarri (1997), "Economic Crisis and Mortality Change in Mexico: Searching for Linkages", Paper presented at the UNU/WIDER Project Meeting on "*Economic Shocks, Social Stress and the Demographic Impact*", 17-19 April 1997, Helsinki.
Boltvinik, Julio and Enrique Hernández-Laos (1991), *La Pobreza y las Necesidades Esenciales en América Latina. El Caso de México*, Proyecto Regional para la Superación de la Pobreza (PNUD), Universidad Autónoma Metropolitana, Mexico.
Boltvinik, Julio and Alicia Puyana (1995), *Economic Reform in Latin America and Its Effects on Poverty Level, The Lessons of Mexico*, Report to International Organisation, Mexico, Unpublished.
Bourguignon, F and Morrison C. (1992), *Adjustment and Equity in Developing Countries: A New Approach*, Paris, OECD.
Breman, Jan (1985), "A Dualistic Labour System? A Critique of the 'Informal Sector' Concept", in Bromley, Ray (ed.) pp. 43-64.
Bromley, Ray (ed.), (1985), *Planning for Small Enterprises in Third World Cities*, Pergamon Press, Oxford, New York, Toronto, Sydney, Paris, Frankfurt.
Bromley, Ray and Chris Gerry (eds.), (1979a), *Casual Work and Poverty in Third World Cities*, John Wiley & Sons, Ltd., Great Britain.
——— (1979b) "Who are the Casual Poor?", in Bromley and Gerry (eds.), pp.3-23.

Brydon, Lynne and Sylvia Chant (1989), *Women in the Third World: Gender Issues in Rural and Urban Areas*, Edward Elgar Publishing Limited, Great Britain.
Bulmer-Thomas, Victor (ed.), (1996a), *The New Economic Model in Latin America and Its Impact on Income Distribution and Poverty*, Institute of Latin America Studies Series, University of London, Great Britain.
_____ (1996b), "Introduction", in Bulmer-Thomas, Victor (ed.), pp. 7-26.
Bustelo, Eduardo and Alberto Minujin (eds.), (1998), *Todos Entran, Propuesta Para Sociedades Incluyentes*, Colección Cuadernos de Debate, UNICEF, Santillana, Colombia.
Buvinic, Mayra (1983), "Women's Issues in Third World Poverty", in Buvinic *et al.* (eds.), pp. 14-31.
Buvinic, Mayra, Margaret A. Lycette and William Paul McGreevey (eds.), (1983), *Women and Poverty in the Third World*, The Johns Hopkins University Press, Baltimore and London.
Camposortega Cruz, Sergio (1992), "Evolución y Tendencia Demográficas de la ZMCM", in Consejo Nacional de Población, pp. 3-15.
Castells, Manuel and Alejandro Portes (1989), "World Underneath: The Origins, Dynamics, and Effects of the Informal Economy", in Portes, *et al.*, pp. 11-37.
CENIET (Centro Nacional de Información y Estadística del Trabajo) (1977), *Encuesta de Ingresos y Gastos Familiares, 1975*, Secretaría del Trabajo y Previsión Social, Mexico.
CEPAL-PNUD (1986), "Magnitud de la Pobreza en los Años Ochenta", Santiago de Chile.
_____ (1992), "Procedimientos para Medir la Pobreza en América Latina con el Método de la Línea de Pobreza", in *Comercio Exterior*, Volumen 42, Num. 4, April, pp.340-353, Mexico.
Chant, Sylvia (1991), *Women and Survival in Mexican Cities, Perspectives on Gender, Labour Markets and Low-Income Households*, Manchester University Press, Manchester and New York.
_____ (1994), "Women, Work and Household Survival Strategies in Mexico, 1982-1992: Past Trends, Current Tendencies and Future Research", in *Bulletin of Latin America Research*, Vol.13, No. 2., May, pp. 202-233.
El Colegio de México, Fundación Friedrich Ebert, and El Colegio de la Frontera Norte (1992), *Ajuste Estructural, Mercados Laborales y el TLC*, El Colegio de México, Mexico.
Consejo Nacional de Población (1992), *Zona Metropolitana de la Ciudad de México, Problemática Actual y Perspectivas Demográficas y Urbanas*, CONAPO, México.
_____ (1993), *Indicadores Socioeconómicos e Índice de Marginación Municipal, 1990*, CONAPO, Comisión Nacional de Agua, Mexico.
Coordinación Nacional del Plan Nacional de Zonas Deprimidas y Grupos Marginados (1982a), *Necesidades Esenciales y Estructura Productiva en México. Lineamientos de Programación para el Proyecto Nacional*, Presidencia de la República, Government of Mexico.

_____ (1982b), *Alimentación*, COPLAMAR, Siglo XXI Editores, Vol. 1, Mexico.

_____ (1982c), *Salud*, COPLAMAR, Siglo XXI Editores, Vol. 4, Mexico.

_____ (1983), *Macroeconomía de las Necesidades Esenciales en México, Situación Actual y Perspectivas al Año 2000*, COPLAMAR, Siglo XXI Editores, Second Edition, Mexico.

Córdoba, José (1994), "Mexico", in Williamson, John (ed.), pp. 232-284.

Cornia, Giovanni Andrea (1987) "Adjustment at the Household Level: Potentials and Limitations of Survival Strategies", in Cornia *et. al*, pp. 90-104.

Cornia, Giovanni Andrea and Frances Stewart (1995), "Food Subsidies: Two Errors of Targeting", in Stewart, Frances pp. 82-107.

Cornia, Giovanni Andrea; Richard Jolly and Frances Stewart (eds.), (1987), *Adjustment With a Human Face, Protecting the Vulnerable and Promoting Growth*, Vol. I Claredon Press, Oxford.

Cortés, Fernando (1995a), "*Tendencias en la Distribución del Ingreso de los Hogares Desde 1977 a 1992. Apuntes Para una Discusión*", Paper presented in the Income Inequality and Poverty Meeting of the Development Crisis in Mexico Seminar, April, Tepoztlán, Morelos, Mexico, unpublished.

_____ (1995b), "El Ingreso de los Hogares en Contexto de Crisis, Ajuste, y Estabilización: un Análisis de su Distribución en México, 1977-1992", in *Estudios Sociológicos*, Vol. XIII, Num. 37, Mexico, January-April.

_____ (1995c), "Procesos Sociales y Demográficos en Auxilio de la Economía Neoliberal. Análisis de la Distribución del Ingreso en México Durante los Ochenta", in *Revista Mexicana de Sociología*, Num. 2/95, Mexico, April-June.

_____ (1996), *La Distribución del Ingreso de los Hogares Mexicanos Vis a Vis los Modelos de Desarrollo*, Mexico, (unpublished).

_____ (1997), *Distribución del Ingreso en México en Épocas de Estabilización y Reforma Económica*, Ph.D. thesis in Social Sciences, CIESAS, Universidad de Guadalajara, Área de Antropología e Historia, Mexico.

Cortés, Fernando and Rosa María Rubalcava (1990), "Algunas Consecuencias del Ajuste: México post 1982", Centro de Estudios Sociológicos, El Colegio de México, September, (unpublished).

_____ (1991), *Autoexplotación Forzada y Equidad por Empobrecimiento*, El Colegio de México, Mexico.

_____ (1994), *El Ingreso de los Hogares*, INEGI, Colegio de México, IIS-UNAM, Mexico.

Coulomb, René (1992), "El Acceso a la Vivienda", in Consejo Nacional de Población, pp. 157-177.

Damián, Araceli (1992), "Ciudad de México: los Servicios Urbanos en los Noventa", in *Vivienda Nueva Época*, Instituto del Fondo Nacional de la Vivienda para los Trabajadores, Vol. 3, Num. 1, January-April, Mexico.

De la Peña, Guillermo; Juan Manuel Durán; Agustín Escobar and Javier García de Alba (eds.), (1990), *Crisis, Conflicto, y Sobrevivencia. Estudios sobre la

Sociedad Urbana en México, Universidad de Guadalajara and CIESAS, México.
De Oliveira, Orlandina and Brígida García (1986), "El Mercado de Trabajo en la Ciudad de México", in Garza, Gustavo and Programa de Intercambio Científico y Capacitación Técnica, Departamento de Distrito Federal (comps.), pp. 140-145.
Dex, Shirley (ed.), (1991), *Life and Work History Analyses. Quantitative and Qualitative Developments*, Routledge, London
Dudley, Seers (ed.), (1984), *Pioneers in Development*, Oxford University Press, England.
Economic Commission for Latin America and the Caribbean (1992), *Social Equity and Changing Production Patterns: An Interacted Approach*, Chile.
_____ (1995), *Economic Survey of Latin America and the Caribbean*, United Nations.
_____ *Statistical Yearbook*, several years
Elbadawi, I.; Ghura and Uwujaren G. (1992), "World Bank Adjustment Lending and Economic Performance in Sub-Saharan Africa in the 1980s", in *Policy Research Working Papers*, Num. 1000, Washington D.C., World Bank.
Escobar Latapí, Agustín (1995) "Movilidad, Reestructuración, y Clase Social en México: El Caso de Guadalajara", in *Estudios Sociológicos*, El Colegio de México, Vol. XIII, Num. 38, May-August, Mexico, pp. 231-259.
_____ (1996), "Mexico, Poverty as Politics and Academic Disciplines", in Oyen, Else and Syed Abdus Else (eds.), pp. 539-566.
FitzGerald, E.V.K. (1996), "The New Trade Regimen, Macroeconomic Behaviour and Income Distribution in Latin America", in Bulmer-Thomas, Victor (ed.), pp. 29-52.
Friedmann, Santiago; Nora Lustig and Arianna Legovini (1995), "Mexico: Social Spending and Food Subsidies during Adjustment in the 1980s", in Lustig (ed.), pp. 335-374.
García, Brígida (1994), *Determinantes de la Oferta de Mano de Obra en México*, Cuadernos de Trabajo Num. 6, Secretaría del Trabajo y Previsión Social, Mexico.
García, Brígida and Orlandina de Oliveira (1994), *Trabajo Femenino y Vida Familiar en México*, El Colegio de México, Mexico.
Garza, Gustavo (1990), "The Metropolitan Character of Urbanization in Mexico, 1990-1988", in Yamada, Mutsuo, *et al.*, pp. 3-30.
_____ (1998) "Normatividad Urbanística Virtual en la Ciudad de México", in Garza and Fernando A. Rodríguez (comps.), pp. 89-142.
Garza, Gustavo and Programa de Intercambio Científico y Capacitación Técnica, Departamento de Distrito Federal (1986) (comps.), *Atlas de la Ciudad de México*, El Colegio de México, Mexico.
Garza, Gustavo and Salvador Rivera (1994), *Dinámica Macroeconómica de las Ciudades de México*, Instituto Nacional de Estadística, Geografía e Informática, El Colegio de México and IIS-UNAM, Mexico.

Garza, Gustavo and Fernando A. Rodríguez (1998), (comps.), *Normatividad en las Principales Metrópolis de México*, El Colegio de México, Mexico.

Genberg, H. (1992), "Macroeconomic Adjustment and the Health Sector: A review" paper presented in the Seminar Macroeconomic Environment and Health, June, 24.

Ghai, Dharam (ed.), (1991a), *The IMF and the South, The Social Impact of Crisis and Adjustment*, Zed Books, London.

_____ (1991b), "Introduction", in Gahi (ed.), pp.1-9.

Ghai, Dharam and Cynthia Hewitt de Alcántara (1991), "The Crisis of the 1980s in Africa, Latin America and the Caribbean: An Overview", in Ghai (ed.), pp.11-42.

González de la Rocha, Mercedes (1988), "Economic Crisis, Domestic Reorganisation and Women's Work in Guadalajara, Mexico", in *Bulletin of Latin American Research*, Vol.7, Num. 2, pp. 207-223.

_____ (1991), "Family Well-Being, Food Consumption and Survival Strategies during Mexico's Economic Crisis", in González de la Rocha and Escobar (eds.), pp. 115-127.

_____ (1993), *The Urban Family and Poverty in Latin America*, paper presented in The Latin American and Caribbean Regional Meeting Preparatory to the International Year of the Family, Cartagena Colombia, United Nations, ECLAC, August, unpublished.

_____ (1994), *The Resources of Poverty: Women and Survival in Mexican City*, Blackwell, Oxford.

González de la Rocha, Mercedes and Agustín Escobar (eds.), (1990), *Social Responses to Mexico's Economic crisis of the 1980s*, University of California, San Diego.

González de la Rocha, Mercedes; Agustín Escobar; and María de la O Martínez Catellanos (1990), "Estrategias versus conflicto. Reflexiones para el estudio del grupo doméstico en época de crisis", in De la Peña, *et al.* (comps.), pp. 351-367.

Gould, David M. (1996), "Mexico's Crisis: Looking Back to Assess the Future", in Randall, Laura (ed.), pp.15-39.

Gregory, Peter (1986), *The Myth of Market Failure, Employment and The Labour Market in Mexico*, World Bank and The Johns Hopkins University Press, Baltimore and London.

Gruben, William and John H. Welch (1996), "Distortions and Resolutions in Mexico's Financial System", in Randall, Laura (ed.), pp. 63-76.

Gurría Treviño, José Angel (1996), "The Mexican Debt Strategy", in Randall, Laura (ed.), pp. 95-102.

Haggard, Stephan and Robert R. Kaufman (1992), *The Politics of Economic Adjustment*, Princeton University Press, New Jersey.

Hansen, Roger D. (1971), *The Politics of Mexican Development*, The Johns Hopkins Press, Baltimore and London.

Harris, Nigel (1990), *The End of the Third World, Newly Industrialising Countries and the Decline of an Ideology*, Penguin Books, England (first edition, 1986).

_____ (1995), "Can the West Survive?", in *Competition & Change*, Overseas Publishers Association, Harwood Academic Publisher GmbH, Netherlands.

Harris, Nigel and Ida Fabricius (eds.), (1996), *Cities and Structural Adjustment*, Development Planning Unit, ODA, London.

Hernández-Laos, Enrique (1992), *Crecimiento Económico y Pobreza en México. Una Agenda Para la Investigación*, Centro de Investigaciones Interdisciplinarias en Humanidades, Universidad Nacional Autónoma de México, Mexico.

Hiernaux Nicolás, Daniel (1993), "La Ciudad de México Frente a los Cambios Económicos: las Nuevas Perspectivas de la Apertura", in Bolívar, *et al.* (coords.), pp.153-184.

Ibáñez Aguirre, José Antonio (1998) (coord.), *Deuda Externa Mexicana: Ética, Teoría, Legislación e Impacto Social*, Instituto de Análisis y Propuestas Sociales, IAP, Universidad Iberoamericana, and Plaza y Valdés Editores, Mexico.

Infante, Ricardo and Emilio Klein (1991) "Mercado Latinoamericano de Trabajo en 1950-1990", in Revista de la CEPAL, Num. 45, December, pp. 129-144.

Instituto Nacional del Consumidor (1987), "Seguimiento de la Situación Alimentaria de la Población de Escasos Recursos (datos preliminares), Area Metropolitana de la Ciudad de México", *Cuadernos del Consumidor*, Mexico, March.

_____ (1989), "El Gasto Alimentario de la Población de Escasos Recurso de la Ciudad de México", in *Comercio Exterior*, Vol. 39, Num. 1, January, Mexico, pp. 52-58.

Instituto Nacional de Estadística Geografía e Informática (1997a), *Indicadores Sobre las Características del Empleo Urbano, 1987-1996*, Aguascalientes.

_____ (1997b), *Sistema de Cuentas Nacionales de México, Cuentas de Bienes y Servicios 1988-1996*, Tomo I, Aguascalientes.

_____ (2000), *Statistical Database*.

Instituto Nacional de Estadística Geografía e Informática and Comisión Económica para América Latina y el Caribe (1993), *Magnitud y Evolución de la Pobreza en México, 1984-1992*, Informe Metodológico, December, Mexico.

Instituto Nacional de Nutrición Salvador Zubirán, (1997), *Encuesta Nacional de Alimentación en el Medio rural*, 1996, México, Vol.1.

Jusidman, Clara (1988), "Empleo y Mercados de Trabajo en el Área Metropolitana de la Ciudad de México", in Puente and Legorreta (coord.), pp. 225-250.

Kabeer, Naila (1991), "Gender, Production and Wellbeing: Rethinking the Household Economy", *Discussion Paper*, Num. 288, Institute of Development Studies, IDS Publications, Institute of Development Studies, University of Sussex, England.

Kannappan, Subbiah (1989), "Urban Labour Markets in Developing Countries", in *Finance & Development*, Vol. 33, Num. 4. IMF/World Bank, Washington D.C., June, pp.47-48.
Krugmann, Harmut (1995), "Overcoming Africa's crisis: adjusting structural adjustment towards sustainable development", in Logan and Mengisteab (eds.), pp.129-162.
Langer, Ana and Rafael Lozano (1996), "Health of Women in Mexico: Current Panorama and Future Prospects", in Randall, Laura (ed.), pp. 333-348.
Levy, Santiago (1994), "La Pobreza en México", in Vélez (comp), pp.15-112.
Little, I.M.D.; Richard N. Cooper; W. Max Corden and Sarath Rajapatirana (1993), *Debt, Crisis, and Adjustment, The Macroeconomic Experience of Developing Countries*, World Bank, Oxford University Press, New York.
Logan, Ikubolajeh and Kidane Mengisteab (eds.), (1995), *Beyond Economic Liberalisation in Africa, Structural Adjustment and the Alternatives*, Zed Books, London & New Jersey.
Lustig, Nora (1992), *Mexico. The Remaking of an Economy*, The Bookings Institution, Washington, D.C.
_____ (1993), "El efecto Social del Ajuste", in Bazdresch, *et al.*, pp.201-238.
_____ (ed.), (1995), *Coping With Austerity, Poverty and Inequality in Latin America*, Brooking Institute and Inter-America Dialogue, Washington, D.C.
Lustig, Nora and Ann Mitchell (1994), "Poverty in times of austerity: Mexico in the 1980's", paper presented in the XII Latin American Meeting of the Econometric Society, Caracas.
Lustig, Nora and Miguel Székely (1997), *México, Evolución Económica, Pobreza y Desigualdad*, Report to the Research Project "Los Determinantes de la Pobreza en América Latina", UNDP, IDB and ECLAC.
Martín del Campo, Antonio and Rosendo Calderón Tinoco (1993), "Reestructuración de los Subsidios a Productos Básicos y Modernización de la CONASUPO", in Bazdresch, *et al.*, pp. 88-133.
Martin, Jean and Ceridwed Roberts (1984), *Women and Employment, a Lifetime Perspective*, Department of Employment Office of Population Censuses and Surveys, London.
Mayer-Serra, Carlos Elizondo (1996), "Tax Reform under the Salinas Administration", in Randall, Laura (ed.), pp. 83-94.
McCrone, David (1994), "Getting By and Making Out in Kirkcaldy", in Anderson, *et al.*, pp. 68-99.
Mingione, Enzo (1994), "Life Strategies and Social Economies in the Postfordist Age", in *International Journal of Urban and Regional Research*, Vol. 18, Num.1, pp. 24-45.
Molinar Horcacitas, Juan and Jeffrey A. Weldom (1994), "Programa Nacional de Solidaridad: Determinantes Partidistas y Consecuencias Electorales", in *Estudios Sociológicos*, Vol. XII, Num. 34, January-April, El Colegio de México, Mexico, pp. 155-181.

Moncayo, Pablo Pascual and José Woldenberg (coords.), (1994), *Desarrollo, Desigualdad y Medio Ambiente*, Cal y Arena, Mexico.
Mosley, Paul (1995), "Decomposing the Effects of Structural Adjustment: The Case of Sub Saharan Africa", in Van Der Hoeven, Rolph and Fred Van Der Kraaij (eds.), pp.70-98.
Mosley, Paul; Jean Harrigan and John Toye (1995), *Aid and Power, The World Bank & Policy-Based Lending*, Volume 1, Routledge, London and New York (first published 1991).
Muñoz, Humberto M.A. (1975), "Occupational and Earning Inequalities in Mexico City: A Sectorial Analysis of the Labor Force", Ph.D. Thesis, University of Texas at Austin, May.
Nelson, Joan M. (1992), "Poverty, Equity, and the Politics of Adjustment", in Haggard and Kaufman (eds.), pp. 221-269.
Nolan, Brian and Christopher T. Whelan (1996), *Resources, Deprivation and Poverty*, Claredon Press, Oxford.
Nussbaum, Martha C. and Sen Amartya (eds.), (1993), *The Quality of Life*, Clarendon Press, Oxford, United States.
Orshansky, Molly (1965), "Counting the Poor: Another Look at the Poverty Profile", *Social Security Bulletin*, Washington, U.S. Department of Heath, Education and Welfare, Vol. 28, Num. 1, January, pp.3-29.
Ortega, Eugenio and Ernesto Tironi (1988), *La Pobreza en Chile, Centro de Estudios del Desarrollo*, Santiago de Chile.
Oyen, Else; S.M. Miller and Syed Abdus Else (eds.), (1996), *Poverty. A Global Review. Handbook on International Poverty Research*, Scandinavian University Press, Oslo.
Pacheco Gómez Muñóz, Maria Edith (1994), "Dinámica del Mercado de Trabajo en la Ciudad de México a Fines de los Ochenta", PhD. thesis, Centro de Estudios Demográficos y de Desarrollo Urbano, El Colegio de México, Mexico, Unpublished.
Pahl, R.E. and Clair Wallace (1985), "Household Work Strategies in Economic Recession", in Redclift Nanneke and Enzo Mingione (eds.), pp. 189-227.
Pánuco-Laguette, Humberto and Miguel Székely (1996), "Income Distribution and Poverty in Mexico", in Bulmer-Thomas (ed.), pp. 185-222.
Please, Stanley (1996), "Structural Adjustment and Poverty-Blotting the Criticisms", *Development Policy Review*, Vol. 15, pp. 185-202.
Portes, Alejandro; Manuel Castells and Lauren A. Benton (eds.), (1989), *The Informal Economy, Studies in Advanced and Less Development Countries*, Johns Hopkins University Press, Baltimore and London.
Prebisch, Raúl (1984), "Five Stages in My Thinking on Development", in Dudley, Seers (ed.), pp. 72-95.
Psacharopoulos, George; Samuel Morley; Ariel Fiszbein; Haeduck Lee and Bill Wood, (1997), *La Pobreza y la Distribución de los Ingresos in América Latina, Historias del Decenio de 1980*, Documento Técnico del Banco Mundial, Washington.

Puente, Sergio and Jorge Legorreta (1988), (coord.), *Medio Ambiente y Calidad de Vida*, Departamento del Distrito Federal and Plaza y Valdés Editores, Mexico.

Randall, Laura (ed.), (1996), *Changing Structure of Mexico, Political, Social, and Economic Prospects*, M.E. Sharpe, Armonk, New York, London, England.

Redclift, Nanneke and Enzo Minginione (eds.), (1985), *Beyond Employment, Household, Gender and Subsistence*, Basil Blackwell, Oxford.

Rendón, Teresa and Carlos Salas (1989), "Employment Structure, Life Cycle, and Life Chances: Formal and Informal Sector in Guadalajara", in Portes, Castells and Benton (eds.), pp. 11-37.

_____ (1992a), "Mercado de Trabajo no Agrícola en México, Tendencias y Cambios Recientes", in El Colegio de México, *et al.*, pp. 13-31.

_____ (1992b), "El Empleo Ciudad de México, 1979-1989", in Bassols Batalla, *et al.* (coord.).

_____ (1993), "El Empleo en México en los Ochenta: Tendencias y Cambios, in *Comercio Exterior*, Vol. 43, Num. 8, August, Mexico.

Roldán, Martha (1985), "Industrial Outworking, Struggles for the Reproduction of Working-class Families and Gender Subordination", in Redclift, Nanneke and Enzo Mingione (eds.), pp.278-285.

Salinas de Gortari, Carlos (1991), *Tercer Informe de Gobierno*, Anexo Estadístico, Presidencia de la República, Mexico.

Samaniego, Ricardo (1996), "Financing City Development", in Harris and Fabricius (eds.), pp. 56-65.

Schmink, Marianne (1984), "Household Economic Strategies: Review and Research Agenda", *Latin American Research Review*, Vol. 19, No. 3, pp. 87-101.

Schteingart, Martha (1997), (coord.), *Pobreza, Condiciones de Vida y Salud en la Ciudad de México*, El Colegio de México, Mexico.

Scott, Alison MacEwen (1979), "Who are the Self-Employed?", in Bromley, Ray and Chris Gerry (eds.), pp.105-129.

Selby, Henry A.; Arthur D. Murphy and Stephen A. Lorenzen (1990), *The Mexican Urban Household, Organising for Self-Defence*, (with Ignacio Cabrera, Aida Castañeda and Ignacio Ruiz Love), University of Texas Press, Austin.

Sen, Amartya (1984), *Poverty and Famines. An Essay on Entitlement and Deprivation*, Clarendon Press Oxford, United States, (First Published 1981).

_____ (1995), "The Political Economy of Targeting", in Van de Walle and Nead (eds.), pp. 11-24.

Standing, Guy and Victor Tokman (eds.) (1991), *Towards Social Adjustment, Labour Market Issues in Structural Adjustment*, International Labour Office, Geneva.

Stewart, Frances (1995), *Adjustment and Poverty, Options and Choices*, Routledge, London and New York.

_____ (1998), "La Insuficiencia Crónica del Ajuste", in Bustelo and Minujin (eds.), pp. 25-65.

Stiglitz, Joseph E. (1998), *More Instruments and Broader Goals: Moving Toward the Post-Washington Consensus*, WIDER Annual Lectures 2, The United Nations University, World Institute for Development Economics Research, Helsinki, Finland.
Thomas, Jim (1993), *The Links Between Structural Adjustment and Poverty: Causal or Remedial?*, ILO-PREALC, January, Num. 373.
_____ (1995), *Survival in the City, the Urban Informal Sector in Latin America*, Pluto Press, London, East Haven CT.
Tokman, Victor (1978), "An Exploration Into the Nature of Informal/Formal Sector Relationships", *World Development*, No.6, Sept.-Oct., pp. 1187-1198.
_____ (1989), "Policies for a Heterogeneous Informal Sector in Latin America", in *World Development*, Vol. 17, No.17, July, pp. 1067-1076.
_____ (1991), "The Informal Sector in Latin America: From Underground to Legality", in Standing and Tockman (ed.), pp. 141-157.
Toye, John (1995), *Structural Adjustment and Employment: Issues and Experience*, International Labour Office, Geneva.
Trejo, Guillermo and Claudio Jones (1992) (coords.), *Contra la Pobreza. Por una Estrategia de Política Social*, Cal y Arena, Mexico.
Tuirán Gutierrez, Rodolfo (1992), "Los Hogares Frente a la Crisis: Ciudad de México, 1985-1988", in Consejo Nacional de Población, pp. 179-201.
Turnham, David (1993), *Employment and Development a New Review of Evidence*, Development Centre of the Organisation for Economic Co-Operation and Development.
UNDP (1991), *Economía Popular. Una Vía Para el Desarrollo Sin Pobreza en América Latina*, Proyecto Regional Para la Superación de la Pobreza, Santafé de Bogotá, Colombia.
Valdés-Ugalde, Francisco (1996), "The Changing Relationship Between the State and the Economy in Mexico", in Randall, Laura (ed.), pp.55-62.
Van De Walle, Erik and Kimberly Nead (1995), *Public Spending and the Poor, Theory and Evidence*, World Bank and John Hopkins University Press, Baltimore and London.
Van Der Hoeven, Rolph and Richard Anker, (eds.), (1994), *Poverty Monitoring, An International Concern*, St. Martin's Press, New York.
Van Der Hoeven, Rolph and Fred Van der Kraaij (eds.), (1995), *Structural Adjustment and Beyond in Sub-Saharan Africa*, Ministry of Foreign Affairs the Hague in association with James Currey Ltd, London.
Vélez, Felix (comp.), (1994), *La Pobreza en México, Causas y Políticas Para Combatirla*, el Trimestre Económico, Num. 78, Lecturas, Instituto Tecnológico Autónomo de México ITAM , Fondo de Cultura Económica, Mexico.
Vernon, Raymond (1963), *The Dilemma of Mexico's Development, The Roles of The Private and Public Sector*, Harvard University Press, Cambridge, Massachusetts.

Villareal, René (1997), *Industrialización, Deuda y Desequilibrio Externo en México, Un Enfoque, Neoestructuralista (1929-1997)*, Fondo de Cultura Económica, Mexico.

Walby, Sylvia (1991), "Labour Market and Industrial Structures in Women's Working Lives", in Shirley Dex (ed.), pp. 197-186.

Walton, John and David Seddon (1994), *Free Markets & Food Riots, The Politics of Global Adjustment*, Blackwell Publishers, Oxford, UK & Cambridge, USA.

Weintraub, Sidney (1996), "Mexico's Foreign Economic Policy: From Admiration to Disappointment", in Randall, Laura (ed.), pp.43-54.

Whitehead, Laurence (1996), "Chronic Fiscal Stress and the Reproduction of Poverty and Inequality in Latin America", in Bulmer-Thomas, Victor (ed.), pp. 53-79.

Williamson, John (ed.), (1994), *The Political Economy of Policy Reform*, Institute for International Economics Washington, D.C.

Woodwar, David (1992), *Debt, Adjustment and Poverty in Developing Countries*, Volume 1, National and International Dimensions of Debt and Adjustment in Developing Countries, Save the Children, Printer Publishers, London.

World Bank (1981), *World Bank Development Report*, Oxford University Press.

_____ (1984), *Mexico Recent Economic Developments and Prospects*, Country Programs Department I, Latin America and the Caribbean Regional Office.

_____ (1987), *Mexico after the Oil Boom: Refashioning a Development Strategy*, Country Programs Department 1, Latin America and the Caribbean Regional Office, June, Washington.

_____ (1990), *Report on Adjustment Lending II*, Washington, D.C.

_____ (1992), *World Bank Development Report*, Oxford University Press.

_____ (1993), *Poverty and Income Distribution in Latin America, The Story of the 1980s*, Technical Department, Latin America and the Caribbean.

_____ (1994a), *Mexico Country Economic Memorandum, Fostering Private Sector Development in the 1990s*, Volume I, Country Operations Division I, Country Department II, Latin America and the Caribbean Region.

_____ (1994b), *Mexico Country Economic Memorandum, Fostering Private Sector Development in the 1990s*, Volume II, Statistical Annex, Country Operations Division I, Country Department II, Latin America and the Caribbean Region.

_____ (1995), *Structural and Sectoral Adjustment, The World Bank Experience*, 1980-1992, Washington, D.C.

_____ (1996a) *Social Indicators of Development 1996*, the World Bank and The Johns Hopkins University Press, Baltimore and London.

_____ (1996b), *Social Dimensions of Adjustment*, A World Bank Operations Evaluation Study.

_____ (1996c), *World Bank Debt Tables, External Finance for Developing Countries* Vol. 2, Country Tables, Washington.

_____ (1997) *World Development Report 1997, The State in a Changing World*, World Bank and Oxford University Press.

_____ (1998a) *1998 World Development Indicators*, the World Bank and Oxford University Press.

_____ (1998b), *Mexico, Enhancing Factor Productivity Growth, Country Economic Memorandum*, August, Mexico Department, Latin America and the Caribbean Region.

Yamada, Mutsuo, *et al.*, *Urbanization in Latin America: Its Characteristics and Issues*, The Raten Merika Toshi Kenkyukai, The University of Tsukba, Japan, 1990.

Zedillo, Ernesto (1995), *Primer Informe de Gobierno*, Anexo, Poder Ejecutivo, Mexico.

_____ (1998), *Cuarto Informe de Gobierno*, Anexo, Poder Ejecutivo, Mexico.

Sources of Data

Instituto Nacional de Estadística, Geografía e Informática (1981), *Censo Industrial, Comercial y de Servicios 1981, Datos 1980*, Aguascalientes.

_____ (1986), *Censo Industrial, Comercial y de Servicios, Resultados Definitivos, Resumen General, Datos Referentes a 1985*, Aguascalientes.

_____ (1986-1994), *Encuesta Nacional de Empleo Urbano*, Databases, Aguascalientes.

_____ (1989a), *Encuesta Nacional de Ingresos y Gastos de los Hogares. Tercer Trimestre de 1984*, Aguascalientes.

_____ (1989b), *Encuesta Nacional de Ingresos y Gastos de los Hogares. Tercer Trimestre de 1984*, Database, Aguascalientes.

_____ (1989c), *Censo Industrial, Comercial y de Servicios, Resultados Definitivos, Censos Económicos 1989*, Datos 1988, Aguascalientes.

_____ (1992a), *Encuesta Nacional de Ingresos y Gastos de los Hogares 1989, Transacciones Económicas de Ingresos y Gastos de los Hogares*, Aguascalientes.

_____ (1992b), *Encuesta Nacional de Ingresos y Gastos de los Hogares 1989, Transacciones Económicas de Ingresos y Gastos de los Hogares*, Database, Aguascalientes.

_____ (1992c), *Encuesta de Ingresos y Gastos de los Hogares 1989, Documento Metodológico*, Aguascalientes.

_____ (1992d), *Encuesta de Ingresos y Gastos de los Hogares 1989, Resultados para el Área Metropolitana de la Ciudad de México y Nacionales*, Aguascalientes.

_____ (1993a), *Encuesta Nacional de Ingresos y Gastos de los Hogares 1992*, Aguascalientes.

_____ (1993b), *Encuesta de Ingresos y Gastos de los Hogares 1992, Resultados para el Área Metropolitana de la Ciudad de México y Nacionales*, Aguascalientes.

_____ (1993c) *Encuesta Nacional de Ingresos y Gastos de los Hogares 1992*, Database, Aguascalientes.

_____ (1994), *Censo Industrial, Comercial y de Servicios, Resultados Definitivos, Referentes a 1993, Censos Económicos*, Aguascalientes.

_____ (1995), *Encuesta Nacional de Ingresos y Gastos de los Hogares 1994*, Aguascalientes.

_____ (1997a), *Sistema de Cuentas Nacionales de México, Cuentas de Bienes y Servicios, 1988-1996*, Tomo I, Aguascalientes.

_____ (1997b), *Conteo de Población y Vivienda 1995*, Estados Unidos Mexicanos, Resultados Definitivos, Tabulados Básicos, Aguascalientes.

_____ (1998), Encuesta Nacional de Ingresos y Gastos de los Hogares 1996, Database, Aguascalientes.
Instituto Nacional de Estadística, Geografía e Informática and Secretaría del Trabajo y Previsión Social (1993), *Encuesta Nacional de Empleo, 1991*, Aguascalientes.
_____ (1994), *Encuesta Nacional de Empleo, 1993*, Aguascalientes.
_____ (1996), *Encuesta Nacional de Empleo, 1995*, Aguascalientes.
_____ (1997), *Encuesta Nacional de Empleo, 1996*, Aguascalientes.
Secretaría de Programación y Presupuesto (1977), *Encuesta Nacional de Ingresos y Gastos de los Hogares*, Primera Observación, Mexico.
_____ (1980), *Encuesta Continua Sobre Ocupación*, Serie 1, Vol. 7, First Quarter, 1979, Mexico.